WISEGUYS, RABBIS, and THE FBI

WISEGUYS, RABBIS, and THE FBI

How one man became the biggest loanshark in New York City, went to prison, and escaped.

J.A. SCHWARTZMAN WITH MEL COOPER

Copyright © 2025 by J.A. Schwartzman and Mel Cooper

All rights reserved. No part of this book may be reproduced, scanned, copied, or distributed in any form or by any means, including digital reproduction, electronic media, photocopying, recording, or by any other information storage, viewing, and retrieval system, including AI systems of any type, without written permission from the publisher. For information please contact CHPworksllc@gmail.com

This story is based on the recollections of Mel Cooper and other characters in this narrative. Events have been recalled as truthfully as possible over the expanse of time, and verified whenever possible. Some names and identifying details have been changed to protect the privacy of individuals.

Published by CHP Works, LLC, New York
chpworksllc@gmail.com
Visit www.wiseguysrabbis.com

ISBN: 979-8-9894726-1-1 (paperback edition)

ISBN: 979-8-9894726-0-4 (e-book edition)

Library of Congress Control Number: 2023921798

Cover Design: Steve Morris

Photography: Jamie Kalikow

Please purchase and circulate only authorized editions with both authors' names on the cover.

For Gabrielle, who inspires me every day.

CONTENTS

	Preface	i
1	Mel Cooper Gets a Break	1
2	Money, the Family Business	10
3	Leaning Towards Happy	14
4	Cooper and the Cartmen	25
5	The Big Rush	35
6	Look the Other Way	41
7	Enter the Rabbis	49
8	The Easy Money Business	62
9	Trouble at the Palace	68
10	The Arrest	95
11	The Trial	105
12	Courtroom Follies	115
13	The World Fades Away	136
14	Terre Haute	147
15	Have a Nice Flight, Mr. Parisi	158
16	Boston Alive	167
17	Welcome to Fort Lauderdale	172
18	Club Miami	186
19	In Again	192
20	Down in the Hole	201
21	Nothing Left	213
22	The Not-So-Merry-Go-Round	222
23	Down and Out in Otisville	231
24	Time Served	234

PREFACE

This is the true story of Mel Cooper. In the 1980s, the US government claimed Cooper was the mastermind behind the biggest loansharking scheme in New York City; Cooper says he was just a businessman. The government claimed his money came from the Mafia; he claimed it came from a group of Long Island Rabbis. Cooper's story is a window on the freewheeling nature of New York in the 1970s and early '80s, where legitimate business and the Mafia shared the city, corruption prevailed, and people of all walks of life mixed easily as money flowed.

This narrative is based on extensive interviews with Cooper, as well as with many of the central characters. It relies on thousands of pages of trial transcripts and legal documents, as well as published autobiographies by individuals who appear in this book. Our interviews included co-conspirators, friends, lawyers, members of the Cooper family, and FBI agents.

Mel Cooper's 1985 trial was part of then-US Attorney Rudolph Giuliani's efforts to clean up organized crime in New York City. The case was one of Giuliani's first attempts to employ RICO Statutes to target the Mafia. Before there was the famous Commission Trial, there was Mel Cooper's trial.

Cooper's story overlaps with the story of another New York businessman prominent in the 1980s. Like his contemporary, Donald Trump, Cooper was fixated on what he refers to as "deals." As he moved from one deal to the next, Cooper involved his family in a network of businesses, building layers of corporations and entities. He used lawyers to insulate himself at every step. He even used the same lawyers as Donald Trump, with Rudolph Giuliani playing a central role in the destiny of both.

But where one dealmaker became President of the United States, the other found himself in prison, in a story of choices and changes that is still being written.

We thank everyone who helped tell this story and express our deep gratitude for their time, honesty, and assistance in allowing us to interview them. We also thank the tireless and talented journalists who covered this story in the New York Times, Long Island Newsday, the New York Post, the New York Daily News, and other publications, including Kenneth C. Crowe and Selwyn Raab, as well as the authors who told aspects of this story in their own books – Michael Franzese and William Clifford Breen.

We thank Marissa Levien, Ann Klefstad, Matt Greenberg, Lisa Berkowitz, Katherine Glasson, Aleph Institute and Richard Silverstien, Shepard Splain, Harvey J. Kesner, Steve Morris, Vinny, Jon Kushner, Jamie Kalikow, Thomas Zweifel, and Marc Dannenhirsch.

1

MEL COOPER GETS A BREAK

"Case dismissed," says the judge.

Melvin Cooper smiles. Sitting at the defense table in the courtroom of the Suffolk County courthouse, Mel turns to his lawyer, Scott Stadtman, and says, "congratulations." Stadtman shakes Mel's hand but there's no time for conversation. A sheriff is waiting to escort Mel Cooper out.

The sheriff leads Mel out of the courtroom and into the hallway, where an elevator takes them back down to the basement. The officer guides Mel to a holding cell, where Cooper has already spent numerous hours over the last month waiting for his minutes in court. It's the fourth or fifth time he's been in this underground cell. This time there are no handcuffs or leg shackles.

"Double jeopardy," the judge had declared. After almost three months, the case was thrown out. Naturally, Cooper is relieved. But he isn't surprised since the State's case against him was an afterthought, an imitation of the Federal charges he faced a year earlier. The loansharking charges brought against him by New York State were as flimsy as a two-dollar umbrella. No one else is surprised at the ruling either, not even the officer who escorted Mel back from the courtroom.

"What happened in there?" he asks.

"They dismissed the charges," replies Mel.

"Yeah, that's what I thought," says the officer. The justice system isn't much of a mystery if you spend enough time inside it.

An hour passes, and Cooper is still savoring the judge's words when the officer returns. He opens the pen door and orders Cooper to follow him out—still no cuffs. He guides Mel past the row of cells to an office. They enter and he directs Mel to a cubicle.

"Wait here," he orders, leaving Mel alone in the cubicle with a skinny Hispanic kid.

Something is not right. Mel should not be here. He definitely should not be here with someone who looks like he's waiting for his mom to pick him up and take him home.

"What are you doing here?" Mel asks the kid casually.

"The judge wants me back in two weeks," says the kid.

The officer returns and tells the young man to follow him. A few moments later he's back for Mel, and then it's on to another room where a sergeant at a raised platform steps down, shoves an index card in front of Cooper, takes a thumbprint, and asks for Mel's date of birth. He gives Mel papers to sign. Cooper has been handed off enough times now to know something is definitely wrong. Don't they know who he is?

Apparently not. The sergeant marches Mel to a door. He opens it, and daylight pours in. Mel squints.

"Have a nice day," the sergeant says, and he ushers Mel outside, into the courthouse parking lot.

"Thanks," Mel answers. "You too."

The officer shuts the door.

Cooper stares at the empty lot. It's just Mel Cooper and the quiet Hauppauge morning. He can smell the May air, the scent of the breeze coming off the Long Island Sound. He can hear the cars passing on the road just beyond the parking lot, the low roar they make as they pass, followed by silence. It's morning but the sun is already bright and gold above the treetops. It's a beautiful, clear day, and Mel Cooper is free.

He looks at the sky and at the trees bordering the lot. Mel is free to walk away after three months in a Long Island jail and almost a year in maximum security federal prison. This is not what he expected considering he had twenty-nine years left to serve on his sentence. Cooper was supposed to have been delivered to the custody of U.S. Marshals. They were supposed to take him back to prison in Indiana.

It is 9:30 am, May 5th, 1986. Someone just made a big mistake and let Mel Cooper out.

Escape from Federal prison is rare. Despite the compelling tales, from Andersonville to Alcatraz, despite the Hollywood blockbusters with star-studded breakouts, it almost never happens. As unlikely as escape is, accidental release is even more unusual. It's like winning the lottery.

When it does happen, accidental release is a humble type of escape, almost always the result of an administrative error. Sentencing orders are lost or never sent. Parole eligibility is miscalculated. One of the most famous cases took place in Texas in 1926.

One day in June of that year, a warden named White told a prisoner named Pearlman his term was about to expire. He would soon be free, where would he like to be dropped off? Pearlman told Warden White there must be a mistake. He owed the government five years and had only served three. The warden said the record stated three years, and Pearlman was free whether he liked it or not. White sent the prisoner on his way, and Pearlman went home and resumed his life.

But Pearlman was correct. There was an uproar when the mistake was discovered, but Mr. Pearlman was never required to complete his sentence. A court decided that sending him back to jail after he had restarted his life would have amounted to cruel and unusual punishment. This mundane incident is the legal precedent for what happens when the Bureau of Prisons accidentally lets someone go.

It may not be the action-packed scene the word "escape" usually conjures. But if you're away for thirty years like Mel Cooper, you take escape whichever way it's offered. When the hapless sergeant showed Cooper the back door, Mel didn't argue.

At the moment Mel stood outside the Long Island courthouse, his former partner Jesse "Doc" Hyman was engaging in a different kind of escape. Doc and Mel had been convicted in federal court in New York City of loansharking, extortion, racketeering, and conspiracy. Charged along with them were seven top Mafiosi from the Gambino, Colombo, Genovese, and DeCavalcante crime families. The US Attorney who had prosecuted them was Rudolph W. Giuliani.

Cooper and Hyman had been arrested in 1984, just as Rudolph Giuliani was making a name for himself as a prosecutor willing to go to any lengths to take down New York's organized crime families and clean up the city. Giuliani had a reputation as a crime-fighter back then, and Cooper's trial, with its 15 defendants, represented one of the Justice Department's first racketeering "megatrials." After being found guilty, Cooper was dispatched to Federal Penitentiary in Terre Haute, Indiana, while Doc was sent to Petersburg, Virginia.

Doc Hyman negotiated his escape directly with the federal government. He agreed to tell the Justice Department everything he knew about the mobsters he did business with in New York, Chicago, Cleveland, Buffalo, and Las Vegas. Doc also knew a lot about a few Teamsters Union officials in Queens who had given him access to millions of dollars in pension funds. The money had disappeared into Las Vegas hotels and casinos.

In exchange for his testimony, Doc was about to enter the witness protection program. The red-haired dentist didn't have the stomach for maximum security prison, and by agreeing to testify, his thirty-year sentence would be reduced to time served. Doc Hyman would rat on his old friends for years to come.

Mel Cooper had also been pressured to make a deal. He had refused. Unlike Doc, Mel had chosen to serve his time, seeking recourse through his appeal lawyer, Thomas Puccio. Until Mel Cooper was summoned East to stand trial on state charges, he had been uneventfully serving his time. Cooper had just completed one year of his thirty-year sentence when he was released to the custody of a Long Island parking lot.

Back in the courthouse, nobody realized a mistake had been made. Mel knew it was only a matter of time before US Marshals arrived looking for him. If he hoped to profit by their error, he would have to put distance between himself and the courthouse. Still, when the impossible actually happens, you take a moment to absorb it.

"I actually looked up at the sky just to see – I don't know – to put some reality to where I was," Cooper remembers. "When I looked up at the sky, I think the feeling was stronger than euphoria. This was after thirteen months, with twenty-nine years ahead of me. All of a sudden, this guy opens the door and says 'Have a nice day,' and that's that. That's the end of thirty years, and that's the beginning of life again, and it's the sky, it's the smell of outdoors. I knew instantly that I can't stand there staring at the sky. I had to move away from the court."

Mel checks his options. He sees a small, two-lane road to the left of the parking lot, and across the road, a DMV.

"I walked quickly, I didn't want to run. I was dressed with my khakis and my sneakers and I had a manila legal file with my legal papers in it. I got across the road to the Motor Vehicles Bureau parking lot." Mel's only plan was to get out of Hauppauge.

In the mostly empty parking lot, Mel spots two men and a woman getting into a small car. He walks over and speaks to the driver, a young black man, nicely dressed.

"How ya doin'?" says Mel in his heavy Brooklyn accent. Then, speaking as a free man for the first time in over a year, he musters whatever normalcy is left in him and continues: "I have an emergency and I have to get to Kennedy Airport."

They stare at Mel as he spins a story about a fight with his girlfriend and his brother's imminent arrival at the airport. Most convincing is Mel's offer of a hundred dollars if they would give him a lift.

"Get in," says the guy. He does not see the number stamped on Mel's pants and the back of his shirt.

Getting a bulky, six-foot Mel Cooper into the back seat of a small, two-door car is not easy. It takes valuable seconds. Time passes in slow motion as they open the doors and push the seats forward so Mel can climb in. At last the doors slam shut.

The driver puts his foot on the gas and is heading out of the lot when he remembers one important task. He turns his right hand upwards towards the back seat. Mel stares at the palm and realizes the man wants his money.

Cooper thinks fast. He explains someone is going to meet them at Kennedy airport with the money. He doesn't actually have the cash with him. The driver puts his foot on the brake.

A moment later, Mel climbs out of the back seat. His escape is not going well.

The case that had put Mel Cooper and Jesse "Doc" Hyman away was called *United States of America v. Vincent Joseph Rotondo*. It was named after "Jimmy" Rotondo, a powerful organized crime captain based in Brooklyn and associated with the DeCavalcante crime family of New Jersey.

Rotondo worked out of the International Longshoreman's Association headquarters in Carroll Gardens. Now demolished, the headquarters of Local 1814 represented dockworkers on the Brooklyn waterfront. After working on the docks himself from 1947 to 1960, Rotondo became an organizer for the union where he supposedly spent half the day on union business and the other half on his own "projects," including running New York operations for the DeCavalcante organization. Rotondo answered directly to family boss, John Riggi, who oversaw the New Jersey Mafia's vast gambling, labor racketeering, extortion, and loansharking operations.

Though Jimmy's affiliations were in New Jersey, he was a player in New York City thanks to his power on the Brooklyn waterfront. Says a neighborhood acquaintance, "Jimmy was a guy that was around a lot. He was a big action guy. He knew fifty different people, had fifty things going on, and made money lots of ways. He was a well-heeled guy, he was a big earner. The more you look like you're important, the more guys bring you deals." Jimmy had a lot of deals. It would soon emerge that Jimmy was skimming massive amounts of money from another union, Teamsters Local 804, with the help of Doc Hyman.

Says Mel, "He was a little under six foot, and he carried himself like a strong guy, in every sense of the word. He was a made guy, he was a captain in his family, and he snapped his fingers and he got things done. He had many people like Doc working for him."

Though Mel and Doc had the most charges against them, Giuliani must have reasoned that naming the case after a mobster would garner more attention than naming the case after, for example, defendant Dr. Jesse Hyman – a Long Island dentist. In spite of the name, Doc and Mel were labeled "the masterminds" behind the enterprise that pulled together defendants in *United States v. Vincent Joseph Rotondo*.

The Justice Department claimed Mel and Doc's company, Resource Capital Group, was a front for the Mafia's moneylending activities in New York City. Thomas Sheer, head of the FBI's New York office, called it a "super-Shylock operation," referencing, intentionally or not, the fact that the two "masterminds" were Jewish; the word "Shylock" has its origin in Shakespeare's *The Merchant of Venice*, in which the antagonist is a Jewish moneylender.

Giuliani stuck to legal terms. The operation "may be the largest and most sophisticated loansharking operation ever uncovered by the Government," said Giuliani in a 1984 article in the New York Times, and he used the RICO Statutes–the Racketeer Influenced and Corrupt Organizations Act–to charge Cooper, Doc Hyman, and thirteen other men.

The mobsters indicted with Mel and Doc cut across New York's Mafia elite. It included several powerful captains from different organizations, each with his own universe of criminal activities. Besides Jimmy Rotondo, there was Michael J. Franzese, captain in the Colombo family and son of jailed underboss, John "Sonny" Franzese. Michael ran multi-million-dollar gas tax scams, and would soon make a name for himself fixing fights in Atlantic City, allegedly with promoter Don King. There was Benedetto "Benny" Aloi, Colombo family captain and son of mob boss Sebastian "Buster" Aloi, who would eventually be jailed for conspiracy to murder, after a career of gambling, loansharking, and trucking rackets; Anthony "Tony Nap" Napoli, captain in the Genovese family and son of "Jimmy Nap", boss of the Genovese family for thirty years; and Carlo Vaccarezza, John Gotti's driver and bodyguard, and part-owner of a restaurant with the baseball player, Rusty Staub. Rounding out the Gambino group with Vaccarezza were two more tough guys, Francesco "Frankie the Hat" Di Stefano, and Leonard Di Maria.

Besides Cooper, Hyman, and the seven wiseguys, Giuliani also indicted six employees from Mel's company including a Great Neck rabbi. According to the indictment, they were all involved in one long chain of rackets.

But Cooper has another story, an alternate version of the government's narrative. It unfolds in a parallel world, where the money used to fund loans didn't come from mobsters at all. The money came from a group of Long Island rabbis and their friends. One of the rabbis was a famous scholar and writer. Another was an Israeli war hero, a Hebrew school teacher, a *mensch*. And in this alternate story, the reason Cooper did not rat or testify was not because he was particularly loyal to the code of his

Mafia partners, as the government claimed; he didn't flip because he had nothing to tell.

As Mel sees it, he was just a financier, a pioneer venture capitalist, a broker, an inspired lender of funds to businesspeople. Yes, the loans Mel Cooper and Jesse Hyman made at Resource Capital Group pushed the limits of legal moneylending. The government called it loansharking. But much like the imaginative executives of Enron and Worldcom and so many corporations to come, Mel called it "creative financing." And like Donald Trump – another up-and-coming New York entrepreneur – Mel surrounded himself with lawyers, relying on the legal system to insulate himself.

"Those loans were a small part of our total business. They represented nine or ten loans out of thousands of loans we did, between equipment, car leasing, and mortgages," says Cooper. "It was a very insignificant amount of clients and dollars. To us, they were "emergency loans"–people who came in and needed money to stay afloat. These people were begging to have this bridge money to get them over a hump." According to Cooper, he and Doc Hyman had done nothing but broker risky, short-term loans to people with poor credit. His clients owned flashy, entertainment-oriented businesses in New York City, and did not have the collateral to take to a bank. And though Mel and Doc's lending rates of 104 percent to 208 percent a year might appear usurious to conservative observers – the legal limit was 25 percent at the time – they were really just a mixture of fees, commissions, and legal charges with some interest added. These fees totaled as much as $75,000 a week, paid in cash which Mel and Doc stuffed into shoeboxes, briefcases, and safe deposit boxes.

As for the victims of his so-called loansharking activities, Cooper laughs at the notion. "The victims all made hundreds of thousands of dollars. Who's the victim?" says Cooper. "It was a situation where nobody was beaten up to get money back, there were actually mortgages set up with each loan. There was a lawyer at every closing. To collect, we used a pen, not a bat."

But where Mel saw rabbis, the Justice Department saw Mafia. According to Assistant US Attorney Bruce Baird: "Resource Capital Group was a front, a front for an enormous loansharking business. It depended on the threat of force and the fear of organized crime to do its criminal business.

"This was a business that got money from illegal union and organized crime sources," said Baird, "a business that threatened, a business that took control of the businesses of victims who couldn't pay." He called Mel Cooper "the small tip of a large, ugly iceberg."

Bruce A. Baird and Aaron J. Marcu were the assistant US attorneys who prosecuted *United States v. Rotondo*. They were sharp young men, well dressed, and dripping with what Mel calls "Ivy League status." In soft-spoken voices they explained to the jury how Melvin Cooper only looked like a businessman: all clean, nice, and legitimate. But like an iceberg, the part beneath the surface was murky, dirty, and dark. If clients didn't pay money on time each and every week, "the real powers behind this enterprise came up, the bottom of this iceberg"–the capos of four New York crime families and their soldiers.

Back in Hauppauge, the tip of the iceberg stood in the parking lot wondering how, with no money and wearing only prison khakis, he could get out of New York.

2

MONEY, THE FAMILY BUSINESS

It's 1982, two years before any thoughts of prison, racketeering, or trials, and outside the window of Mel Cooper's office are lots of trucks. They're all tractor-trailers except for one forty-foot aluminum container, and they're sitting in the parking lot of Mel's glass office building at 2001 Marcus Avenue in Lake Success.

In a few years, the FBI will come in and shut the place down, but at the time, Cooper has never heard of Rudolph Giuliani, and Terre Haute might as well be Tehran, that's how unlikely Mel is to find himself there.

The trucks outside his window are used but still beauties. There's a powder-blue Autocar with a double sleeper, and next to it, a 22-speed Peterbilt with a Detroit engine–lime green with chrome stacks and footrails. The owner-operator who's leasing the Peterbilt is on his way out to Long Island to pick it up. The trucks belong to Etna Leasing, one of the many businesses owned by the Cooper family.

Besides Etna, there's Cooper Equities, Cooper Commercial, M. Cooper Motor Leasing, and Resource Capital Group. Except for the last of these, all are run by a combination of brothers, uncles, sisters-in-law, and cousins in the immediate family of Mel Cooper.

The other tenants in this expensive suburban business park are not happy about having a truck stop in their backyard. As Mel himself says, "It didn't add much to the whole ambience." But Etna Leasing is in the business of providing money for overland truck leasing, and the parking lot is where pickup and delivery takes place.

One of Mel's employees, a man named Alan Albenga, handles the transactions with the truck drivers. Mel remains in his posh office, doing what he does best: thinking about money. How to get it, how to spend it, how to make more of it.

Cooper sits at an oversized desk while salesmen, accountants, lawyers, and the occasional rabbi run in and out of his office. They're all there to obtain Mel's judgment on some business matter – a new loan, lease, or sales lead – but at the moment he's on the phone with his son's teacher. His son is in trouble again at the Jewish day school he attends on the upper East Side of Manhattan.

Mel tries to get back to business, but as soon as he hangs up his girlfriend calls. His personal life is a stew of complications, and demands fly at him from all sides.

Not only do trucks crowd the parking lot and clients fill the reception area, but somewhere in its respective marina, hanger, yard, or lot are a boat, two planes, and a few thousand automobiles. The boats and planes are collateral Mel has seized from clients who could not pay back the money they borrowed from him.

Mel's lending company – Resource Capital Group – provides brokered loans for the purchase of income-producing equipment. If you're in business and need a bulldozer, a dentist chair, or blow-mold injection equipment, Resource Capital Group is the place to go.

Since they opened their doors in 1973, the company has made bigger and bigger loans for increasingly expensive equipment. All of the Cooper enterprises, in fact, are in a constant state of expansion, thanks to Mel Cooper's driving motto: "More, bigger, faster." His compulsion to open more companies, expand to more offices, and uncover more opportunities has created a constellation of enterprises all focused in one way or another on lending money.

To Cooper, lending money is the logical way of getting rich. You can scale up easily, and the overhead is low. Explains Cooper, "You can get on a phone and talk an eight-million-dollar deal or you can talk a fifty-thousand-dollar deal, it's the same telephone, the same piece of paper. It can have eight million written on it or fifty thousand. That's the money business." Once you know how to do a money deal, one zero more or less is no big deal.

Mel is director of operations. As the oldest of six siblings, together with his twin brother, he's naturally gravitated to a position of leadership. Or perhaps he's the one who's hungry enough, willing to take the greatest risks for the biggest payoff. After many years in the money business, Mel has acquired a certain decisiveness. He can size up customers in minutes, instantly identify the weak link in a contract, or spot a moneymaking opportunity and pounce on it like a cat on a waterbug. When people come to Cooper looking for a loan, he can tell right away whether they're good for three million or not worth risking three hundred.

"I can sit down and read, most of the time, what the person's about, what's on the person's mind, what his motive is. Within minutes I can have a judgment. I can be wrong. But I have a judgment and make a decision."

Customers don't always know they're being sized up. In fact, with all the chaos in Cooper's office, it often seems as if Mel is not paying attention at all. Cooper is a big man with sleepy, heavy-lidded eyes that make it hard to tell what he's looking at, unless he's particularly interested in something; then they open wide enough for you to see his brown eyes. He's tall and strong, with a triangle-shaped upper body that looks as if he's been lifting weights. Before his thirty-year conviction at age 38, he was a little softer, a little more boyish. He did not yet have the streaks of gray in his hair or the kind of muscular build you get from spending hours a day in a prison gym. Still, at six feet tall, Mel Cooper resembles nothing as much as a powerful, unstoppable bear. Mel Cooper moves relentlessly towards opportunity. You cannot stop the man from making money.

Even at 5 years old, Mel Cooper was interested in commerce. He collected bottles on Rockaway Beach to earn money for Italian ices and candy. He would cash in Coke bottles for two cents each at Gabe's on the boardwalk. Eventually Mel realized he could enlist other kids in the task, pay them a penny a bottle, and keep the rest for himself. His candy money doubled.

It may sound like an episode of "Our Gang"—a society of enterprising kids setting schemes in motion on the streets of New York—but Cooper's is a post-war story, the third chapter in the wave of European immigration that characterized the early twentieth century. For baby boomers with

American-born parents, there is no Great Depression to remember, none of the exhausting struggle with poverty that had characterized immigrant life. The Cooper family knew how to make ends meet.

Wealth and the accumulation of it was a constant theme in Mel's early life. While other families were saving money so they could join a beach club, buy a Buick, or send a kid to college, the Coopers were figuring out how to get rich. And while other young families were saving for a house in the suburbs, the Coopers were buying apartment buildings and looking for investments. In the Cooper household, there was always something about money. And in an echo of a family dynamic that still haunts Mel Cooper, if you had deals, you had love.

3

LEANING TOWARDS HAPPY

East New York was a fine place to bring up a family when Sam Cooper moved there in 1946. There were wide streets, convenient trolley cars, comfortable houses, and first-rate shopping on Pitkin Avenue in nearby Brownsville. East New York had been settled by Jewish and Italian immigrants who had left the tenements of lower Manhattan for the private houses and amenity-filled apartments of Brooklyn. The new buildings had elevators, fancy lobbies, and modern kitchens with refrigerators instead of iceboxes. By 1946, Brownsville had become the largest, most established Jewish community in the borough.

But Brownsville's reputation was mixed, thanks to the headline-grabbing criminal activities of "Murder Incorporated," and characters like Abe "Kid Twist" Reles, "Pittsburgh Phil", and Louis "Lepke" Burkhalter, who operated from neighborhood candy stores and luncheonettes. By the time Mel was born, these men were gone, but there were new gangs like The Brownsville Boys, as well as up-and-coming Latin gangs. East New York, just next door, was comfortingly uneventful.

The Coopers lived in a two-family brick house on Snediker Avenue. There was a candy store down the block, and shops like Sam's Pickles and Julie's Barbershop around the corner. The yellow house in which Mel Cooper was born belonged to his grandparents. Mel's parents, Sam and Naomi, lived downstairs, his grandparents upstairs. Mel and his fraternal twin, Barry, were born in 1947 soon after the couple moved to East New York.

Four years later, Jeffrey arrived, then Mark, followed by his sister Fern. The Cooper children had several years between them, and Mel was just leaving the house when his youngest brother David was born.

In spite of the two-family houses and leafy streets, East New York was unmistakably urban. You might find a factory or a busy dairy a block away from a row of houses. It was a mixture of businesses, factories, and residences that stretched in one direction along Linden Boulevard and in another along New Lots Avenue. On streets named after states and cities—Pennsylvania, Georgia, and New Jersey Avenue—life unfolded around the rituals of Orthodox Jewish life. On Friday nights, the Cooper family attended Young Israel Synagogue. After Saturday morning services, the rest of the weekend was spent playing games like Monopoly and Risk, running in the backyard, or on special occasions, going into the city to see a movie—*The Ten Commandments*, for example—with a stop at Chock Full o' Nuts for a cream cheese, raisin, and walnut sandwich.

It was a way of life typical in New York City after World War II, where American culture mixed easily with the traditional, and Mel could move from punchball, stickball, or basketball to his Yeshiva studies with ease.

As far back as he can remember, Mel Cooper had a powerful association between money and pleasure, money and food, money and freedom.

"I remember being in the playground at school and there was this guy with a silver metal pushcart outside the fence, and he would be selling potato knishes, and I mean, I never see these type of knishes anymore, they were oblong with thin skin, and I used to stand by the fence, and I used to just smell it because I didn't have the seven cents. I mean, it just smelled fantastic, and he would take the big metal salt shaker and put salt on it and pass it through the fence. I just remember that I was always looking for the seven cents to get those knishes."

As a young child, Mel recalls a family where money was scarce. "I never got the impression that we had any money because things were pretty meager. We used to have meals, and we'd split up a chicken. No matter how many kids, we'd just divide the chicken up more. And my father would give little pieces of bread. So we didn't overeat. My mother would never buy candy and things like that. She may have once in a while bought a Yankee Doodle, and given one to each kid."

The Cooper men preferred to be in business for themselves. Mel's grandfather had come to America somewhere around 1910. With his sons Sam and Jack, he started a business in 1947, the year Mel was born. Their company, Cooper Tank and Welding, would soon flourish, but initially every penny they had went into the business. Cooper Tank specialized in steel fabrication. They made the huge oil and water tanks that went into New York's basements, and they capitalized on the citywide change from coal to oil heating in the 1950s. Cooper Tanks removed the coal-burning systems that once kept New York City warm and replaced them with steel oil tanks.

Their success in the steel business allowed the Cooper family to move to Far Rockaway in 1959 when Mel was 12 years old. It was an investment as much as a move, since the family bought a three-story apartment building and became landlords. The building on Dorian Court became known as "his mother's building." She was the driving force behind the family's business and the move to expand.

With a busy house full of boys—Mel's sister was not yet born—Sam was not averse to pulling out the belt and smacking his kids when they made trouble. As the oldest and most independent, it was Mel who usually got the worst of it.

"He was tougher with me than with everybody else. I used to have problems, where I used to get beat up a lot from my father," Mel recalls.

The fights often started over food. Mel would sit down for dinner and announce he didn't plan to eat. "My mother was not a good cook. She'd make her and my father rib steaks. We might get a shoulder steak, and she'd overcook it, and then she would take it out and leave it on the counter and then she would start to make the french fries. Everything would come cold, and I wouldn't like it, and she would then start screaming to my father. Then he would inevitably come after me with a belt, and typically, my mother would encourage my father to come after me. Then, when he did, she would yell about what he's doing to me. There were times when I'd run under the bunk beds, and he'd take a two-by-four and start jabbing me. One time he broke a bridge chair over my back. I remember he threw me out of the house one time. I was sitting at the table and he told me get out of the house, and I didn't have shoes on and it was snowing outside. Until I apologized I would have to stay outside."

Cooper's childhood was punctuated by physical and emotional rifts, which somehow do not interfere with his memories of a pleasant childhood. Says Mel, "it was leaning towards happy."

"I ran away with two friends of mine one time. Just like a hobo, I left with a stick and a thing, a bandana, and I left a note under my pillow that said I ran away with Larry Hecht and Sam Lefkowitz. We jumped on a freight train, and we went to New Orleans.

"I was young, I think I was about fourteen, and I remember between the three of us, we didn't have much money. We met in Manhattan, and we went into Macy's and stole some books so we could read on the train, some soft-cover books. Then we bought a ticket to New Jersey on the Hudson Tubes. Then we jumped on a freight train in Jersey City.

"We ended up in New Orleans, and we stayed there for two or three days and I called up my house and my mother begged me to come home, and we ended up going home. That was one time."

Even more telling about the atmosphere in the Cooper household was Mel's singular notion of independence. At an age when most kids are begging their parents for a bigger allowance, Mel decided he simply did not need his parents' money anymore. It happened when he needed bus money one day. The family had just moved to Far Rockaway. Mel and his brother attended the Hebrew Institute of Long Island, a Jewish Yeshiva lodged in four white mansions about a mile away. The bus cost a nickel with a school pass. After several days of travel and snacks, Mel found he needed more bus money.

"What did you do with the dollar I gave you?" his father asked. He demanded an explanation.

"From that point on," recalls Cooper, "I said I'm never going to ask him for money again because I have to explain. So that was the end of that. I started working."

Mel understood at twelve years old, that if you took money from people, they had a hold over you. They could push you around. Money got you freedom. The more money you had, the freer you were. And the way you knew you were free was by spending the money on the things you wanted. As a kid, that meant buying candy and soda; later in life it was cars and condos.

Mel would walk to school and go without lunch if necessary, but he would not take anything from these people. Mel did not ask, and his parents did not offer. And so the business of earning a living began.

His first paying job was at the Washington Hotel in Belle Harbor, Long Island, at the age of thirteen. They hired him as a bellhop and later, a busboy over the Passover holidays. "It was a small religious hotel. People pulled up in their car, and I took about six or seven bags out of the station wagon, and I had to carry them all up the stairs."

There was babysitting and other childhood jobs. The jobs became more serious when Mel started to spend his summers in upstate New York at the hotels of the Catskill Mountains. At the New Roxy and Pineview, Cooper worked his way up from bellhop to waiter, and finally, to lifeguard at the famous Concorde Hotel.

The Concorde was the peak of luxury for Jewish vacationers who left New York for "The Mountains". It was a grand hotel, a resort paradise, and a summer camp rolled into one. The opulent Concorde had a nightclub, Olympic pool, and a lobby designed by the architect, Morris Lapidus, that made guests feel they had wandered into a Hollywood movie. Food was served in endless portions according to Kosher dietary laws.

Entertainment was a central part of the "Borscht Belt" experience and ranged from local *tummelers* who mingled and told jokes by the pool, to talent like young Barbra Streisand and Bobby Darin, to comedians Lenny Bruce, Woody Allen, and Mel Brooks, to jazz greats like Duke Ellington. Mel's job entailed keeping an eye on the kids in the pool while their parents lounged with sun reflectors or played cards and mahjong. On Saturdays, Buster Crabbe, Hollywood's original Tarzan, spent the day as the guest swim coach. There was time off for trips to town, girls, and mischief, like the time Cooper and a buddy stole Mel Tormé's tuxedo.

Serving plates of gefilte fish and brisket and teaching kids to swim was a fine way to get a taste of what real work was all about, but Mel had learned a different lesson watching the Cooper family men build their steel company; the only way to make real money was by working for yourself. As a teenager, Mel took his first steps towards entrepreneurship.

At 15 years old, before he could even drive, he began buying German and Italian motorcycles from classified ads. He fixed them up and sold them, riding them up and down the small private street in front of Dorian Court. A passion for bikes and cars was not unusual in New York in the 1950s and '60s, when you could drag race down the empty streets of Sunset Park by the docks or cruise Bay Ridge, the Shirelles or the Tokens on the radio. As soon as Mel got his license, he bought his own car, a 1960 red Triumph TR3, followed a few years later by an Austin-Healy.

For his next business venture, at 17, Cooper and a friend bought thirty used police cars at an auction, patched together twenty good cars, got two-way radios, and started a gypsy car service called Sweet Rose. Mel had an acquaintance who worked at a gas station on Fulton Street. Roosevelt Fosky knew his way around a car engine. Mel enlisted Roosevelt to run the car service.

Roosevelt lived in Bedford-Stuyvesant. By the early 60s, "Bed-Stuy" had transformed into a neighborhood so rough, even the police didn't like going there. Racial tension was high but as far as Mel was concerned, that had nothing to do with making money. Mel and his friend Barry decided Bedford-Stuyvesant needed a car service, since yellow cabs wouldn't go there, and with Roosevelt as the manager, they rented out their cars for $21 a day.

The business progressed nicely. By this time, Mel was driving a Lincoln Continental, a burgundy convertible with suicide doors. Cooper would go by Roosevelt's office every night in his Lincoln to pick up money and chew the fat. The sidewalk across the street from Sweet Rose's office at 68 Lafayette Avenue was a popular hangout, lined with bars. Recalls Mel, "What happened was, I was coming over with a Lincoln, and picking up money from this black entrepreneur. Even though they were our cars, Roosevelt was starting to feel he's running this business. So one day he said to me, 'I'm not going along with this anymore.' He actually started reaching for a gun. I picked up a chair and hit him." That was the end of Sweet Rose.

"I always had a few things going. Buying and selling motorcycles. The car service. Then we shipped tires to North Carolina for recapping." Mel also sold shirts from the trunk of his car, irregulars purchased from his friend, Artie Klaus, whose father made Oleg Cassini double-knit shirts and Prince Igor ties. Again, he would drive over to Bedford-Stuyvesant, pull up, open his trunk, and charge $15 for shirts he had bought for $5. He was always swamped with buyers. "It comes from my childhood. I never wanted anyone to tell me I can't have something. And I understood you need to have something to offer in order to make money. You need something, it could be anything, apples, milk, anything, as long as you have something you can sell. So that's the key. I liked being in business. I only needed some mechanism to step up on, to use as a diving board. Selling a thing, selling money, even selling intangibles, which is done in financing."

And just like that, Mel realized he had something to sell right in his own backyard. Mel's father, Sam Cooper, was running what had evolved into a booming steel business. Despite the strain between them, his father invited him in.

It wasn't just ambition; Mel had met a girl.

He met Miriam Moneta at the New Roxy Hotel in the Catskills a year earlier, while he was still working as a waiter. She organized social events at the hotel. "She was pretty and nice, and she was from Brooklyn, from 15th Avenue. She had black hair. We started to date. I was about 19 when we got engaged. We were about to get married, and I needed a little more stability. I felt I needed a little more than selling things from the back of my trunk."

His employment with Cooper Tank and Welding began humbly enough. "In the beginning I was just sweeping the floors and carrying steel. Then I was driving on the truck, delivering oil tanks and installing them in the basement of buildings, and working with the guys to rig up smokestacks." He attended Brooklyn College at night, and worked for his father by day.

"After I was there about eight or nine months, I wanted to do something a little more productive." He wanted to go into sales. His father said no. First of all, there was Mel's cousin, who had been in the business five years and still worked in the factory. Mel couldn't just leap right over him. Then there was the question of money; Mel started in the business making $40 a week. It had gone up to $75 when he married Miriam in 1968, then to $125. Mel wanted more, but the senior Cooper wouldn't change the arrangement. "My father, I really believe, felt I was competition. I asked him if I could go into sales and make a commission when I sell something, and he said no."

Sam finally let Mel go into sales, but only as a salaried employee. Mel attacked his new role with energy. Besides selling oil tanks, he sold steel containers to sanitation and trash hauling companies in New York City's five boroughs, New Jersey, and Long Island. Within four months of starting to sell, Mel had brought in so many orders Cooper Tanks had to add a night shift. The growth continued.

When they started their business, the Coopers had invested in a wooden building on Seagal Street in Greenpoint, on the border of Bushwick. Now they bought another factory next to the original one and added more men. Within less than a year, production was at capacity. Orders were backed up eight months. It was impossible to sell equipment with that kind of delivery. All Mel could do was make the rounds of customers and tell them their orders were on the way. Mel begged his father to further increase production, but Sam had no intention of rushing into uncertain expansion. Says Mel, "He was afraid. It was like, you have a grocery store, and suddenly it turns into a supermarket. But he wouldn't keep up with the demand."

Two things were becoming apparent as Mel got deeper into the family business. First, his father was distressingly complacent and not particularly interested in risk or change. And second, his mother was ready to do business.

"I would speak to him, to my father, about expanding and he would say, 'Let me mull it over tonight and I'll give you an answer tomorrow,' and he did this many times. Finally, I realized when he used to mull it over, in reality he was asking my mother for the answer. After she told him what to do, he would come back with the answer. So after a certain point I would go home to my mother and ask her directly if she would look to expand."

Thus began a lifelong relationship of counsel and collaboration between mother and son. Mel would regularly report to his mother Naomi, looking for the approval and advice he was not getting from his father.

Opportunity appeared again in the form of a whole new business. "One day a guy named Harold Fried came into the office saying he worked for General Electric credit. He was looking to finance our customers when we sold containers or compactors to the garbage companies. He said he would like to finance them through General Electric Credit. We gave him the first deal for about $110,000 and he told us how he did it. So I sat down with my father and I said, 'This looks like a good business, why don't we go into the finance business?'"

His father said no. Sam Cooper controlled a profitable business. He controlled 30,000 square feet of real estate in Bushwick, and hundreds of customers. And he controlled his son, a salaried employee. Why change a good thing?

It was 1971, Mel was 24 years old, and ready for action. Mel assumed, with a nod to their unspoken competition, that his father simply did not want him to make any real money. Mel decided to go into the finance business. "I went over to this friend of mine, who I used to be partners in the cab company, and said 'Why don't we start a finance company?' He listened, he liked it."

Mel started his business with his friend Barry Septimus and Barry's brother-in-law, Sidney Hirth. Each took a third of the business. They called the company CBS Leasing, and started offering a variety of leases for income-producing equipment to the same customers Mel had been selling containers to just the week before. They worked with banks to finance the equipment, and made money by charging the customer more in interest than CBS Leasing was paying the bank.

With this arrangement, Cooper continued to sell oil tanks, compactors and containers, only now he offered his customers finance and leasing deals as well. The arrangements with the banks were varied, there were tax leases, leveraged leases, equipment leases – all of which Mel learned about as he went along. Within the first six months they had generated a million and half dollars in sales, earning between $150,000 and $200,000 in profit for the three partners.

This kind of return was not lost on Naomi, who listened carefully to Mel's reports of the leasing business every weekend when Mel and his wife stopped by their home. After a year she decided she was ready to do more than just listen.

One Sunday, she and Sam sat down at the kitchen table with Mel. "Okay, the family is ready to go into the finance business," Naomi announced.

"I already have a finance company," Mel replied. By now he had established lines of credit with twelve different banks.

"Get rid of it," she said. After a lecture on the importance of family and the meaning of loyalty–you went into business with family, not friends–Mel bought out his two partners.

It took some finesse to buy his way out of CBS Financing, which Mel did by convincing Barry and Sidney they couldn't handle the business without his salesmanship. Cooper took the existing loans and bank contacts, and renamed the enterprise Cooper Funding Ltd. He expected to split his new family business into two equal parts–50 percent for himself and 50 percent for his father and uncle. But as they sewed up the details of the arrangement, Sam Cooper sprung a surprise on Mel. "No, no," Sam said, "we're not dividing it fifty-fifty. We have to divide it four ways, we have my brother Jack and his son Joel, and you and me." Mel's share went from a third of CBS Leasing to a quarter of Cooper Funding.

He learned a big lesson from this encounter. "When you're dealing with family it's not like dealing with strangers. I was put under a whole layer of guilt. They had been putting pressure on me to turn over the finance company, or else I couldn't work for Cooper Tank anymore. That was the message.

"I learned that people are out for themselves with really very little regard for others. Even if it's family."

There was no turning back now. They hired a secretary, found some salesmen, and built offices above the steel plant on Sam Cooper's property, which they decorated with the latest in office decor–wooden office furniture and a chocolate brown shag rug. Cooper Funding was open for business.

The company took off immediately. They quickly branched out, diversifying into funding anything that qualified as income-producing equipment, from printing presses to mainframe computers. With constant expansion and spectacular growth, there was no time to look for meaning in life. There was only time to take the next step forward. At 21 years old, Mel Cooper was married and out of the house. By 25, he was running a funding company. By 26, he had started M. Cooper Motor Leasing, then Cooper Equities. By 28 he was directing a multi-million-dollar family of companies.

"I was in a race. I wanted to finish first from everybody. I wanted to get married first, I wanted to have my kids first, by the time I was 25, I wanted to be finished with the whole thing, and obviously I didn't know what I was doing."

"The jobs were not fulfilling to me, they were just a stepping stone to the next step. I always thought that you've got to climb up a ladder." Mel's life was characterized by total focus on getting up that ladder. Everything he did was becoming a means to an end. It didn't matter what he financed or to whom he lent money, as long as it was a good deal.

Moving so quickly, it didn't occur to Mel he might be losing sight of some important details, like the fact that many of his finance deals came from the sanitation business. It was an industry increasingly associated with organized crime, and under constant surveillance by the FBI.

By the 1970s, carting was controlled by the Mafia. The closer Mel got to the guys he did business with, the more he came under the scrutiny of the law enforcement officials watching them. Mel didn't think about it. He moved forward, towards an increasingly explosive mixture of risk and opportunity.

4

COOPER AND THE CARTMEN

Sam Cooper's container division, Kleen-tainer Corp., made five-, six-, seven-, and eight-yard steel containers. While Leach, a manufacturer of "rear loading refuse collection bodies"–a fancy name for garbage trucks–supplied commercial trash collectors with trucks, the Coopers had taken the bold step of producing uniquely large containers. Everyone in the carting industry wanted them.

Their industry-wide access meant the family's finance business, Cooper Funding, was first in line to offer financing to almost every carting company in New York. And in the 1970s and '80s, that meant Mel Cooper was doing business with a different kind of family enterprise–the organized crime families that dominated garbage collection in New York.

While New York City takes care of residential sanitation, private companies compete to remove commercial trash. This competition began in 1956, when New York City privatized the hauling of commercial waste. This quickly put New York City and Long Island's commercial trash collection or "carting" into the hands of hundreds of small, family-owned businesses, mostly run by Italian Americans. These small carting companies organized themselves around legitimate trade associations which were quickly infiltrated by organized crime. Commercial carting provided a low-profile, small-business environment that turned out to be perfect for rackets like bid rigging, protection, extortion, and price inflation.

The Genovese, Gambino, and Lucchese organizations dominated sanitation. Trash haulers had no choice but to respect the rules of the Mafia-run sanitation associations and unions, and participate in the cartel known as the Property Rights system.

Under the Property Rights system, each carter exclusively owned a collection route. That route and all the stops along the way were his alone to work or sell. Customers could not change carters, shop for prices, or bid out work. From the biggest corporation to the smallest storefront, they were married to the carter assigned to them, and divorce was not an option. The carter could charge whatever he wanted for the route within the guidelines of the cartel, making New York City trash collection prices the highest in the country.

The cartmen paid fees to various trade associations who, in turn, made sure no one stepped out of line. Nonmembers were kept out of the game, and except for the occasional garbage truck that went up in flames or some beaten drivers, by the 1970s there was little resistance to the system. The mob had total control.

Customers who didn't play along faced the threat of labor disruption. A strike by the drivers meant trash would pile up on the customer's sidewalk for as long as it took to rekindle enthusiasm for the cartel-assigned service. When that didn't work, there was the spectacle of rotting garbage dumped in front of their premises, vandalism, or a note or phone call inquiring about the welfare of the customer's children. The ultimate penalty – death – was reserved for local carters and family members who tried to buck the system; men like Robert Kubecka and Donald Barstow who were murdered in 1989 for refusing to respect the cartel, and for taking their complaints to law enforcement authorities.

In this atmosphere, actual waste disposal itself was often a sham, as significant amounts of toxic materials found their way into New York's rivers, landfills, and dumps.

Mel Cooper got along well with his mostly Italian customers. Even as far back as CBS Leasing, it was Mel who knew how to talk to customers while his partners Barry and Sidney handled the back office.

It's not that Mel was tough. He had been in Jewish day schools and Yeshiva all his life, where a rough day at school meant getting heckled at a spelling bee. And though there were gangs in East New York, Mel did not participate in them. But his adolescent years running the car service in Bedford-Stuyvesant, selling motorcycles, and peddling shirts from the trunk of his Lincoln had made him streetwise. It didn't take him long to learn how things worked in the sanitation business.

"There's a sanitation association, and there's the head of that association. The head of the association is the one that dictates how much routes should cost, who's going to take routes, who's going to get routes, who's going to be able sell the routes, and the association gets money back. There was a guy in charge of the association, Jimmy, and this is the way the whole thing runs. Anybody that had a problem would go to Jimmy to resolve it."

Jimmy–James "Jimmy Brown" Failla–was a capo in the Gambino family and President of the Association of Trade Waste Removers of Greater New York for over thirty years. It was Jimmy Brown who managed disputes and conflicts, and functioned like the chief judge of a trash court meting out justice, until he was convicted of conspiracy to commit murder in 1994.

Mel knew Jimmy Brown and Bernard Adelstein, president of Teamsters Union Local 813, which represented drivers. He knew Sal Avellino, Lucchese family member who, with Lucchese boss Tony "Ducks" Corallo, controlled the Private Sanitation Industry Association of Nassau/Suffolk. Mel knew "Matty the Horse" Ianniello, underboss in the Genovese family and owner of Consolidated Carting. From National Carting to Rosedale Carting whose owners would become notorious in the '90s for toxic waste dumping on New York's Belt Parkway, Mel Cooper did business with them all.

Mel's take on this is strictly practical. "It's business. I'm in the business of selling containers, I'm selling processors. Financing their trucks, selling them trucks." According to Mel, his involvement did not go deeper than this. He sold and financed equipment, period. He didn't do favors, he didn't make unsecured loans. And as with other customers, he didn't let anyone skip payments.

And yet while not directly involved with Mafia business, he certainly became acquainted. "You can't help it. You sit down and a lot of time you'll see certain people, and we couldn't really sell because we were already backed up eight months, and so I was just there bullshitting with these guys. I'd make my rounds, and I'd hear, this is going on, that's going on. They might go over business about this family or that family, and things would come up."

Mel learned who to talk to if a carting company was not paying. He overheard things that made him a valued bearer of news at the bullshitting sessions. "I had a product that was in great demand because our containers were like the Cadillac of containers, so I was always welcome. And because they knew I would go around to all the cartmen, they wanted to hear, what did the other guy say, or what's going on with this one or that one. Because it's still competition."

Mel delivered more than just gossip. He was smart and had a knack for spotting the legitimate potential of any business situation. After he officially launched Cooper Funding, Mel became drawn to money-making opportunities offered by these acquaintances. "I wanted to take their connections and turn them into legitimate benefits."

When someone needed an on-the-books loan for a legitimate business venture, they could go to Mel. One wiseguy would introduce him to the next, who might need financing for a fleet of trucks or a container. Mel became particularly friendly with Victor "Little Vic" Orena, a capo in the Colombo family. Vic observed Mel's instincts for uncovering profitable business opportunities, and he introduced Mel to various associates including Tommy Gambino, Carmine "the Snake" Persico, and others.

Says Mel, "Vic was very modern in certain ways, he wanted to get himself involved in legitimate businesses. With his connections, he could very easily help my business grow." Little Vic was only a few years older than Mel, and was one of the more enterprising, up-and-coming young Mafia captains. He was moving beyond the classic Cosa Nostra enterprises like bookmaking, protection, and loansharking, into more sophisticated areas. Later, Little Vic would later become family boss while Persico was in prison. It was Vic who helped set off the bloody Colombo family war of 1991 that killed at least ten people.

"Many times I offered to try to put something legitimate together. They had access to a lot of different things and businesses. But instead of thinking, how can I swing the law, sneak, or smuggle, I was sitting down and saying, 'Listen, you could take the same business, and we can do all the financing, millions of dollars, and you could make a nice commission." So I was trying to put them into something legitimate.

"Like one of the accounts that Vic had was a certain trucking company. Today, I think that company is one of the biggest truckers around. The owner was a good friend of Vic's. We helped turn this guy into a business with 400 trucks, which is a huge amount. We financed his first two trucks in the '70s. Each truck is like $90,000, then you got trailers. The guy had warehouses in different parts of the country. He started with two trucks and the reason he got so big, in my opinion, was he got 'introduced.' He didn't just knock on doors and try to get business. He was put into it and Vic introduced me to him.

The other one was Consolidated Carriers owned by Tommy Gambino in the garment center. He had some good routes. There's a classic example of how to make money in the trucking business when you can't lose.

"My stuff with Orena was all legitimate. He was introducing me to finance deals on which he made a commission." And like any good salesman servicing an account, when the customer called, Mel came running.

"Vic would say 'okay, I'll meet you at such and such a restaurant. That's where all his friends were. He'd say 'I have to see you in an hour, I have something.' So you gotta go. Or 'I'll meet you in two hours at Monte's on Carroll Street,' so you go to Monte's on Carroll Street, that's where they all hang out, that's where Junior is, and Allie Boy, and that's where the whole Colombo gang normally hangs out, otherwise we would meet at Stella's in Queens, which is also an Italian restaurant. It's always 'I'll meet you there at 8 o'clock' and he would typically walk in an hour late at best, and there were a few people waiting, and it's like a whole goddamn ritual that I never cared for. The more I could stay away from these meetings, the more I liked it. These meetings, to me, were a waste of time. I could accomplish the same thing that we accomplished in three meetings in a ten-minute phone call."

Once there, however, there was no walking away. "They didn't just sit there and discuss crimes. It was like, okay, we're all friends, and Vic would pay for the dinner, so it would make everybody feel there's a certain allegiance. It's all part of a whole scene, you meet, everybody's together, these guys are doing this, they're doing that, and of course if you have a problem, Vic would like you to come and tell him about your problem. That's something I'd try to shy away from as well because you never finish paying for that."

Mel frequently found himself in the company of Colombo family boss Carmine Persico Jr., who built a reputation as one of the most ruthless figures in New York's Mafia. "Vic was shrewd, but when I spoke to Junior–there was a guy you definitely don't want to owe a favor to. Vic is one thing, and Vic is not a pushover, but this guy Junior will make Vic look like a nursery schoolteacher."

"Junior Persico invited me up to his ranch one time, which is the furthest place I would want to be. It's upstate someplace, where he had horses. I never went. That guy, he's got the right name. 'The Snake.'" Which leads Mel to his general take on the world that thrived in 1970s New York: "When it comes to wiseguys," says Cooper, "there's a touch of psycho in all of them.

"They can't take their minds off the streets. They can't see a situation and keep it on a correct track. In order for them to see benefits, it's got to be turned into a pile of shit. In fact, the one thing I found interesting is these guys had tremendous entrees into business, but they had such tunnel vision that they could only see the stuff that was crooked, that didn't have a straight line to it. But if they just looked at what they had… In other words, I was able to see what they had and what they could turn it into.

"On the other hand, some of them are more brains than brawn. They're all quite smart in their own way. They're all quick and they have their own justice system, they know their own laws, they're very sharp at cornering a situation. They know the street."

Mel got to know Sonny Franzese, powerful underboss in the Colombo family and an object of obsession for the Justice Department. He was even better acquainted with his son, Michael Franzese, self-described "Yuppie Don" who was also a capo in the Colombo family. Michael was famous for his Monday night parties at a club called Casablanca out on Long Island, to which Mel Cooper had an open invitation. Cooper in turn helped Franzese obtain financing for his Mazda dealership. "I wanted to keep a certain distance, although sometimes they make it difficult."

"Michael had a business in Long Island. We had our office in Lake Success. As it turned out, someone from Franzese's circle got in touch, and said he's interested in doing some financing on a dealership.

"He called me a lot with different things and introduced me to different people who needed financing. Financing was a common denominator between him and other people."

Introducing legitimate money-making opportunities to most of Mel's Mafia customers did not turn out to be as easy as he had hoped. Cooper's instincts and observations told him this was a dangerous world, and worse, an unprofitable one. Still, a side of him was attracted by the action, the bravado, and above all, the cash flow.

This push and pull was best embodied in Mel's relationship with a man named Joe Lombardi of Citywide Sanitation in Brooklyn, whom Cooper describes as "a business associate who wanted to be a pal but was not a pal."

Joe Lombardi brought Mel finance deals from other garbage men, friends, and knockaround guys. The deals were not big but they were on the up and up, and Joe was worth the price of admission. Recalls Mel, "He did some crazy, crazy things. He went with his truck one day to Canal Street where they have the diamond stores. He hooked up the back of his truck with a cable to a second story window, and they pulled a safe right through the window. This was a guy that wouldn't think twice about beating the hell out of somebody, but if he was driving his car and he saw an injured bird on the side, he'd stop the car immediately and go pick it up and take it to a vet.

"Joe Lombardi brought in business from garbage guys, and one day they brought in a bakery deal. We made an appointment to go meet these people at the bakery. So we're driving down New Utrecht Avenue in Brooklyn, and I think we made a U-turn, and all of a sudden five or six detectives in different cars converge on my car, and they jumped out of the cars with the guns pointing at the car and they said 'Get your hands up.' So I put my hands on the roof, and meanwhile, this idiot is doing something under the dashboard, he's fumbling around under the dashboard doing I don't know what, while they're were screaming to put our hands on the car. I said 'What the hell are you doing, put your hands up.' So they ended up coming over, they handcuffed us right away, and at first I thought, My God, they're really cracking down on traffic violations.

"I didn't know what the hell was going on. Anyway, it turns out they had a warrant out for him for hitting his wife or his girlfriend in Jersey, so they took us both to the precinct, they let me go. They kept him, and I think, the next day or two I spoke to him. But the first thing I thought was, my God, all this for a U-turn."

One of the problems with canvassing a Mafia cartel for business was that the industry was under investigation by the FBI. Mel's business connections with New York's wiseguys did not go unnoticed.

"They knew my name from early on because of me going around to these different garbage companies that they always had under surveillance. So my name got around. They keep files on everybody. And they had files on many of the carting companies that I went around to for years, so sure, they had pictures and write-ups and everything." Mel was not troubled.

But he was more deeply involved than he realized. Cooper had begun to adopt the norms of the organized crime families he did business with, one being that there are always two ways of doing things, the legitimate way and the illegitimate shortcut. Call it a growing sense of amorality–a detachment from the laws that make other people think twice, or too much time doing business with guys like Joe Lombardi and Little Vic–but like his Mafia clientele, it was increasingly easy for Mel to bend the rules.

"I definitely think there was some groundwork laid by doing business with the sanitation industry. You can't get from here to all the way over there..."–and by "there" Mel means his conviction for loansharking–"... without starting to walk first." Increasingly, rules were something one followed at one's convenience. Opportunity became opportunism.

By the end of the 1970s, Mel was one of the top financiers to the carting industry. "With Cooper Funding, not only was I financing the cartmen when they bought their trucks and equipment, their containers, we would also help them refinance their equipment to buy routes. We raised money for them to be able to buy routes. So we were a funder of routes with creative financing."

Because of the Property Rights system, a garbage route was extremely valuable. "If someone wanted to sell their route, it sold at forty or fifty to one, for one stop. If a stop brought in a thousand dollars a month, that stop was worth forty or fifty thousand dollars. If you have a hundred stops, you have a big route, so this was a very profitable business. These are millionaires, everyone that owned a truck and had a route was worth millions of dollars – but it was worth that because there was protection. You think about people in the garbage business and say, 'he's just a garbage man,' but these guys drove around in Rolls Royces and had magnificent homes and boats."

Banks were not enthusiastic about entering this world. Sanitation was a gray area where too many questionable practices played central roles on a carting company's financial statement. You can't put extortion and price-fixing on a balance sheet. The gray area became Mel's specialty.

He worked out any number of deals to help the sanitation industry purchase routes and equipment using methods normal banks eschew. Cooper began to leave certain conditions unwritten; exaggerate assets; loan money for the purchase or sale of equipment that ultimately never changed hands; use collateral that didn't exist. Cooper claims most deals were fundamentally legitimate, but the Justice Department did not see it that way.

In 1973, and again in 1976, the FBI investigated Cooper Funding, issuing subpoenas to Bankers Trust, Chemical Bank, and National Bank of North America to review records regarding Cooper Funding's leases. After reviewing Mel's relationships with various banks as well as over 400 Cooper Funding documents, the FBI linked Cooper to major organized crime figures within the Colombo and Gambino families. No charges were ever filed. In the 1985 exposé, Poison for Profit: The Mafia and Toxic Waste in America, Alan Block and Frank Scarpitti call Cooper Funding an "organized-crime-backed equipment leasing operation" and a "front for mob loansharking in the waste industry." Mel Cooper was referred to as "the notorious front man."

Through it all, Mel insists he had no relationships with these men beyond finance and leasing. If his customers were not always above board in the use of his funds, it was not his problem. If someone obtained $50,000 to buy a garbage truck and that money ended up distributed as "street money" – loanshark loans – it was not his affair. Apparently, more than once, that's exactly what happened.

"There is hardly a significant carting firm linked to organized crime …that did not do business with Mel Cooper," Block and Scarpitti conclude. "Indeed there is hardly one which didn't have its hands in the toxic waste business so far reviewed that wasn't a Cooper client or partner. Put all that together, and one wonders why the FBI investigation into the affairs of Mel Cooper was put into an almost interminable holding pattern."

While the government, the FBI, and a few enterprising journalists were busy trying to figure out why someone named Mel Cooper seemed to appear Zelig-like at every significant investigation and surveillance event in the sanitation business, Mel Cooper was constructing a thriving finance business where loans arranged in documented packages with above-board lenders were being used for illegitimate gain, including the maintenance of the Property Rights system.

As far as Mel was concerned, his live-and-let-live philosophy of business was a winning formula. It was a business philosophy that would come back to haunt him.

5

THE BIG RUSH

By the end of the 1970s, Mel's business interests were unfolding in several directions. One path cut through the sanitation business and encompassed his deepening involvement with the Mafia. A second path traveled through the world of legitimate loans and leases brought in by Cooper Funding and other businesses. A third represented his foray into "trash technology" or the pyrolysis business.

Pyrolysis is a scientific process that attempts to convert trash into oil or gas. Incorporating the Latin word for "fire," pyrolysis is contemporary alchemy in which garbage is converted to oil or gas through a catalytic process using ultra-high heat without oxygen.

Putting his toe in the waters of venture capitalism, Cooper, together with four partners, invested in an early effort to exploit the process. They had heard about a company in Orange County, California, called Deko Energy. One of the main investors was the actor John Wayne. They flew out to California to see the pilot plant.

"There was a factory with a big sign that said 'Deko,' and you walked inside and there was a one-ton pilot plant that was actually in operation."

The plan was, once all the bugs were worked out, Deko would scale this model up to a 150-ton system. Recalls Mel, "I was standing around and taking photographs of the system and everything about it, and it was fascinating to see the garbage going in, oil going out. It was like there was a little monkey pouring oil at the end or something. And all of a sudden somebody puts their hands around my neck, and I turn around, and it's John Wayne. And I said 'How you doin'?' There was a big sign on the wall said, 'No Photographs,' and he saw me with the camera."

"You're not taking pictures, are you?" said Wayne.

"No, I'm waiting to take a picture with *you*," said Mel, and with that, the group marched outside for photos.

Mel and partners arranged to meet with the project's three decision-makers: a man named Orval Gould who built the system, John Chambers who had designed the system, and John Wayne, who was funding the project. "We ended up making a deal that required us to sell the first pyrolysis system in order to acquire the rights for the east coast. We formed a new company called BW Energy Systems." They issued five million shares of stock—a million for each of the five partners—and set up shop in New York City.

"Around the time we started BW, everything was really flourishing," recalls Mel. "We opened up Cooper Funding offices in California and Texas, we opened up the car leasing, we opened up the mortgages. Things were just booming."

By then, Cooper Funding had moved to its upscale corporate headquarters in Lake Success, having outgrown the offices above the factory on Seagal Street. Mel wanted the kind of place where million-dollar clients could feel at home. Lake Success offered the sophistication Mel craved: a gleaming black glass-and-steel building in a manicured industrial-park setting. No longer within shouting distance of a Bushwick steel factory, Cooper's neighbors on Marcus Avenue were law offices and real estate firms.

Mel's new office had a credit department, cubicles for fifteen salesmen, a conference room, and large offices for all the Cooper executives including an in-house lawyer. Mel was starting to look the part of the entrepreneur. The deals had grown bigger and now Mel financed everything from oil rigs to airplanes. By 1980 the Cooper family was poised to expand into real estate. But there were problems. As the business grew, Mel's personal life was falling apart.

In 1979 he learned his wife Miriam was having an affair. "I used to go to California and Texas a lot, and we also had an office in Puerto Rico. So

I used to travel. Once a month I would go to LA and spend a few days there." His wife was growing tired of a husband home only long enough to do laundry and start packing again. "During that period, she used to pick me up when I came in on the red-eye at Kennedy Airport, at 6 o'clock in the morning. Then after a number of months she asked me if it would be okay if I took a cab from the airport because it was really early for her. That was the first sign of things to come."

Seeing less and less of his wife, Mel suspected something was going on and he hired detectives. The youngest of their three children, David, was a baby at the time. Mel wanted to know what Miriam was doing with David when she took him out for hours at a time. "I got a call from the detective one day that she had gone to meet a friend. She got involved with a guy she knew before we were married." Mel was devastated. He saw his marriage turning into what he calls "a cheap five-cent novel." His previously pleasurable work life evolved into all-day agony, punctuated by reports from detectives on his wife's infidelities, and the lingering knowledge he would have to go home to unbearable tension. "I decided to confront him. I went out with my friends, and the guy was holding the baby, and we ended up dragging this guy out of the car. I took the baby away and gave him to my friend because he hardly had any clothes on and it was freezing out. It ended with Miriam taking the guy to the hospital."

In April of 1980, Mel left the house. In September, right after his older kids came home from summer camp, his wife called him up and said, "Come get your children." Mel got custody of his three children, now 3, 8, and 11 years old.

"I was with a girl at Guerney's Inn in Montauk. I got a call Sunday, saying that my wife had just dropped off the kids by my father's house in Long Island, saying she didn't want to see them again. So we took a drive over to my father's house from Montauk and I had a Mercedes convertible, and I put the three of them in the car and I drove to New York.

"I had a one-bedroom apartment on 72nd Street and Third Avenue. It was a Sunday, so we went upstairs. I knew I had to get some mattresses and stuff. Over the next couple of days I was able to get a housekeeper that was able to stay and watch them, and I registered them at the Park East Day School. We moved to an apartment in a building called the Solo Building, on 66th Street and Second Avenue, with a pool on the roof.

"My wife wanted her freedom. She claimed that she wasn't meant to be a mother. She didn't want to have to support them, she didn't want to be stuck taking care of them."

Adding to the stress, Mel had a bad feeling about his BW Energy deal. With his extensive connections in the sanitation industry, Mel had taken the lead in finding local trash companies willing to invest in the first pyrolysis plants. He sold the first plant to a conglomeration of garbage companies, and they had already built the first fifty-ton plant. But Mel had become so consumed by his collapsing marriage that he hadn't paid attention to his investments. He had placed the operation, a well-financed entity with endless potential, in the hands of partners who, Mel observed, spent more time and money on lunches, trips, and office décor than on business. They talked up projects in Puerto Rico, another near Kennedy Airport that would eventually allow the company to go public. But nothing ever materialized.

Meanwhile, after a few months with kids in the house, Mel could barely focus on work. "Everybody would be lining up at the door to come in and ask questions, and I'm sitting there staring at the ceiling." Cooper needed help.

All Mel's brothers and sisters were already involved in running some aspect of the family businesses. He would have to bring in someone from the outside. He recalled a few months earlier, at the end of 1980, one of Little Vic Orena's friends had referred a man named Jesse David Hyman to Cooper Funding.

Hyman was a dentist and he had come to Cooper for a loan to buy dental chairs. Jesse Hyman, or "Doc" as he was known, owned three dental clinics in Long Island, Manhattan, and Buffalo, and had developed a thriving practice, thanks to his dental contracts with various trade unions.

Jesse Hyman had visited Mel at Cooper Funding. Being men of similar ambition, background, and age–they were both in their late 30s–Mel and Doc had been impressed with each other. Doc even expressed interest in Mel Cooper's business. "If you'd ever like to do something together, call me," Jesse had said. Now, in desperation, Mel called Doc at his Long Island office.

Despite his nickname, "Doc" Hyman had already moved far beyond his career as a dentist. He had been putting together deals for ten years by the time he met Mel, and referred to himself as "a self-taught financier." He was especially adept at putting together large financing deals. In 1975 he had tried to buy La Hacienda, a Las Vegas hotel, from Allen Glick, on behalf of a group of investors who also happened to be members of organized crime families. With another group he had made a bid and purchased the Santa Fe Downs Racetrack in New Mexico. Shortly before he met Mel, Doc was involved in the purchase of The Westchester Premier Theater, famous for being the front for a huge racketeering scheme which used high-profile performers to attract investors. In 1978, he was the target of an FBI investigation into the laundering of organized crime money through his Buffalo Dental Clinic. He was linked to mobsters from coast to coast.

Mel and Jesse met again, this time to discuss how they might work together. "He had light freckles, curly hair, he was about 5 foot 11. He was dressed like a stockbroker and wore glasses." Doc projected confidence. And Mel liked what Jesse had to say; Doc could easily buy into Cooper Funding. One of Doc's more appealing qualities was that he had access to enormous amounts of money–always helpful in the funding business. The two men worked out a deal.

Doc Hyman would buy out Mel's father, uncle, and cousin. He would purchase their shares of Cooper Funding for $500,000 dollars. This was a significant amount of money in 1981, equivalent to $1.5 million in today's dollars.

In the process of making this deal, Mel learned something else: Jesse Hyman seemed to have unlimited access to union pension funds. Doc explained to Mel he had a relationship with a man named Forrest Bedell, founder of an investment company called Penvest. Since Jesse was not licensed in financial services, Doc was not allowed to handle or invest large institutional funds. He brought his financial clients to Penvest. Forest handled the money for him. Doc supplied the investment advice.

The money Doc would use to buy into Cooper Funding was Teamsters Union money. Mel had been in business long enough to know nobody has unlimited access to Teamsters pension funds without the help of friends–the same kind of friends Mel had made in the sanitation business.

Mel learned Doc Hyman's friend and partner in his investment efforts was Vincent "Jimmy" Rotondo, the Brooklyn Longshoreman's Union official, and the future namesake of Mel's indictment. Jimmy answered directly to John Riggi, boss of the DeCavalcante organization.

Jimmy worked behind the scenes in both Doc's investment projects and his dental clinics, bringing in the lucrative union dental contracts and making introductions to funding sources. They had worked together for years; Jimmy Rotondo opened doors that Doc could not have opened alone.

For some people this might have been troubling. Mel chose not to think about it. Doc had money. It wasn't Mel's affair where it came from. Mel applied the same principle that guided his relationships in the garbage business: don't look too closely, stick to business, and let denial do the rest.

In April of 1981, Doc became co-owner of Cooper Funding. Soon after, they changed the name of the company in honor of their new shared enterprise. They called it Resource Capital Group.

6

LOOK THE OTHER WAY

With Doc in the office, Mel found he could pay more attention to his three kids and their new living arrangements. Jesse Hyman eased into the business, making himself a well-liked presence not just in his executive capacity, but as a stabilizing influence throughout the business.

"Doc was an organizational type of guy," recalls Mel. "He was shrewd and knew how things worked. Doc liked problems, and he liked solving them." He was fair and generous when it came to resolving conflicts, and people throughout the organization welcomed him.

By the end of 1981, Mel and his sons had settled into their two-bedroom apartment on East 66th street. Even though he had a house full of kids, recalls Mel, "I was still very meticulous. Everything had to be just so. I remember I was growing orchids." Now, in addition to Mel's leather furniture, artwork, and plants, his apartment was full of toys, schoolbooks, and games. A housekeeper cooked their meals, and each morning she took the boys to school few blocks away.

"We used to go to shows and movies. We used to go to Brooks Brothers and get clothes for the kids. In the summer, we used to go on a boat I had in Long Island. It was called *Engulf and Devour*. I took the name from a Mel Brooks movie, *Silent Movie*." Mel was nothing if not consistent in his effort to dominate.

Now in his thirties, Mel's unspoken drama between himself, his mother, and his father continued. Every Sunday Mel stopped by his parents' house to bring his mother up to date on the latest developments in the business. Naomi's relationship with her son had deepened over the years as he fulfilled their shared vision. Some might say he was her favorite. Strong and smart, she egged Mel on to ever more daring feats in the world of finance.

Mother and son would sit on the couch in the living room, now in Lawrence Bay Park, and discuss the new companies Mel was setting up. His weekly updates barely masked his need for approval. Recalls Cooper, "She would say, 'Oh, that's terrific,' and she would look to have my father impressed, or get involved with me in different things I was doing. She would always want to find out what's new in business."

Appreciation was not forthcoming from Mel's father. According to Mel, his father would usually dismiss Mel's ideas, though he was happy to take credit when the opportunity came his way. "I used to take my father into a lot of the companies. It's interesting, we opened up probably four companies, and I had all my brothers and my sister and my uncle and my cousin working there, and we used to go to the synagogue and my father's friends would come over to him, and say 'Wow, you're really an incredible guy and you opened up these companies and your kids are all working for you, and it's really incredible,' and on and on, and he'd take the recognition, and a lot of times I'd be standing with him. And so this would bother me a little bit.

"I remember distinctly that the next company we opened up was Cooper Motor Leasing, I said 'No, we're going to make this M. Cooper motor leasing,' and this way when someone says, 'Hey Sam, that's really good what you did,' I could say, 'Hey, gee, how come it's M. Cooper Motor Leasing? It's interesting that we called it that, M. Cooper Motor Leasing.'"

Just as things began to stabilize, Mel received another blow. At his son's bar mitzvah, Mel noticed his mother slurring her words. Soon after, Naomi Cooper was diagnosed with ALS.

Her deterioration progressed quickly. Within a year, Naomi Cooper was confined to a wheelchair, unable to use her hands or stand up. She could hardly speak. ALS, or *amyotrophic lateral sclerosis*, is a neurodegenerative disease. It wastes the nerve cells of its victim, destroying those that control muscle movements. Eventually, muscle control is lost until involuntary functions like breathing and swallowing are affected, even while a sufferer's mind remains intact.

Seeing his mother and mentor reduced to helplessness was unbearable. Mel simply refused to believe he was powerless, even when faced with an incurable disease. If his collapsing marriage had been a blow that delivered him to utter distraction, his mother's illness became an obsession. Mel was determined to find a cure for her illness, and if he couldn't find a cure, he would find a relief. Anything to stop the slow annihilation.

During this time, Mel Cooper's only pleasure was the time he stole to work with Doc Hyman. To Mel, Doc had all: creativity, connections, ambition, plus a smooth demeanor Cooper lacked. He savored the company of his bright new partner. Mel could be rough when he chose to, boosting his pure Brooklyn accent to street-level intensity at a moments' notice. Doc was low-key with an easy manner. "Doc brought in funds, he helped implement things. Doc made life easier all around," recalls Mel.

Furthermore, Doc was turning out to be a maestro when it came to deal-making. Give him almost any set of players and circumstances, and he could produce a perfectly orchestrated symphony of interests. When Doc put a deal together everybody made money. "You couldn't say no to the guy. He knew how to put something together. He had so much creativity."

Which did not mean that they were the kind of deals you learn about in business school. While Mel already knew about Doc's Teamster connections, he learned the full nature of Doc's involvement with the Mafia gradually, over the course of meals, meetings, and more. He learned, for example, the degree to which Jimmy Rotondo was a silent presence in all Doc's activities.

Mel recalls, "Not too long after Doc came on board, he explained that Jimmy is his partner in the dental clinics. Not officially of course, but that's why he was able to get all these Teamster accounts. Jimmy brought them in."

Mel learned about Jimmy's power on New York's waterfront, how he dexterously managed a variety of interests between New York and New

Jersey. He used his position in the International Longshoreman's Association to determine who worked and who didn't, and what it would cost to keep the Union out of certain situations.

Like Doc, Jimmy enjoyed a reputation as a family man, a nice guy not particularly caught up in the fast life or involved in the partying that characterized New York City in the 1970s and 80s. According to one of his acquaintances, "He didn't run around at night, fool around with women, or keep a high profile. Jimmy was a gentleman."

Mel agrees. "He was more of a gentleman than The Snake, although they're all psychopaths. So it's just a question of what it takes to get to that level of their personality."

Jimmy Rotondo introduced Doc Hyman to influential union officials, including John Long, Secretary-Treasurer of Teamsters Local 804, and John Mahoney, Secretary-Treasurer of Teamsters Local 808, both in Queens. After Jimmy made the introductions, Jesse Hyman, the well-spoken professional, made his deals.

Doc occasionally took Mel with him to meetings with union officials. "Most of the time Doc went by himself, but I went with him one time, someplace by Northern Boulevard near the scrap yards. That's where the Union office was. Doc got out of the car, and he went in for a while and came out. He didn't advertise it, but he walked in with a package that I assume was cash. He definitely wasn't bringing him lunch. So many things were going on, this was just one of many, many things, and I was amazed at how he structured this whole thing to begin with.

"Doc felt that he was a man of power, and when he came in he was walking and talking like he had power, quiet power behind him, so he was able to say things, do things, have things done. He was a sharp guy. He wasn't ostentatious, he was not showy. He was conniving. He knew he had money because of who was behind him.

"A clear example is he wanted to come into the finance business with me, and he paid a lot of money. Where do you think that money came from? The people behind him. If it's good for them, it's good for him. He's done this in a lot in different situations, and it put him in a very strong position to negotiate. He was very confident about everything he wanted to do."

Mel was particularly impressed by Doc's relationship with Penvest.

Doc paid union officials kickbacks, and in exchange, they would let Doc Hyman and Jimmy Rotondo invest their pension money. But pension funds, by law, are not allowed to make loans to private individuals. For Doc and Jimmy to secure union funds, they had to first move it through a legitimate investment agent like Penvest.

Forrest Bedell was a classic, white-shoe investment expert, a serious, church-going man who had mastered every nuance of denial in order to get involved with Jess Hyman. He lived on Sutton Place, ran his investment company out of an office on Fifth Avenue, and since 1980, had convinced numerous investors to entrust their life savings to him.

In exchange for "taking Doc's advice," Forrest would get a percentage of the loan money he distributed for Doc, which he then used to make his own loans.

"Doc was very imaginative. I mean, he's the guy that comes up with these deals, and I used to laugh when I would sit there with him and Forrest. Doc would come up with a way where Forrest ends up with $300,000 for a loan he wants to make, and Doc arranges to get the money from the Teamsters to go into Forrest's investment fund, where Doc then borrows seven million."

Cooper explains, "Doc knew how to structure something, to give you a deal you can't refuse, in other words, he knows what Bedell wants. Forrest was looking to make some of his own conservative loans. So Doc would arrange for him to get a small piece, as long as Forrest arranges to send 90 percent of the money over to where Doc wanted. Doc would say, okay, if you lend thirty million dollars, we give back a million and you could lend that million. By the time this guy was finished he had to count his fingers."

Doc and Jimmy steered the loan money to Las Vegas hotels. Some of the older hotels like the Sands and the Dunes had a difficult time securing loans due to their history of close ties to organized crime. Penvest offered these hotels large loans at reasonable rates. Doc and Jimmy got a twofold return. First there were the "fees." Closing fees, management fees, broker's fees, and finder's fees add up to a lot on a thirty-million-dollar loan.

Then there were the unwritten conditions the borrowers had to meet. As a condition of each loan, Rotondo got to place people in certain key positions: casino jobs, head of coat check, bellhops, waiters, even chefs, for example. These inside positions, in turn, gave Jimmy access to a staggering number of rackets and schemes.

"I remember going to Las Vegas, and meeting with Morris Schenker, arranging for millions of dollars in mortgages for the Dunes Hotels, then arranging for people in different positions in exchange for a favorable rate. Everyone Jimmy and Doc put in there was able to give the Mafia entree into the Dunes."

The hotels got cash they needed to expand, and they got it at a low rate which they repaid–sometimes. Doc and Jimmy got substantial fees for the transactions, and a doorway into unending schemes. Forrest Bedell got his play money and fees. The union officials who steered their pension funds to Penvest got generous kickbacks. Says Mel, "These loans were a great deal for everyone involved. Doc and Jimmy got so much. It got skimmed off as they went. The unions who actually lent the money got the smallest interest you could get."

Says Mel, "They tried to dot the i's and cross the t's but it wasn't ethical anyway you looked at it." Still, almost everyone was happy, particularly the mob, who netted a nebbishy, red-haired Jewish dentist for a front.

The people who would ultimately pay for Doc's deals were the losers at the end of the line: the union members whose money was loaned at substandard rates with hefty fees extracted, and the hotel employees and union workers who were on the receiving end of shakedowns, extortion, loss of opportunity and seniority, and a host of other labor racketeering practices.

Even as he learned the details of Doc's connections to organized crime, Mel still had no idea of how deep those connections went. In fact, Doc's Mafia partnerships preceded Jimmy Rotondo by years. Doc was involved in racketeering schemes in Cincinnati, Cleveland, Buffalo, New Jersey, and New York, moving money and union contracts through his dental clinics with the help of kickbacks and bribes. He had been accused of arson, caught scamming lottery ticket sales, and been associated with a who's who of East Coast and Midwest mobsters, from Cleveland hitman John "Curly" Montana to Buffalo's Carl Rizzo. Rizzo helped Hyman get his start with union dental contracts. Anthony Dominic Liberatore, another Hyman associate, was a player in the Cleveland mob, involved in labor union corruption, murder, bomb-making, and more. Jesse Hyman had even met with Meyer Lansky to discuss legalized gambling in Florida.

"Doc was entrenched up to his neck when he came to me," says Mel. "He was plugged in pretty good."

Cooper was no boy scout after ten years of dealing with New York's carting industry. He could talk business with any wiseguy in the tri-state area. Mel didn't hesitate to stretch the truth to obtain funds or make arrangements that went well beyond what could be put on paper. He knew the financing game so well he could put together a loan with Monopoly money and make it look real. Some thought he was already a crook, given his Cosa Nostra clientele.

But through it all, Mel claims most of his loans were basically legal, with legal interest. He may have behaved unethically at times, but as Mel puts it, "unethical is not necessarily illegal." And he had his principles: he didn't like violence, he didn't get involved in favors, and he stuck to his main passion: making money.

On the contrary, Mel claims, "Before Doc, we disliked having anything to do with wiseguys as far as business goes. It just doesn't work." Referring to the mob's idea of partnership, says Cooper, "You can't go into a business with them. You tell the guy, 'here, you're my partner,' and then you have to give him 90% of what you're doing. I mean, it's just not profitable.

"I had meetings with Little Vic, so I had already learned by that time, the less I have to do with them the better. But there are times when you want to be able to say, 'Hey, can you help me out with this situation,' if you can't avoid saying that. If you can avoid it, then you're better off avoiding it, because that one favor is going to cost you. It's never forgotten. But I had my lesson before I met Doc. I learned I don't want to go there unless it's really necessary. It was always my intention to stay as far away as possible. Keep it platonic, if you will.

"But there's no question about it, there's certain things you can do with that power behind you, making it easier to march into something. There's doors that open that wouldn't otherwise open, that'll open easier, and other doors that wouldn't open at all, but that you can go into now, just by mentioning a name."

Mel and Doc's nuanced approach to their mob connections made for business principles built on shifting sand. Their mixture of pragmatism and denial allowed them to run their business with a fair amount of unchecked self-deception. Both men had a history of playing fast and loose with the law and they got off on the excitement of seeing what they could get away with. They loved risk, and the longer they got away with rule-bending, the greater the risks they were willing to take. It was a match made in heaven; Doc's daring and Mel's drive; Jesse's connections and Mel's ambition.

Doc began to use teamster money to finance some of Resource Capital Group's loans, the more difficult ones that banks would not approve. In their first year together as Resource Capital Group, Ltd., with this new source of funds, Mel and Doc made several high-risk loans from $500,000 to $1.5 million each. At the same time, they continued to broker loans for Cooper Funding's conventional clientele, relying on an assortment of banks for the money. Doc and Jimmy continued to funnel money through Penvest.

Says Mel, "I remember how Forrest looked when I first met him, and I remember how he looked a couple of years later, when he lent out all kinds of money, and people went back to him and said 'where's the money?' This guy was just a wreck. It was a comical scene to see how this guy looked like he aged twenty years."

The Teamsters would never see most of their money returned. The funds dwindled or disappeared entirely. The other investors in Penvest, all hardworking New Yorkers who had trusted Forrest Bedell with their life savings, would lose it when, one after another, Penvest's loans collapsed. Forrest Bedell would eventually be hurled into Chapter 11, along with an FBI investigation. But first, Mel and Doc were about to take a risk that would change their lives forever.

7

ENTER THE RABBIS

Doc and Mel never called what they were doing "loansharking." At Resource Capital Group, it had lots of other names: Emergency Money, Special Loans, Short-Term Loans, Interim Money. In fact, initially, these loans were not different from what many credit cards, check-cashers, payday lenders, and other short-term lenders offer: ultra-high-interest loans designed to last only a few weeks, thus evading the definition of usury while charging exorbitant rates.

Whatever Mel chose to call his illegal loans on any given day, they started when a man named Don Kulick came to Mel Cooper for a loan. The two men had done business before. Three years earlier, Cooper Funding had lent Don $75,000 for his lumber business, Jo-al Lumber, in Suffolk County. This time Don wanted to open a restaurant in Soho.

"He comes in and says he wants to borrow a quarter of a million dollars for a place called 'Wings on Wooster Street.' He had drawings and everything, and it was going to be a grand opening, and they were going to have actors and actresses and garment center people go there. And the whole place is going to be pink."

Kulick showed Mel the floor plans; the place would have two floors, a huge dining room, and a piano bar with a pink grand piano.

In his mid-forties, with graying hair and horn-rimmed glasses, Don Kulick was hyper, hustling, and hardworking, and Mel had always been impressed by his industriousness. There were other investors in Wings on Wooster, Howard Finger and Michael Asen. Mel got the group financing for a quarter-million dollars at a conventional rate of 9 percent a year.

But by October of 1981, they needed more money. Kulick had no more collateral and no way to guarantee the risky loan. Mel said he would give Don the money he needed but it might have to come at a higher-than-normal interest rate—*if* he could find the funding.

This offer was not lost on a part-time employee named Chaim Gerlitz. As Don and Mel discussed the matter, Gerlitz hovered in the doorway of Mel's office, waiting for a break in the cascade of activity.

A chubby man in his early fifties, Gerlitz worked as a salesman for Resource Capital Group, hoping to supplement his modest income as a religious teacher. He had been ordained as a rabbi in Jerusalem where he was born, but now taught Hebrew school and served as a cantor at synagogue in Great Neck. He was no stranger to business, however, and had worked in economics for the Israeli government. Chaim fit in a few days a week selling the funding and brokerage services of Cooper Funding.

Gerlitz had come to Mel Cooper through another employee, also a Jewish scholar. Mel had a symbiotic relationship with New York's ultra-orthodox community, one that mirrored all his loving bonds: money was the hub around which relationships revolved. Cooper would set up profitable business arrangements for rabbis and *Chassids*. The religious men would work for Cooper, doing sales and making deals under Mel's guidance. Mel constantly found innovative ways to involve religious men in his business, to their benefit and his. Later in life, in the telecom business, Mel would be the first to issue certain Chassidic communities their own long-distance phone cards, in an act of *Tzedakah* or charity, giving away free long distance minutes that could then be refilled at a profit, which Mel would share with the rabbis who distributed them. Cooper's philosophy of charity is captured by the Chinese proverb, "Give a man a fish, and he'll eat for a day. Teach him how to fish and he'll eat forever." Mel taught rabbis how to fish.

Cooper gave Chaim Gerlitz a cubicle in the center of the sales division. From there, Gerlitz made calls, sent letters, and mailed out what he referred to as "paraphernalia."

Gerlitz was persistent and likeable, and his fractured Israeli-accented

English was never an obstacle. But despite his efforts, after five months he hadn't made a single sale though he had almost closed several multi-million-dollar deals that ultimately fell through. Since he was working for commission only, "almost" equaled failure.

In September of that year, Mel had called Gerlitz into his office, and said he had one more chance to make it at Resource Capital Group. Mel explained he planned to offer a new product: Emergency Loans. These loans would be offered to customers who had applied for a regular loan, but needed money fast while Cooper Funding tried to place their loan with a regular bank.

Says Gerlitz, "He realized that I am becoming a little bit frustrated. He told me that they are going to create a new department. There was a variety of real estate, new ventures, restaurants—this kind of people, who are looking for loans—and in order to hold them down so they should not go to any other place, the emergency loans will help them to continue to stay in business."

The Emergency Loans would last from six to sixteen weeks. There would be collateral, a second mortgage on a house or a car. All Chaim had to do was bring in investors willing to fund the loan. In return, Gerlitz would get half of the 10% closing fee. Having overheard Don Kulick, a respectable looking fellow, say he needed money fast, Gerlitz saw a chance to leap head first into Mel's new venture.

"Mel," said Gerlitz, "Excuse me, can I talk to you for a minute?" His eyes were wide.

Cooper got up from his chair and asked Kulick to wait, he'd be right back. Out in the hall, Gerlitz presented his idea. "I was overhearing that you need money quickly. How much do you need?"

"The guy needs $75,000," said Mel.

"I have people in Great Neck that would maybe lend the money short term," said Gerlitz, with a single-minded intensity Mel had never seen before.

"How much would they charge?"

"Let me research it. Maybe 10%? It's a friend, and he's looking around for a good investment." Gerlitz explained the friend had written a book and made a lot of money. "He's also working at the synagogue." This clinched it for Mel.

"Let me talk to Don and see if he's interested."

Gerlitz added in a whisper, as Mel stepped back into his office, "You have to guarantee it as well." This meant Mel would have to guarantee the investors would get their money back. Thinking quickly, Mel calculated what it would take to get Don Kulick his money.

Back at his big desk, Mel said to Kulick, "Something came up and I think I can get the money. But maybe you should go somewhere else, this is very expensive money." Given what he would need to charge, Mel was unsure whether Don's reaction would be interest or outrage.

"How much is it?" asked Don.

Mel explained the formula: The money would cost 20% for a period of ten weeks, or 2 percent a week.

"I'll take it," said Don.

"He didn't even think about it," recalls Mel. "Within a week and a half, we closed the loan. There was a lien put on Kulick's house for the money." $75,000 went to Don Kulick for Wings on Wooster. Immediately, the promised interest and fees started rolling in.

Chaim Gerlitz's friend turned out to be a rabbi as well. Rabbi Lionel J. Toledano was a world-renowned scholar, a highly respected expert in the history of persecuted Jews who had escaped Europe by way of South America. He had written several popular books on the subject, and often took tour groups to Argentina, Cuba, and Brazil to explore the Jewish culture that thrived there. Rabbi Toledano also worked at a synagogue in Great Neck.

Says Mel, "After the first $75,000 loan from Rabbi Toledano, very quickly Kulick came back and said he needs another $100,000. Gerlitz asked Rabbi Toledano to come in and talk to us, just to talk about the business, see our office, our customers, just to generally get an idea of who we were." The next day, Rabbi Lionel J. Toledano sat in Cooper Funding's offices, listening as Mel Cooper described the sure-fire return the Rabbi and his wife, Leah, could make as backers of Cooper Funding's totally legal emergency loans.

Mel explained to Rabbi Toledano his calculations were based on short-term, high-interest rates that would return something for everybody. The loans would be secured with houses and property. Best of all, Mel explained, the interest payments would come every week. There would be no waiting around for a long-term payoff. This was the kind of investment that would put money in the rabbi's pocket right from day one.

Mel showed the Toledanos the loan documents, the contracts and paperwork, assuring them it was a legitimate investment. He advised them to show the paperwork to a lawyer. The Toledanos showed it all to their lawyer, who, after several calls to Mel, gave his blessings to the undertaking.

The Toledanos would be rewarded with 1 percent a week or over $4,000 a month. Again, Mel would take his cut of 10% from the loan, and the loan would supposedly last ten weeks. By limiting loans to ten weeks, they would remain well within the legal limits of funding. Gerlitz would get 5 percent of the closing fees, which included a variety of charges, fees, incentives, and commissions. But no matter how he broke it down, Cooper knew this rate skirted the legal guidelines.

In 1982, New York State permitted interest charges of up to 25 percent a year, a little less than half a percent a week. Don Kulick's loan of 2 percent interest a week would add up to almost 20 percent over two months, a high but not outrageous sum considering his loan was designed to be short-term. But projected over a year, this amounted to 104 percent, making it illegal in the extreme.

"I was in the finance business long enough to know it could be questionable," Mel admits, adding, "Actually, I knew it, I knew it right from the beginning. I knew it was usury, according to the lending limits. But I had experience with this stuff, going back. I was involved in certain loans years before this, when I was living in Lawrence, and there was a gas station there. I was involved in something similar when I was making certain smaller loans at high interest rates. This was not my first rodeo. But I thought it was basically taking real estate as security, and the no one would be threatened because I was taking real estate as security. It was safe.

Cooper took the package to Don Kulick who again said yes. Kulick desperately needed the money for food, payroll, and contractors. He was confident Wings' plentiful cash flow would cover him. Cooper didn't tell the rabbis their investment was potentially illegal. Instead, Mel drew up papers for a conventional loan of 24 percent a year, and left the actual conditions of the loan – the weekly 2 percent interest payments – off the documents. The interest payments were an unwritten understanding between himself and Don Kulick, sealed with a handshake.

Mel made sure a boatload of collateral was signed over in the loan documents, including what is known as a *chattel mortgage* for all the property that belonged to Wings. If the restaurant defaulted, all their fixtures, chairs, china, and silverware, as well as a mortgage on one of the partner's houses, would go to Lionel and Leah Toledano. Mel and Doc also took a 15 percent stake in the restaurant. Cooper brought a lawyer to the closing, and he and Kulick signed the official, if imaginative, loan documents.

"If I had used my head I would have walked away," says Cooper. "That year, Cooper Funding, with its main focus on income-producing equipment, did over a hundred million dollars in sales. The car leasing division, the mortgage division, and the truck leasing were going strong.

"But this was an opportunity to make a loan and take equity in a restaurant. It was a nice diversification from where we were in the drab money business, lending money for equipment. It was exciting, this type of loan. But if I would have had three minutes to think about it, I should have walked away from that, right from the first loan. I didn't need this, I just didn't need it."

But Mel didn't walk away. Gerlitz recalls the day Rabbi Toledano came to Cooper Funding with the money for Don Kulick's second loan. "It was on a Friday, I remember. He came in with two checks from Shearson/American Express for $100,000."

The transaction with Don was a formal and professional exchange attended by Mel Cooper, Jesse Hyman, Lionel and Leah Toledano, and one of Mel's in-house lawyers. At this perfunctory meeting, Leah Toledano, a short woman with black hair, handed Don Kulick the checks she had tucked away in her purse. The paperwork was signed with all security designated to Lionel and Leah Toledano, and 5 percent of the loan money going to Chaim Gerlitz as part of the closing fees. Thus Mel Cooper found himself in the loansharking business with a cantor, a rabbi, and a rabbi's wife.

When you're loaning money at illegal interest rates, it's not done with billing statements mailed on company stationery. When you're picking up $2,700 in interest a week, someone comes to get it. That someone was

Al Albenga.

Oscar "Al" Albenga or "Al Senior" as he was known around the office, was a friend of Little Vic Orena. Vic had sent him to Mel Cooper. Though Mel didn't like doing favors, he usually found work for friends of Little Vic. They were guys who knew how to get things done.

Al's job at Cooper Funding concerned the overland truck business. It was his job to sign up the drivers, make arrangements to bring in the trucks, and handle all transactions between Cooper and the drivers.

"That was his cup of tea," says Mel. "He wasn't very sophisticated in the leasing business and didn't have a great understanding of finance. He came across more like a street guy from Brooklyn. And he had a background of street guy from Brooklyn."

Now living in Massapequa, Long Island, Al had worked for Local 3 of the Electrician's Union but had injured his back. He needed work that did not involve lifting equipment. He had been a "knockaround guy" most of his life with arrests and acquittals over the years for loansharking and gambling. Short, bald, about fifty years old, Al was as tough as they come, yet he also found the mob world something of a joke. Like Mel, he ridiculed it even as he benefited from his connections.

Al used his tough guy act for convenience, particularly when it came to collecting money. But says Mel, "He was not as official as he tried to impress on you. Not like a regular wiseguy. He was more of an actor."

He knew what to say to get people to pay, and this led to his increasingly central role after Cooper Funding became Resource Capital Group. "Al was in charge of collecting the weekly money from the loans. He would make sure that the monies came in as they were due."

Albenga's job collecting interest became increasingly time-consuming, and with Mel's permission, he brought in his son to help. Alan Junior was 27 years old when he came to work at Cooper Funding, where he served as driver, messenger, and more. It was Alan Junior's job to pick up the interest payment at Wings on Wooster.

Al Senior's tactics consisted of ruthless persistence and veiled threats. At Mel's direction, there was little tolerance for late payments, and this philosophy was passed on to Alan Junior, who was more polished, but who would go back as many times as necessary in the course of a day until a customer's weekly interest payment was made.

"Albenga and his son were not there to dust the windows, they were there to collect the money, so they had their previous tactics of having talked to people. But in these cases, they knew that these loans are all protected by real estate and collateral, and we don't have to use any tactics other than a lawyer."

Recalls Nick Mercorella, the former manager of Wings on Wooster, "Alan used to come in on Friday night to pick up the money. It wasn't always available when he came in. He would come back the second time. Sometimes he would come back the third time. Sometimes he would wait until we had cash available or until the messenger came from downtown.

"I felt it did not look good in that type of establishment I was running, that people were well aware that the gentleman was waiting for money… and I did not want my customers to see that."

Others noticed Alan Jr.'s presence. It even made it into a New York City guidebook called *New York Underground*, by Sharon Churcher, published in 1985 as a guide to the seamier side of the city. It included Wings on Wooster, noting "A thug attired in jeans and a T-shirt appeared regularly at Wings to collect the vig, distracting some diners from their boneless braised duck in raspberry vinegar." This was Resource Capital Group's collection department.

The weekly stack of cash from Don Kulick produced a well-timed addition to Cooper's pocket money. With three sons in the house, immediate gratification cost more than it used to. If Mel wanted to jump in the car and take the kids skiing or to a Broadway show, it would cost him. When Don Kulick mentioned he had a friend who was looking for a loan similar to his own, Mel was interested.

The friend's name was Frank Deutsch. He was an accountant by trade with opportunities in the shipping business. Deutsch wanted to buy a steamship in South America, explained Kulick. Mel offered Frank Deutsch $450,000 in a series of loans at 2.5 percent a week–one point for Cooper Funding, one point for the Toledanos, and half a point for Don. The interest payment alone came to be $11,250 per week. Adjusting for inflation, that is the equivalent of over $32,000 a week.

The word was out that money was available–expensive money, but very large amounts of it. By word of mouth, over a period of a year and a half, other customers found their way to Resource Capital Group, all of them desperate, and willing to sign almost anything.

There were at least ten different customers with up to four loans per customer. They all borrowed money from Resource Capital Group in an arrangement similar to Don Kulick's. The customer understood that above and beyond the documents he signed showing an interest rate of 24 percent a year, he was obligated for weekly interest payments which varied from 2 percent to as much as 4 percent per week, plus fees. The fees usually amounted to 10 percent of the loan itself. The loans were collateralized by real estate or property, and when the collateral was insufficient, Resource Capital took equity. The loan papers were written so that all collateral was designated to the funders of the loans. Soon, a number of Mel's customers held paper that illustrated their debt to Lionel and Leah Toledano. The customers understood that the loans were emergency funds–interim, short-term loans with a life of 30 to 60 days–while permanent bank funding was arranged.

Curiously, the permanent funding never seemed to come through.

These customers paid their weekly interest payments with a check or cash, which was picked up by one of the Albengas. One of them would stop by in person, often with yet another assistant collector–a young man freshly out of prison named Joey Lipari. At the customer's request, they would leave a receipt: a Resource Capital Group business card noting the customer's payment had been received. Later, these receipts would be used by Mel Cooper during his trial in an attempt to prove that these loans were entirely above board; after all, who ever heard of a loanshark giving receipts?

The cash from these loans began to flood Mel's pockets, his briefcase, his desk. By 1982, Mel and Doc were collecting $75,000 a week, and it wasn't just the interest. As Cooper explains, "Every closing also had a 10 percent fee, so if you close a $400,000 loan, it's a $40,000 fee. That's taken out of the loan money. So that goes into the pile. There were loans over three points, even a couple for four. I mean, there was never a day I went home without my pockets bulging with cash.

"I had a shoebox in my closet, and I put cash in there. I wouldn't have time to go to the bank. I never went to the bank without fifty thousand there, and I always went like once or twice a week. So I would just put the money in a shoebox and within a couple of days there would be fifty again.

"I remember, one day I get a call from the Park East School, saying that my housekeeper didn't come to pick up my son, David. I was in Long Island. I said, I'm going to leave and come pick him up. So I was driving back to the city, and on my way I said to myself, 'Wow, where the heck is the housekeeper? Either she's dead or my money is missing.'

"Sure enough, I picked David up, I went home, the housekeeper was gone, and the box of money was gone. The housekeeper was from Sweden, so I hired detectives and Interpol, but I did that because that's the thing you're supposed to do when someone steals from you. The part that bothered me the most is that it didn't bother me that she stole $30,000. It really didn't bother me."

The housekeeper went back to Sweden and within a few days, the box was full again.

Says Mel, "Money was not an object. I didn't think twice if I had to buy a suit or eight suits or a shirt. I was buying Giorgio Armani Black Label like someone buys oranges at the fruit stand. I mean, I went in and I'd say, 'Give me that one in blue, and that one in gray.' I had closets full of shoes and shirts and ties. The ties and shoes, I would get from London.

"I would spend $40,000 on a Lalique coffee table. I would buy Lalique ashtrays, Lalique statues, Lalique wine bottles. I loved Lalique. Then I bought paintings. I was driving a Bentley 2000 Azure, all-black convertible. I used to go to the corner, there would be a crowd around the car when I had the top down. I ended up selling it. In New York it was too difficult. You get a scratch, you have to bring it into the Bentley showroom, and they would be wearing white coats like a doctor.

"I think I had no limit. I was dating a number of beautiful girls. I was always with someone beautiful, smart, talented, funny. They had different positive qualities. We flew to different places like Rio De Janeiro for Carnival, I flew to Mexico, to Acapulco. St. Maarten was a place I frequented. I liked girls with a great sense of humor.

"I did everything I could imagine I'd want to do. No matter what it was I wanted, I was able to do it. There was nothing holding me back from any enjoyment. I never did drugs, but I would drink, but I didn't even drink much, I wasn't a big drinker. Women were my weakness, but even there,

I was very picky, and when I found someone I liked, I would stay with them.

Unlike Mel, Doc did not direct his energy towards enjoying life in New York City. Discreet and low key, in the evenings he went home to his wife Arlene in Roslyn, or so he claimed; later, his wife would accuse him of extensive infidelities. But during their time together at Resource Capital Group, Mel did not get involved in Doc's personal life and the two did not socialize. "We did a few things, not a lot. Maybe a couple of times he went out with me. We went to a show once or twice. I wasn't his good buddy, he had his life, I had my life."

Doc was busy building his business. He still had a dental practice patronized by the Teamsters locals who prepaid their dental insurance and needed service. And he and Jimmy Rotondo were busy deepening their ties to various unions.

Meanwhile, out in Great Neck, Rabbi and Mrs. Toledano were pleased to see their investment in Cooper Funding producing results. Not only were their interest checks coming every week as promised, but they had already received their principal back on several loans. Furthermore, Mel Cooper had given the Toledanos the right to issue a Note of Demand which meant at any time, the couple could request their money. The loans appeared to be as secure as Mel promised.

Mel made it clear to the Toledanos that his need for liquid investment funds was unlimited. Rabbi Toledano began to tell others about the opportunity presented by Mel Cooper through his dear friend Chaim Gerlitz, and he put together a small group of investors consisting of family and friends.

These investors came from Great Neck and beyond. There was Lionel Toledano's first cousin and his son, an actor and producer in California. Rabbi Toledano's legal advisor joined in with money of his own, and the circle slowly expanded to include others in the Toledano clan including a rabbi in Israel, a cousin in Florida, and friends from Great Neck. By spring of 1982 their investment had grown to almost a million dollars.

Chaim Gerlitz was ecstatic. It didn't matter whether you called his share–a finder's fee, co-brokerage, or commission–every loan represented more income. His daughter was getting married soon, and he needed the cash to pay for the wedding. Gerlitz went into the office daily to check on the progress of his loans. He started a ledger to track the status of the loans. To add intrigue to the business, he began to refer to Rabbi Toledano as "Cuba" in his ledger, in a nod to the Rabbi's expertise. Each week Chaim moved money between Mel's Lake Success office and Great Neck, notating the visit in his ledger. He delivered checks and cash to "Cuba" and brought more investment money back to Mel.

Did these investors know what they were getting into? According to the Toledanos, they may have found a good thing, but they had no idea it was illegal. After all, they had seen the paperwork and contracts, and a lawyer had approved it all.

Mel Cooper disagrees. "I can't tell you for sure, but I would think that they knew because some of it was a little cloak and dagger. In my opinion, Toledano is smart enough to have understood that these were not conventional loans. As a matter of fact, a lot of the loans were cash, because Chaim wanted his 5 percent right away. Chaim brought in the cash and he'd come running into our office to give us the money. Toledano was getting one percent a week. You don't have to be a mathematical genius to know there's something wrong with that. I would say Toledano definitely knew. That's how it looked to me."

As for Gerlitz, in Mel's opinion, "He knew exactly what it was. He came in at the beginning, the first loan was with him. It's how we got started in this.

"Gerlitz liked to make money, but he wasn't an evil person, by any means. He's a nice guy, he really is. He was looking to do things to improve his income for his family, he didn't mind working two, three jobs. He's a salesman of anything–pots and pans or whatever you have to sell. If you're in a conversation and you mention something from North Africa, he'll say 'What do you have there? I can do it, I can handle it, I can sell it.'"

Chaim Gerlitz, meanwhile, expanded his own coterie of investors. Just as Rabbi Toledano shared his investment opportunity with relatives, Gerlitz brought in a young man from Mexico, the nephew of his wife.

Moshe Mendelson was the chief cantor of Mexico City, and he had come to New York City for a wedding. At his uncle's insistence, the young man made the acquaintance of Mel Cooper. Before he left New York, he had invested $33,000 with Cooper—$25,000 for a loan to a Brooklyn dress shop, and another $8,000 going to a pinball arcade on Fulton Street in downtown Brooklyn.

And Mel spread the good news to his own family. Soon, Mel's father and brothers had put money into Resource Capital Group's Emergency Loans. Mel told everyone their investments were legal.

Doc Hyman also brought new funding sources to Resource Capital Group, including Jimmy Rotondo and his Teamster friends. And he began to expand lending opportunities for Resource Capital Group. After all, if Rotondo was putting money into Resource Capital Group, he could certainly offer some ideas about where that money should go.

Meanwhile, Mel used the sea of cash to invest in property. He bought a condo in the Hamptons. "Everybody was happy making money," says Cooper. "The rabbis, my father. I mean, they were all happy. Money was coming back, and it wasn't bad for anyone."

This happy band of rabbis and investors, including Jimmy Rotondo and a union treasurer from Yonkers, had almost three million dollars out in illegal loans by summer of 1982.

8

THE EASY MONEY BUSINESS

Peter King liked to brag that it cost him $8,000 just to start the engine of one of his racing boats. He kept these boats in a Babylon, Long Island marina operated by a man named James Feynman.

King liked to race what are known as "scarab boats"—sleek, high-performance racing crafts. Besides his scarab boat, he had two Mercedes, a few more boats, and no income. On his loan papers, however, Peter King claimed he was a founder of Calvin Klein's fashion business, and listed his job income as $350,000, though he was unemployed.

James Feynman's sidekick was "Frankie G" Castagnaro, the "G" standing for "Gangster." Frankie G was a member of Michael Franzese's crew. Through these connections, Peter King found his way to Mel Cooper.

James Feynman made the introduction to Peter King, and in January of 1982, King borrowed $100,000 at a rate of 3 percent a week. In April, King borrowed an additional $65,000. Each loan exacted a hefty fee, and a portion of each interest payment went to Feynman. To secure the loan, Feynman used his own property, and gave Cooper a mortgage on his marina as collateral. Every Tuesday and Thursday, Alan Albenga Jr. and Joey Lipari stopped by the marina to pick up the interest payments totaling over $4,000 a week.

King was typical of the customers Resource Capital Group attracted to their emergency loans: nervy businessmen who had exhausted other money sources and no longer had the standing to get money from banks. These customers were high-risk and had bad credit. Despite their dismal financial status, they had the *chutzpah* to ask for half a million dollars, then lie, falsify, or exaggerate in order to get it. Many had no intention of actually paying the money back–something banks realized long before these customers came to Mel.

Another customer, Donald Brindley, a friend of Doc Hyman, wanted money to buy a huge parcel of land in Texas. As usual, before going to Resource Capital Group, an attempt had been made to structure a deal involving multiple participants and several banks. Nothing had materialized. When Brindley, who was based in Iowa, became desperate for money, Resource Capital Group came to the rescue, giving Brindley a loan of $400,000 at a rate of 1.5 percent a week, assuring him the conventional funding would come through within 30 days. But the permanent financing did not come through, and Brindley continued to make interest payments of $6,000 a week.

With Donald Brindley, Frank Deutsch, and Don Kulick now making weekly interest payments, Mel and Doc decided they needed someone to keep track of the over $1 million in special loans. Cooper and Hyman enlisted Elaine Haber, Al Senior's niece, to keep a ledger tracking all the loans, interest payments, and distributions. Later this ledger would serve as a handy catalog of all Doc and Mel's illegal activities.

Little by little, one borrower led to another, and soon a number of smaller fish in the form of local businesspeople found their way to Resource Capital Group. There was Elaine and William Reisman and Phil Levenberg of Champion Roofing who needed money for a home improvement business; Mikael Nevruzian, a merchant who needed a bridge loan for the purchase of oriental rugs; and Thomas Rajkumar who owned a building on Amsterdam Avenue and needed money for repairs. They all needed cash fast and had limited assets. All of them signed loan papers showing an interest rate of 24 percent a year, but on the side agreed to pay anywhere from 2 percent to 4 percent interest a week, signing over mortgages and property as collateral. All were told permanent financing would be coming soon. Many miscalculated the difficulty they would face in returning high-interest loans. Greed and need made for bad business decisions. Soon, all were having trouble paying back the money they had borrowed from Mel Cooper and Doc Hyman.

To incentivize the borrower to pay, Al Albenga would issue ambiguous threats. When Peter King failed to make some of his weekly interest payments, Al Senior told King that the money he received came from Brooklyn. More explicitly, he threatened to break his legs.

When Donald Brindley found he could not keep up interest payments after four months, Al Albenga Senior began calling Brindley in Iowa. He informed Brindley that Mel's collectors were part of the "biggest non-uniformed army in the country," and he threatened to drag Brindley back to New York City. Soon after, Brindley's wife started getting threatening phone calls.

Even Don Kulick miscalculated how hard it would be to run a restaurant, pay for all the steak and braised duck, the weekly salaries, the taxes, and still come up with cash for Cooper Funding every week. Mel had little sympathy.

"Let's look at the first loan," says Cooper, using Kulick as an example. "A guy came in, he wanted a quarter of a million dollars. We gave him a quarter of a million dollars. I told him, that's as much as I can get for you. He came back a month later and said 'I need more money.' I said 'I can't get you any more money.' He stood there for a half hour begging and pleading for money until the rabbi who was waiting at the door said 'I can get him some interim money.' Now is this a guy that I was twisting his arm? Look at the first loan, and none of them are much different. Is this a guy that I pushed the money on?"

Many of the people Mel loaned money to were his equal when it came to bending the law. If Doc engaged in healthcare fraud and corruption, and Mel had eased into loansharking, their customers were as likely to gamble, steal, or blow their money on drugs as they were to spend it on business. Some, like Frank Deutsch, used their borrowed money to make street loans of their own. Many turned out to be liars, hustlers, and crooks.

Loansharking, gambling, theft, drugs – it often meant organized crime was just around the corner. Sylvie Goldstien, for example, the owner of a dress shop in Brooklyn called "Sylvie's", borrowed only $35,000 from Resource Capital Group, but the project seemed to involve half the mobsters in Brooklyn. She owned the shop with her boyfriend, a man named Walter Fagin, and they sold fur coats as well as dresses. Recalls Mel, "They were initially recommended by a guy named Stanley Gramavot, and Jimmy Rotondo wanted them to have what they needed, so Doc was involved in making sure they would get their loan. We went to their place because there was an urgency to try to accommodate them. I met with Sylvie Goldstien, her boyfriend Walter Fagin, and Stanley."

Fagin was a convicted felon, a low-level hustler who had gone to jail for insurance fraud, grand larceny, and more. Though they were a terrible prospect by any measure, according to Mel, Jimmy Rotondo had a financial interest in the place. Mel and Doc lent them money, calling it a short-term loan until conventional financing could be arranged.

"Walter was stubborn and a tough kind of businessman, and not very appreciative, and he showed his dissatisfaction with being given this money. We gave him $35,000. After a few payments the place was in trouble, and then they had an insurance theft, and the fur coats were all gone. So they collected insurance money and didn't pay back the loan."

Stanley Gramavot was a low-level associate in the Colombo family, and when the loan payments went unpaid, the problem moved up the chain of command. First, Tony "the Gawk" Augello appeared, suggesting the smart thing to do would be to pay Mel and Doc back. When that didn't work, matter then went to Colombo family capo Benny Aloi, resulting in a series of sit-downs, store visits, and discussions.

Benny, Jimmy, Mel, Doc, Stanley, Tony – there wasn't enough blouses and furs in Brooklyn to justify the interests that clashed over Sylvie's. That loan served as a testimony to the inefficiency of illegal activity: if everyone wants a piece of the action, eventually, there is no action.

Why didn't Jesse and Mel walk away from these deals? Like most people who like risk, they didn't dwell on what would happen if something went wrong. They simply didn't say no to opportunity that promised the rush of fast returns, higher stakes, and more excitement. Mel considers this one of his own personal flaws, a mistake he's repeated over and over throughout his life. He describes it as "extending yourself, reaching out, exposing yourself, living on the edge."

"It's taking a risk because you like the risk," says Mel. "It's not because you wanted more money. It's not greed. It's exposure for the thrill of it.

The money was obviously a fringe benefit but that was not the main thing. I didn't need twenty companies. It was that I had to be able to say I have twenty companies."

As for Doc, the question of how a well-educated dentist could be drawn into a business that required him to hand out bags of cash in diners and union offices, that can't be answered by money alone. Perhaps it goes back to Mel's observation that there's "a little bit of psycho" in all of them, including Doc. Or maybe Doc was just a groupie who loved the "Mafia aura" and enjoyed the power trip of letting people know who was behind him, which was something he did often.

Doc told people he knew Tony Accardo, the Chicago crime boss. He knew Jackie Cerrone in Cincinnati. He bragged he had invested money in Las Vegas on behalf of Sam "The Plumber" DeCavalcante. There were few people who didn't know he had worked with Meyer Lansky, because Doc told everyone – except, it seems, his wife, Arlene.

Or maybe, for a man trained as a dentist, it was simply more fun flying around the country negotiating for Las Vegas hotels, theaters, and racetracks, than it was staring in people's mouths.

And Doc was smart, not just a "puffer" – a nobody who boasts and exaggerates. With Mel by his side and Jimmy Rotondo behind him, Doc had become a player in his own right with a gift for making everything he did look and feel legitimate. Both he and Cooper ignored the massive potential for problems and focused instead on the huge sums of money in play, big profits, and best of all, the chance to get into businesses more glamorous and dynamic than "the drab money business."

"There were restaurants involved, there were clubs involved, we took our clients out to dinner at Wings on Wooster Street all the time, we had credit over there. We were partners so we just charged it to the account."

In February of 1982, Mimi Sheraton reviewed Wings in the New York Times, and observed, "The dining room suggests a dream-world Art Deco ocean liner. The romantic room, with its pink walls, rose-velvet banquettes, serpentine streak of blue neon across the ceiling and fantastic, stylized fabric-flower sculptures, is a stage that inspires appropriate costumes from its cast of diners...But best of all, Wings is a beautiful restaurant where very good food seems to be the rule." Wings on Wooster was doing well.

Mel was also part-owner of a disco called Melons on 16th Street.

Owned by Mel's old sanitation business acquaintances at Golden Gate Carting in Brooklyn, Melons occupied the top floor of a building overlooking Irving Place in Gramercy Park, and it attracted a hip, late-night crowd. With a little equity, you had a limitless tab. Show up any time and there's a table waiting for you, your favorite drink – in Mel's case, a Manhattan – brought without asking.

"We went to a place called Club A all the time, Tommy Agro's club on 61st off First Avenue. We used to go there a lot. We had meetings at least once or twice a week either at Stella's or once in a while, at Monte's. That was with Little Vic. "Doc had his own projects and had to run over to Fourth Avenue in Brooklyn many times to meet Jimmy. There was a little club over there where they would meet. And we would take customers out to dinner at Gallaghers or Sparks or the Palms.

"There was a pizza place on 116th Street where Joe Biasucci hung out – he was another union guy who put money into these special loans – and we'd meet a few people there. We had the limousine, we had our driver, we would go to the mountains skiing, we would rent a house in Vermont with my girlfriend and the kids."

For Mel, the perks of funding restaurants and nightclubs, as opposed to bulldozers and sixteen-wheelers, meant no more staring through a chain link fence like he did as a boy, figuring out how to get the money for the good stuff on the other side. They brought the good stuff right to his table. He had made it.

Sylvie's, Peter King, Frank Deutsch, Wings – each loan had its own story, but the biggest story was a club called The Cowboy Palace in the old Diplomat Hotel on 43rd Street in Manhattan. It was a head-on car-crash of a scheme, the vision of a young hustler named Tom Duke. For Mel and Doc, it turned out to be quicksand, dragging down everyone who went near it.

9

TROUBLE AT THE PALACE

It was 1982 and disco's days were dwindling. Nothing had replaced it yet, but a young man, Tom Duke, managed to sell a few investors on his vision of the Next Big Thing. It was called the Cowboy Palace, and it was going to be the biggest nightclub since Studio 54.

Duke had come to Cooper through Mel's Dallas office. The manager told Mel he had a customer who wanted money for a New York nightclub.

"Tell the guy to call me in my office," Mel told him. A few weeks later, on July 14, Tom Duke went to see Mel Cooper and Jesse Hyman at Resource Capital Group.

Tom Duke was a trim yuppie, a local boy from Northport, Long Island who had been living in Miami as a nightclub owner and restaurateur. His most recent venture, a hotspot called Miami Miami, had burned down. He had inaugurated his next project, the Cowboy Palace, in October of 1981 with two lesser partners and friends named Butch Gorgone and Charlie Diverna. Together, they formed a free-spending entourage that was making itself known in New York City. They had raised $125,000 over several months, but that was hardly enough to fund Duke's ambition to make a splash in New York nightlife.

On the day he went to see Mel Cooper, Tom Duke was not happy. He had come out from the city by limousine to see Mel, only to be made to wait for an hour. The neat young man in the white shirt and khaki pants had to sit in the reception area, like everyone else there to see Mel Cooper.

When he finally got in to see Mel, he pitched his idea for his country and western night club. Tom Duke described it as a "major nightclub holding 2,000 patrons" and showed Mel an elaborate rendering. The Cowboy Palace would have both style and substance; it was New York City meets Nashville, and the top acts would perform there. From the moment it opened its doors, the Cowboy Palace would pull in twelve million dollars a year, according to Duke.

"It was a beautiful potential," recalls Cooper, "there were three floors with balconies and bars on every floor, and there was going to be, like, an old-fashioned nightclub with tables. I liked the idea, I would do one of those today. Willie Nelson was going to be opening night, but then there was going to be a theme of, like, old-style gangster films, with floor shows."

The Cowboy Palace was already under construction in the former grand ballroom of the Diplomat Hotel on West 43rd Street in midtown Manhattan. "Tom Duke said he needed to borrow $750,000 to finish it. I explained to him that we don't make unsecured loans." Cooper agreed to give Duke $440,000 in a series of loans, funded by Lionel and Leah Toledano, but only if Duke could bring Mel some collateral.

At their next meeting Tom Duke brought his collateral in the form of a red-faced, Rolex-flashing Irishman named William Clifford Breen. Known as "Billy", Breen was older than Tom Duke, in his fifties. He was as hard and gritty as Duke was smooth and slick: ruddy-faced, dissolute, pudgy, and wearing jewelry and clothes that managed to be simultaneously wildly expensive and tacky. According to Breen himself, his first words to Mel's secretary after being made to wait half an hour in Resource Capital Group's reception room were, "Hey, Sweetie, do me a favor. Tell those motherfuckers to get their asses out here or I'm going to start kicking the doors in, okay?" Whether he actually said it or not, it's true to Breen style: rough, tough, and cinematic in the retelling.

Says Cooper, "Duke came in all excited that he had someone who was putting up properties so he could conclude his loans. I asked Breen, 'What do you have, what properties?' and he started to rattle off, he has a property in Texas, a property in Virginia, a number of single-family homes in different states, Florida, California. We started to ask him what's the value of the property, what's the mortgage on it, and that was the initial meeting.

He agreed to go and get the paperwork and copies of the deeds so we could follow up with the title searches in different states and see how much could be lent against these properties to the Cowboy Palace. He was pledging these properties so that Duke could get his loans." It seemed Tom Duke had found a partner.

Mel's first take on Billy Breen was simple: "He seemed like an Irish drunk."

Billy Breen was introduced to Mel and Doc as "William Clyde Walker," a wealthy Irishman and property owner with the Provisional Irish Republican Army. The reasons for the pseudonym was that Breen had another occupation: professional informant. Billy Breen had spent most of his life engaged in criminal activity into which he then invited the FBI. Depending on the agent you ask, he's a self-employed vigilante, compulsive liar, undercover pro, or psychotic scumbag. Breen has been banned by entire state law enforcement departments, thanks to the mayhem and criminality he leaves in his wake. Later, the FBI would deem him "out of control."

On the other hand, when he was a little more in control, he was instrumental in busting one of the country's top marijuana smuggling rings in South Florida, putting away traffickers Jimmy Chagra and Bobby Piccolo. Over the years, Breen helped bust thieves, drug dealers, bookmakers, and fences, at the very same time he made a living at these enterprises himself. Millions in drugs, cash, and merchandise have flowed through Billy Breen's hands, although he claims he doesn't do it for the money. He wants justice.

"I'm a catalyst," Billy Breen is fond of saying, "a law-and-order guy." Breen wants drug dealers, criminals, and lowlifes put away. But while he puts away drug smugglers, he does it by moving drugs himself, once bringing a 60,000-pound shipment of marijuana into South Carolina. While he claims he helped solve the 1979 assassination of a Federal district judge and the attempted murder of an assistant US attorney, it was Breen himself who introduced the client to the hit man. The year he met Mel Cooper, he pled guilty to conspiracy to distribute marijuana in Wisconsin.

To accomplish his mission, Breen does not wait for crime to come to him; he seeks it out and eggs his targets on. Unfortunately for Mel Cooper, Billy Breen set his sights on the Cowboy Palace, even though there was nothing about the club that could not be said of many New York nightspots: construction was funded by expensive private loans, executed and staffed by Mafia contractors. Without even knowing Cooper and Hyman, Breen already had two words for them: "greaseball shylocks." The anti-Italian, anti-Semitic moniker didn't trouble Breen.

Said Breen, "I was working with the Organized Crime Bureau in Florida, and I was asked if I was interested in taking down a shylock in New York City, and I says, 'positively.' And I didn't care how I took him down." Before you could say "Hawiya"–allegedly, Breen's FBI code name based on his signature rapid-fire way of spitting out "How are you?"–Breen was gunning for Cooper, Hyman, and everyone they knew.

The Cowboy Palace occupied several floors in the Diplomat Hotel. The entrance was one level up from the lobby, on the mezzanine. Stepping off the elevator, one faced a plate glass door, and beyond that a reception area. There were a few desks and telephones, and in the back, a single, large private office. To the left of the reception area, a lobby was under construction which would eventually include a ticket booth and coat check. One level up was the club itself, taking shape in the grand ballroom.

Billy Breen liked the idea of infiltrating the Cowboy Palace. Not only would he finally get a chance to break into the highest stakes game around–organized crime in New York City–at worst, even if nothing panned out, he would find a way to rip off the shylocks themselves for fifty thousand dollars. It would come in handy since he owed the Internal Revenue Service $49,000.

Breen had found his way to Tom Duke through a man named Maury Joseph, another FBI informant. Call it professional courtesy–one informant reaching out to another–but after their introduction through an agent named Lloyd Hough of the Metro-Dade Organized Crime Bureau, Joseph offered to put Breen in touch with what he described as "the mob's loan-sharks" in New York City.

From the start, Breen found Maury Joseph an untrustworthy lowlife who "would double-deal his mother"–no small thing coming from a man who admitted he had not earned a legal day's pay in decades. When they met, Joseph was infiltrating a Caribbean drug ring. He suggested Breen come in and help him with the bust, then failed to deliver one correct tip. According to Breen, Joseph suggested they let a shipment of drugs into the country and split the profits.

Joseph's next plan was to help the FBI round up a bunch of loansharks in New York City. Joseph had the funds to make it happen; he dressed Breen up in an Adolfo suit, bought him a first-class ticket to New York, and checked him into the St. Moritz Hotel, with no further details on who they were there to meet.

Maury Joseph brought Billy Breen to the Cowboy Palace on July 23, 1982 to meet Tom Duke. Breen and Joseph stepped into the uproar of workers nailing sheetrock, laying down carpet, and hanging lights. The plan was still unclear to Breen, or as he said to Joseph, "I thought we were gonna take down a bunch of greaseball shylocks? What the fuck's going on?" Joseph explained the deal to Breen: get involved with Tom Duke and you get involved with the shylocks. Tom Duke appeared from the chaos.

They quickly got down to business. Believing Breen was just a freelance hustler looking for a chance to put his money to work, Duke proposed his idea: Duke would use Breen's property as collateral for a loan. Duke would borrow against the properties, first obtaining inflated appraisals. Once the money started coming in, Duke would buy the property from Breen at an outrageously high price, earning Breen a "big, fat profit." Duke would pay Breen weekly and give him a 7 percent stake in the Cowboy Palace. A title company in Duke's pocket would make sure the ownership of Breen's properties never actually changed hands. A little fraud, a little forgery, and Breen's four properties in Virginia, California, Florida, and Texas would keep the Cowboy Palace in business.

The thing about loansharking is it doesn't feel like a crime. The enthusiasm of the borrower creates the illusion everybody is happy. Everyone participates willingly. The fact that the borrower is usually driven by desperation or mindless greed is not the lender's problem. As Mel says, "No matter what you tell these people, they needed the money at the time. Their choice in many cases was to take the money or to have their business go under. They chose to take this loan.

"When you borrow the money, it's 'I'll pay you back the way I'm supposed to.' But a week after you borrow it, when your payments are due, you have all kinds of reasons why you shouldn't have to pay." Proclaims Mel, "But they *needed* this money, they *wanted* this money." And no one wanted and needed money more than Tom Duke.

On the day Tom Duke brought Billy Breen out to Resource Capital Group, Breen was excited. Believing he was meeting real mob loansharks, he decided to play full tilt gangster. After he threatened the secretary, he entered Mel's office where Mel, Doc, and the Albengas, father and son, were waiting.

He strode up to Doc, and hissed, "Who the fuck do you think you are? You never make me wait."

Mel rolled his eyes, having seen his share of hotheads. "Oh, for Chrissake."

Mel turned to Tom Duke and said, "Tommy, take him into the conference room and cool him off. I've had enough aggravation for one day." When Breen calmed down, the meeting began.

Watching Doc and Mel in action on his first visit to Resource Capital Group, Breen assessed his targets. Taking Doc for the more enterprising of the two partners, Breen took a different tack and decided to use criminal charm. He took Doc aside and discreetly let him know he was in the market for illegal goods. Did Doc have any stocks or credit cards he wanted to get rid of? Breen claims Doc Hyman told him about six million dollars' worth of diamonds a friend named Curly Montana was trying to unload. Breen told Doc he would check around and see if there was any interest.

Thanks to Doc's "puffing", Breen got a good idea of Mel and Doc's circle of friends. He had already heard about Curly Montana, the Cleveland hit man, in their brief acquaintance. At another meeting, Doc let other names drop, even boasting to Breen about his friendships with various Mafia capos. Breen learned Doc and Mel were good friends of Michael Franzese, the enterprising young Colombo capo. Since Mel Cooper's early days providing financing, Michael had developed what he referred to as a "far-reaching criminal domain." It was so far-reaching, that a range of U.S. law enforcement agencies had come together to form a "Michael Franzese Task Force."

As planned, Breen signed over his property. Billy Breen's Virginia house was worth $50,000. It had been appraised for $95,000. Duke got his $440,000 loan at a rate of 2 percent a week, less the usual fees and commissions.

In 1982, $440,000 went far. But as construction at the Cowboy Palace proceeded, it was already clear that Duke's money was going into more than just nails and sheetrock.

"Tom Duke used to come by in a limousine with his crew, his friends, whatever, and he would have plenty of coke laid out in the back, and he would be snorting it all the way from Manhattan to our office in Lake Success," says Cooper. "He would come into the office all stoned and say, 'Hey, I need a few hundred thousand more. I gotta get this thing going, I need more money.'"

After the meeting, Duke would shuttle back to Manhattan to his temporary home in a suite at the St. Moritz Hotel on Central Park South, where the hotel doorman would usher the clean-cut Duke into the hotel's white and lemon-yellow lobby. There were nightly dinners out on the Upper East Side, after which Duke would retire to his suite, enjoying a lifestyle that cost the young man, not yet thirty years old, five thousand dollars a week. Meanwhile, tradesmen were not being paid and Duke had already missed interest payments.

Though he hardly seemed like a good bet, he continued to talk up the Cowboy Palace like a pro and borrow more money. Duke's main skills seemed to be charm and confidence. Duke may have convinced Mel and Doc that the Cowboy Palace was a good investment, but more likely, they thought Duke himself was a good investment. Mel did not generally care whether his borrower's dreams came true. "Am I going to get my money back? That's my only instinct, not whether this guy is going to succeed or not. In other words, I didn't give any of these guys more than a fifty-fifty chance to succeed. That wasn't what I was trying to analyze," says Cooper.

But considering Duke's free-spending habits, one might wonder if they would see their principal returned, much less a completed Cowboy Palace. After a few months, Mel and Doc were starting to wonder the same thing.

"He gave us whatever stories fit at the time. At the beginning it was all about how he was going to get this Cowboy Palace going, with the rendering that he had, and it's going to be a beautiful thing, and it's going to happen in 90 days, or in 120 days, he'll have it all up and operating. Very optimistic."

By the end of August of 1982, Duke owed Mel and Doc $12,000 a week in interest. And as part of the loan package, Resource Capital Group had taken a 27 percent stake in the Cowboy Palace.

With his mouth watering at what he believed was going to be a case of massive proportions and rewards, Breen decided it was time to get the FBI involved. Though he had gotten the lead from the Miami office, the FBI was not yet officially involved with his activities. They had no knowledge of his plan to develop a case against Mel Cooper and Doc Hyman. Since he had no contacts in New York, Breen called his friend, Special Agent Joe Gersky in the Las Vegas office, who steered him to Special Agent Jerry Lang in New York City. Breen phoned Agent Lang.

Special Agent Lang listened to what Breen had to say and told him it sounded like he was on to something. Unfortunately, Lang had just been transferred out of town; another agent would have to follow up. It took a few days of being passed around the office but Breen found his way to Special Agent Bob Mathews, who promised he would look into Resource Capital Group and see what the FBI knew about them.

Finally, after several days a response came: "We never heard of them. There's nothing there. Go home, kid."

"Sometimes an agent might just say that, or maybe he just wasn't looking in the right place. We definitely knew about Resource Capital Group," says Special Agent Walter Stowe, Jr., who was in the FBI's Organized Crime division of the New York field office at the time. Not only did he know about Resource Capital Group, claims Stowe, but Mel Cooper already had a solid reputation among the Feds as a loanshark. Still, Resource Capital Group was not an active target for the FBI, not until Walt Stowe met Billy Breen in early October of 1982.

They were introduced by a small-time loanshark and informant who told Stowe about Mel and Doc's operation. The informant allegedly said to Stowe, "Why are you wasting your time with me? Go after some big fish." He referred Stowe to Billy Breen.

Stowe had already been working for the FBI for ten years. While he did not find Breen particularly trustworthy, he decided Billy was on to something with the Cowboy Palace. Says Stowe, "Billy's world was not a strictly factual world. Billy was a hustler. Billy was also a great storyteller. I said, 'Billy, what can you do for me?' and he said, 'I'll introduce you,' so Billy brought me in as the guy watching his money.

"Our story was we had money from the IRA"—the Irish Republican Army—"and I was in right away. That story kept me out of trouble because nobody wanted to mess with the IRA."

A few days after they met, Walt Stowe accompanied Billy Breen to the Cowboy Palace. Breen introduced Stowe to Tom Duke as "Walter Johnson", a financial whiz whose job it was to keep an eye on Breen's money. According to their story, Walter Johnson was both a tough guy with the IRA and an accountant. Tom Duke bought the story. The FBI was inside the Cowboy Palace.

Stowe and Breen put in full days whenever they could at the Cowboy Palace. They manned the office, took calls, and gradually handled more and more of the club's finances. Stowe's goal was to gather as much information as possible on the Mafia-connected characters associated with the Cowboy Palace.

Tom Duke, meanwhile, was slowly receding from day-to-day operations, coming in later mornings, leaving earlier at night, allowing Breen and Stowe to push ever deeper into the business. In Duke's estimation, the tall and handsome Stowe appeared to be a trustworthy and brainy advisor, and Duke was soon referring to Walt Stowe, AKA Walt Johnson, as "my accountant."

If there was any doubt as to Stowe's credibility among the rest of the team, it was put to rest by Breen who barked, "He's with me," whenever Walt appeared, leaving no room for discussion.

Breen and Stowe had a front row seat from which they could observe the comings and goings at the club. Given Mel and Doc's long-standing associations with the Mafia, the Cowboy Palace was an opportunity to do favors, and they brought in old friends in construction, handing out contracts for everything from carpeting to catering. Concessions were in high demand, and they went to friends of Jimmy Rotondo, Doc, and Mel.

Recalls Mel, "These people had peripheral interest. Michael Franzese had the cigarette concession. It was all legal. I think Michael was also trying to get more, the coat concession, and he was always talking to Doc about getting more involved. Michael was a real aggressive guy, and he was looking to get a foothold in the club. He saw that as being a winner."

Breen could not have been more thrilled. It was like Mafia stargazing.

Besides Franzese, he spotted Tony Napoli, a Genovese family capo who ran a limousine service and supplied Duke with the cars he kept on hand night and day. He saw Tommy Pecora from New Jersey, Benedetto Aloi, a capo in the Colombo family, and at Tom Duke's favorite hangout, a steakhouse called Rusty's on 73rd Street and Third Avenue, he met Carlo Vaccarezza, Frankie "The Hat" Di Stefano, and Lenny Di Maria, all Gambino family associates, and part of John Gotti's crew.

Rusty's was owned by baseball player Rusty Staub, who at the time, still played and coached for the New York Mets. Duke and his buddies ate at Rusty's as often as five nights a week. Duke always picked up the tab for this inner circle of pals and investors who had a kind of youthful enthusiasm that had long since passed by Billy Breen. Breen loathed them all.

Rusty's was a lively hangout with a buzzing singles scene but Breen found himself attracted to Vaccarezza and his cronies who used the restaurant as a base for their bookmaking operation. To insinuate himself into the group, Breen began making $1,000 bets on football games.

Money was in motion, flowing into parties, dinners, tips, drugs, gambling, and limousines. But the Cowboy Palace was going nowhere. By the end of October it was obvious that Tom Duke was clueless, hustling, or high. Each time Mel and Doc stopped by to see how their investment was proceeding, they were dismayed to find almost no progress.

Breen, meanwhile, saw organized crime everywhere, and began to sabotage any serious construction that had been completed, buying time to collect more data for his big crime bust. He didn't want the party to end, and approached the situation with a mind-boggling level of grandiosity. Breen was convinced he was going to "dismantle one of New York's most lucrative rackets and decimate the city's organized-crime families," as he put it. Maybe it was his history of mental problems showing itself, or maybe it was Breen's drinking habits, but like the club, Breen himself was in a holding pattern. Tom Duke gave him the nickname, Billy "Drink-All-Day-and-Night." When Breen wasn't scheming, he was loaded.

Duke himself did not seem particularly concerned by the delays. Despite his vision of the Cowboy Palace generating millions of dollars, obtaining the loan money itself seemed to be his only goal. Most of what came in to build the club would go right out again to pay for Duke's lifestyle, with some of each loan going to Billy Breen as a payment for the property he had put up. Evenings were spent at Rusty's or Studio 54, dropping thousands a night on alcohol and drugs, hotels and dinners.

The lack of progress in the Cowboy Palace didn't seem to bother anyone except Mel and Doc. After yet another loan for which Breen put up his Texas property, Duke owed Resource Capital Group $14,000 a week in interest. He was behind in his payments. He had not paid his hotel bill. Contractors and tradesmen were lined up at the door threatening to rip up the carpet or take down the curtains if Duke didn't settle. He had even stiffed his brother-in-law, William Lupone, whom he had hired to do construction.

Lupone had grown up with Tom Duke in Northport, Long Island. He purchased materials, tore down walls, did electrical work, and loyally tried to execute Duke's vision for the Cowboy Palace, even as chaos unfolded around him and checks bounced.

As an old friend, he felt it was his job to look after Duke. He even confronted Mel Cooper and company one day as they toured the Cowboy Palace.

"Why are you guys giving Tom cash? Cash is like water. It goes right through his fingers. If you have a business, you have to have controls. There are no controls. There's no accounts, no documentation, nothing."

After three months of cash infusions from Resource Capital Group, the Cowboy Palace had little to show for it. Lupone was only stating the obvious. No one answered him.

Finally, Al Albenga spoke. "We know. Tom has been throwing hundred-dollar bills to the doorman at the Grand Hyatt." He was clearly upset.

"This is not how you run a business. This is ridiculous," said Lupone.

Al Senior replied, "Don't worry, we are putting our people in."

A loanshark does not typically insert himself into his customer's business. He doesn't usually engage contractors or figure out how to get the lighting guy paid. But as part owners of the club, Doc and Mel started doing just that. They did what they could to move the Cowboy Palace forward, signing checks and paying contractors directly using Duke's loan money.

Says Mel, "We see this kid pissing away money on limousines, living in the St. Moritz, and coming in high as a kite, and we'd take a look at the

Cowboy Palace and it's not moving. We wanted to get the place open."

Duke barely bothered to hide his indifference to Mel and Doc's interests. Stowe remembers sitting with Tom Duke in the back of a limo as Duke boasted about his plans to burn Resource Capital Group. "He told me that when he got the nightclub open, he was going to tell Resource Capital to forget about their previous deal, that he would pay back the money that he had borrowed from them when he got around to it, when the club generated the funds. He said that he felt that they would be unable to press the issue with him, because, as he put it, 'they were too high profile.' And Duke said that since the documents he had used to secure the loans were forgeries, they would not be able to enforce the loan in court. And he also said that he hadn't paid any vig on the loan in two weeks."

Duke even seemed to take pride in his debt. He told Stowe, word was out on the street that Duke was the biggest debtor in New York City, but that he was also the best payer.

Says Stowe, "He said also, at the time, that the vig on the loan had been suspended for three weeks because Mel Cooper and Doc Hyman knew they would never get their money out of the club unless it opened. He said that they were beginning to have some problems with the people behind them, because of his failure to pay back the loan."

The "people behind them" were none other than Rabbi Lionel J. Toledano and his relatives. They had put together a special group for the Cowboy Palace loan. When Duke fell behind in his interest payments to Resource Capital Group, Lionel Toledano's weekly checks stopped coming. If Duke didn't pay Mel, Mel didn't pay the rabbis. It was that simple.

Rabbi Toledano became frantic, calling Chaim Gerlitz daily trying to find out what happened to his money. Gerlitz went to both Mel and Doc, desperate to find out when the payments would start again, but he only got vague answers.

Believing Doc Hyman to be the more compassionate of the two partners, Gerlitz went to Doc's office to ask the question he dreaded; what happened if a customer didn't pay?

Trying to calm Gerlitz, Doc explained there were only two options: They could take the legal route and foreclose on the loan, or they could negotiate a settlement with the customer. This hardly satisfied Chaim.

Continued Doc, "What I'm telling you is that you're protected against loss of money. Okay? The time that you're going to get it, is involved in time of foreclosure and in doing everything with it. Okay?" This seemed clear enough to Chaim until Doc added, "Then, if you foreclose, and the guy sues you back and countersues you, you're going to wind up in the courts for nine months to a year, okay?"

It was the first time Gerlitz understood the reality of the phony loan papers. Continued Doc, "They have to understand they're getting their money back, and whatever's owed them in interest. But they just can't..." Doc paused. "Things like this, you just don't go and file a suit. Then they'll start making claims of usury."

Chaim closed his eyes, shutting out the reality of the catastrophe in which he was now involved.

Doc Hyman did not tell Chaim Gerlitz that besides the threat of foreclosure, Mel Cooper and Doc Hyman had developed other, more unorthodox ways of dealing with borrowers who did not pay: Al Albenga Senior and Junior. Along these lines, as promised, Resource Capital Group now had someone new looking after their interests.

A young man named Anthony Capo appeared at the Cowboy Palace. He told everyone he was Jimmy Rotondo's nephew. He said he had been sent to Resource Capital Group by his uncle to keep his eye on the project and make sure everything was moving. Recalls William Lupone, "Towards the end of 1982 they put in Mr. Capo who was there every day. He was in the office sitting, watching everything, making sure everything was done right."

Walt Stowe recalls telling Capo one day, as they watched construction drag on, "Billy wants me to keep track of what's going on because he can't be here all the time."

Capo's response was "I do the same for my people."

While Anthony Capo kept his eye on the Cowboy Palace, Mel and Doc tried to motivate Tom Duke to finish the Cowboy Palace construction using still another method they had perfected: grinding their customers down to desperation. Additional bank loans they promised Duke had never materialized. Loans designed to last ten weeks went on month after month. Duke was strung along with the promise of more cash, then made to wait for hours in the Resource Capital reception area. And to make it clear who was in charge, Mel and Doc regularly bounced checks.

Says Stowe, "What they would do is suck these people along until they were totally desperate. They dragged it out, saying 'We'll help you, we'll get you the money,' until the person would agree to almost anything. I once heard someone pleading with them for money." Clients would call day after day in an increasing frenzy.

Tom Duke was not happy with this way of doing business. He would go to Resource Capital Group's Long Island office to pick up his checks only to have them bounce the next day. He would show up for an appointment only to be told the checks weren't ready, come back another day.

On October 27, frustration and greed collided on a variety of fronts. Mel and Doc had given Duke yet another loan—$90,000 in checks, which promptly bounced. Frustrated, Duke went out to Resource Capital to see his financiers. As usual, he had to wait in the reception area until Mel summoned him. By the time he went in for his meeting, Duke was livid.

Waiting for him in the office were Cooper, the two Albengas, and Anthony Capo. Though Duke knew Capo from the Cowboy Palace, in reality, Anthony Capo was little more than a young thug from New Jersey with a short fuse and an easy way with violence. He had everything it took to become a killer, as would happen two decades later when he assassinated a crime family boss. Billy Breen remembers him as a "petulant, ambitious young hood."

Tom Duke swept in and started to berate Cooper. Recalls Mel, "Duke began to complain about some bounced checks. He was complaining. But he wasn't responding to the fact that he owed money."

Duke then began to rage about Doc Hyman.

"You have a problem?" said Mel. "Talk to Doc."

"Fine, where is he?" said Duke.

"Hang on," said Mel, "I'll get him on the phone." Jesse Hyman was out of the office. A few moments later the phone rang. It was Doc, He knew there was a meeting with Tom Duke, and had planned to call in.

"Here's the phone," said Mel, "Tell him yourself."

Duke began to speak but Doc interrupted him. Duke fell silent. Everyone watched as Tom Duke listened to Doc. No one was quite sure what Hyman had said, but everyone heard Duke's reply: "Go fuck yourself," said Duke.

Anthony Capo did not share Doc and Mel's distinction between violence and the threat of violence. He got up, walked over to Tom Duke, and slapped him with full power. Duke's head snapped back. He was stunned. Anthony Capo hit him twice more until blood dripped onto Tom Duke's light blue shirt.

Duke returned to the Cowboy Palace pale and shaken, his face swollen. "He was scared to death," says Walt Stowe, "They terrified him. He was really smacked around and came back all bloodied up."

As usual, Mel's memory of events is more benign. Says Cooper, "The whole thing was for show. I went along with it but it was Al Albenga's idea. Doc and I went along with it. They arranged the whole thing in advance because Duke was getting out of line. We felt we had to straighten out Tom Duke. We planned to incite him, to have him get annoyed, and then hit him. So Duke was complaining about something, and talking a little negatively about Doc. They wanted to teach him a lesson, so they set this up so whatever he said, they would end up slapping him."

They thought Tom Duke was the kind of guy who only needed a taste of what might happen if he didn't straighten out. But roughing up Tom Duke set an unfortunate train of events in motion. Duke was now scared. Agent Stowe believed things were getting ugly at the Cowboy Palace, so he helped arrange a "sit-down" at Rusty Staub's steakhouse to clear the air. He planned to attend the meeting wearing a recording device.

Tom Duke showed up that night at Rusty's with his usual entourage: Maury Joseph, the universally disliked hustler, Billy Breen, Walt Stowe, and Charlie Diverna, Duke's friend and investor. There, they met the Albengas, father and son. As usual, they all found themselves waiting for Mel and Doc.

The group sat at a large table in the front window of Rusty's. Unaware their conversation was being taped and that a number of the diners in the restaurant were armed, undercover FBI agents, they quickly turned to the matter at hand: Tom Duke getting roughed up at Resource Capital Group, and the difficult financial situation in which he found himself.

Al Albenga tried to get Tom Duke's advisors to understand, this is how Mel and Doc do business; the pressure would never let up.

"They're grinding him out," said Albenga, addressing Billy Breen.

"They're taking it all," Billy said. "They're giving him a little bit and taking it all. Am I right or wrong?"

Albenga explained again, that's how Mel and Doc did business, like it or not. "Mel Cooper wants his money on the minute," said Al. He acknowledged that Cooper and Hyman would purposely hold up the loan proceeds every time Duke went out to Long Island for money.

"They're trying to kick a guy down so he can't pay. Now is that fair?" asked Stowe, "Is that decent?"

"In their philosophy, it's decent," said Al. "I've been in the money business most of my life and I'm used to loaning money man to man. If I didn't collect, it was either him or me. Resource Capital does business a very different way. When I went over there, when I was put there by somebody, I learned a whole new system. It's like a poker game, they play a good game of poker."

After circling over the topic for a while longer, Tom Duke tried to turn the conversation back to getting the club open. But Maury Joseph, who had a knack for saying the wrong thing at the wrong time, brought up Capo's slap.

Albenga tried to avoid the subject. "Look, if you don't like the way they do business, go somewhere else for the money. That's what I'd do." Albenga was not about to bond with lowlifes like Breen and Joseph. But Maury insisted, asking Al again, "What would you do if it was your kid who got slapped?"

"You want an answer? I'd go get a gun and kill Tony. That's what I would do, I would kill him," bellowed Al. He turned to Duke and said, "You're asking me what I would do, my friend? That's what I would do if anybody hit my fucking son. You can do the same thing. Go get a gun and kill Anthony....If you got the balls to do it, then do it. If not, you are going to get smacked again. Alright?"

Recalls Walt Stowe, "Alan went ballistic. The restaurant had been really crowded. He became agitated. He stood up in the restaurant and began speaking in a louder voice and pounding the table." Quietly, patrons began leaving the restaurant.

Just then Mel and Doc's limousine pulled up. Through the window, the group could see they had brought Anthony Capo with them.

"What the fuck is he doing here?" said Duke, seeing Capo.

Recalls Stowe, "Tom Duke became very, very nervous, very agitated and said that if Anthony came in, he was going to leave. And at that point, Al Albenga went outside to talk to the other three."

But Doc, Mel, and Capo marched into Rusty's, and as promised, Duke and his friends walked out, leaving Walt Stowe and Billy Breen alone with Mel Cooper and Doc Hyman.

Mel and Doc proceeded to have one of the most damaging conversations they would engage in while under surveillance. Trying to make it clear to Breen and his accountant what was at stake in the Cowboy Palace, Doc went on a spree of self-importance.

"We went to a lot of people, we're on the hook to a lot of people for this money," began Doc. He wasn't referring to the rabbis. He started talking about his friend Tony in Chicago–Tony Accardo. "He's a friend of mine because I handled all their money in Vegas," said Doc. "It's a small circle. Every union guy knows one another, every bookmaker knows one another all over the country."

"There are people involved here," said Mel. "We're looking at a hundred people behind this table."

"You gotta remember, we got people behind us who could blow your fucking head off," Doc added, sealing his fate.

Tom Duke never returned to the table at Rusty's.

The next day, a contingent from Resource Capital Group paid a visit to the Cowboy Palace. Mel and Doc were flanked by their collectors Al Albenga, Anthony Capo, and Joey Lipari, as well as their attorneys, Gil Greenberg and Ed Zujkowski. The seven of them stepped through the glass doors of the Cowboy Palace and headed to Tom Duke's office.

Though they were supposedly there to look at the books, Tony, Joey, and Al were hardly accountants. "We went down there to work something out, and maybe we wanted to make a certain impression," Mel admits. "But that's all, it was just a visit to sort out business, to decide how they're going to proceed."

Recalls Agent Stowe, "I was in my office when the whole crew marched in." He believed they were there to take the Cowboy Palace from Tom Duke. "I was afraid they had come for trouble."

As always, the smallest activity took endless meetings and negotiation, and time passed as Walt Stowe and Tom Duke met with various members of Mel's contingent. Stowe had told the group they could not all go into the back office together or it would be just like the evening before. "Tommy would get frightened and leave."

Eventually, with most of the young hotheads outside, the group settled in Tom Duke's office to discuss what it would take to get the Cowboy Palace open. As Stowe feared, Mel and Doc demanded that Tom Duke sign over the remaining shares of the Cowboy Palace.

Duke refused, doing his best to play the tough guy. "You know, a lot of people have been watching me, and some very, very close friends are involved," said Duke, "and they said 'Any problems, please speak to me,' and I said 'fine.'"

Al Albenga responded, "You shouldn't even mention that terminology. It's not your fuckin' ball game."

"That league, I can't stand, maybe because I don't understand it."

"All right, so see?" said Albenga.

"But they ain't about to see me hurt," said Duke. According to Al Albenga, Tom Duke trying to sound tough was about as convincing as Walt Stowe trying to sound like a gangster. Albenga considered Stowe a hick, and Tom Duke an idiot.

"They're showing you respect by sitting down with you. But you have an obligation," Al explained.

There was more back and forth. Two hours later, the Resource Capital Group left, having accomplished nothing. They never knew that Stowe had arranged for a team of FBI agents to be ready outside the building in case something went wrong.

When Stowe came in the next day, he found a small note stuck to his desk. "Walt Johnson is an FBI agent," the note said. It also said "Billy Clyde Walker is Bill Breen. Bill Breen is an agent working for the FBI. Bill Breen is self-centered. Bill Breen is an egoist."

The notes were the handiwork of Maury Joseph, who had figured out Walt Johnson's secret and decided to let the world know. Joseph had been an ever-present hanger-on at the Cowboy Palace, though no one knew his exact financial role. Stowe assumed he had some stake because by then, no one put in time at the Cowboy Palace for the sheer fun of it. Perhaps Maury, like Breen, spotted financial opportunity, and wanted to take FBI agent Stowe out of the picture.

Walt Stowe immediately reported to his supervisor at the FBI. "I told my supervisor I was going to beat the shit out of Maury Joseph."

"You're off the case," said Damon Taylor, who decided Stowe had gotten a little too involved.

FBI Agent Stanley Nye took over the case. In contrast to Stowe's one-man undercover operation, Nye launched a full-scale surveillance of the Cowboy Palace, Cooper Funding, and Resource Capital Group. Using hidden cameras, wiretaps, and more, the FBI began to surveil anyone who had anything to do with Resource Capital Group, including the Cooper family businesses at the Lake Success office and each of the customers they did business with. The FBI set up Michael Franzese with an undercover agent in Atlantic City, just as Franzese began to make a name for himself in sports betting. Jimmy Rotondo was taped at his Brooklyn social club. Recorders were put into Sylvie's, capturing hours of Mafia jawing on tape. The crew at the Babylon Cove Marina–James Feynman and Frankie G– were surveilled as they spent the day hanging around the docks, trading dirt on Resource Capital Group.

In the end, the FBI had 47 days worth of videotape, wiretaps, audio recordings, and surveillance of hustlers, con artists, wiseguys, and low-level gangsters, all of them gossiping like a bunch of junior high-schoolers about Mel Cooper and his dentist partner, Doc Hyman.

The FBI dug in just in time to capture the final chapter of the Cowboy Palace debacle. By the time Agent Nye took over the case, Breen was panicking. Mel Cooper had sold Breen's Florida property, the third property he had pledged as collateral. Breen had wrongly believed the transfer of property to Mel and Doc had not actually taken place. Apparently, Resource Capital Group had taken his property and turned it over to a Long Island rabbi.

Still in contact with Breen, the FBI told him to stay away from the Cowboy Palace, things were getting too hot. Agents Damon Taylor and Art Krinsky told Billy Breen to leave immediately. Breen ignored them. Breen was also ordered to stop talking to Tom Duke, which he also refused to do. The FBI considered Tom Duke a crook, an arsonist, and a thief.

As for Duke, he was fed up with his financiers, and started looking elsewhere for money. First, he went to Tony Napoli whose company, Anjo Limo, had been supplying Duke with the cars that shuttled him everywhere. Napoli was allegedly a capo in the Genovese family. A genial guy, Napoli was always on the lookout for opportunity.

"Tony Napoli's father was a big guy, Jimmy Nap," according to one of his contemporaries. "Tony took care of the garage for them on Grand Avenue in Brooklyn. He was a mechanic. He was like, a captain, an influential, powerful guy. Everybody spoke very highly of the father."

Tom Duke told Tony Napoli that for $100,000, he could have a third of the Cowboy Palace. As far as Duke was concerned, there was no limit to how many times you can sell the same 33 percent.

Duke then went to Carlo Vaccarezza of Rusty's. Carlo had introduced Duke to Lenny Di Maria and Frankie "The Hat" Di Stefano. Duke told them he needed money. Duke didn't tell them about they money he owed Doc Hyman and Mel Cooper. They agreed to give Duke $15,000 at 3 percent a week to start him off, with a promise of more to come. Now, heavy hitters in the Gambino family were involved.

Doc and Mel were desperate to salvage something from the Cowboy Palace. Not only did they owe the rabbis in Great Neck a fortune, Jimmy Rotondo had invested in the Cowboy Palace, and they owed him money as well. Mel and Doc tried to bring in their own union workers to finish the job.

But Breen only escalated his efforts to undermine the Cowboy Palace. He still had faith in his plan to take down all of organized crime in New York City, and he continued to engineer accidents in the form of flooded carpets, torn-down drapes, and broken mirrors.

When Doc Hyman found out Duke was trying to get street money from other lenders, the checks from Resource Capital Group stopped coming once and for all. Doc gave Billy Breen the news on one of his visits to the Cowboy Palace in early November. Billy wanted to know what happened to Tom Duke's most recent round of funding.

"Oh, I'm sorry, Billy, listen, this kid went to a lot of. . . uh, he ran into some people obviously," said Doc.

"What do ya mean when you say he ran into people?"

"Well, he ran into some wiseguys, okay? We're stopping all the checks that we issued to him the other day, we're stopping payment on it and we're putting a demand note now."

Tom Duke was proving to be a skilled con artist, able to hustle the hustlers. By borrowing street money from competing sources, he was causing chaos. By early December of 1982, things got so bad that the various families agreed to meet.

Observed Walter Fagin, co-owner of Sylvie's, who talked to Doc Hyman often, "Things had reached such a state of disarray, of confusion, of people yelling and screaming at one another, that five families had a sit-down as a result of what was happening in the Cowboy Palace situation."

They met at Gallagher's Steak House on 47th street in Manhattan, and this time there were no FBI agents or wannabe tough guys. It was the real thing. Michael Franzese went on behalf of Mel and Doc. Di Maria, Vaccarezza, Di Stefano, Jimmy Rotondo, and Tony Napoli attended as well, each representing their family's interests.

Recalls Mel, "They met because they were concerned that Tom Duke was on his sixth or seventh loan, and things were out of control. People were complaining. Rotondo was the one that was really on top of this thing, and he was responsible for everything Doc was doing, for any problems Doc caused. So the meeting was a way of letting Rotondo know he better get control of everything going on.

"Jimmy was making money off Doc with the Teamsters and the dental clinics, but he wasn't the only one. A number of them were making money because Doc and Jimmy had brought into the Teamsters. They wanted to know what's going on with Doc, and let Rotondo know he's responsible for anything that happens."

The meeting was a warning. Get a grip on the Cowboy Palace and make sure all the other projects—the Teamster money, the various rackets, Doc's Las Vegas investments—stayed on track.

"They were hearing things that made them uncomfortable. That maybe Tom Duke and Billy Breen were being watched. They already had their suspicions," recalls Mel.

The other interest the disparate group shared was their desire to get the Cowboy Palace open. Unaware of Breen's sabotage, they still had hope, not to mention plenty of sunk costs. At the meeting, they agreed they would each would take an interest in the Cowboy Palace, and work together to get it open.

But it was too late. In December, Tom Duke got an eviction notice ordering him out of the premises at the Diplomat hotel. The liquor license, under the auspices of the previous operator, was about to expire. According to Billy Breen, snake and fink Maury Joseph, went to the landlord – a Mrs. Salzman – behind Tom Duke's back to negotiate the lease himself. Tony Napoli also wanted to take over the Cowboy Palace lease but was stopped when the police raided Napoli's club and arrested everyone for illegal gambling. Billy Breen, hoping to cut his losses, got a tip about a drug deal and left town. And Rudolph Giuliani was poised to change everything about the way the mob did business in New York City.

Mel Cooper and his twin brother Barry in 1949

Mel and brother in 1960

Mel with three sons after his divorce

Mel out and about in 1970s New York

Mel Cooper with Naomi and Sam Cooper, 1981

Jesse "Doc" Hyman   *Oscar "Al" Albenga*   *Chaim Gerlitz*

Rudolph W. Giuliani

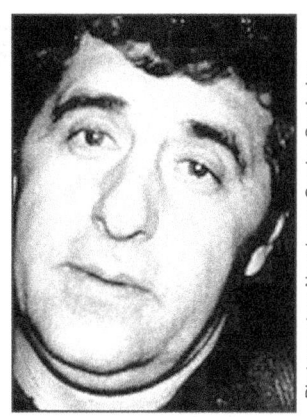

Above: "Little Vic" Orena

Below: Michael Franzese

Cooper with son, before conviction

Above: Anthony Capo

Sara Krulwich/The New York Times/Redux

Above: Judge Leonard B. Sand in 1985.

Above: Special Agent Walter Stowe Jr.

Mel and sons on his boat, "Engulf and Devour"

10

THE ARREST

On the morning of February 3, 1983, Mel Cooper was in the living room of his apartment on 66th Street, getting ready to head to the office. The phone rang.

"They've just picked up Doc," said Al Albenga on the other end.

"So I guess I can expect a visit," Mel replied.

"Yeah, I think so."

"I'll call you back."

Mel hung up the phone. There was no time to talk. Moving through the apartment with focus, Mel gathered his confidential papers, ledgers, books, and a shoebox full of cash, and stuffed them into a laundry bag.

He called the housekeeper who had just returned from taking his sons to school.

"I need you to do something for me," said Mel, handing her the laundry bag. "Take this and go across the street to the bank on the corner of Second and 65th. Wait for me there. I'll be right down. I just have to take care of something."

Mel wanted to exit the building empty-handed should the FBI be waiting for him.

The housekeeper took the bag and went downstairs as requested. Mel walked through the apartment, wondering if he had forgotten anything. Steeling himself for what was about to happen, he grabbed his keys and left the apartment. Downstairs, he stepped off the elevator, took a deep breath, and walked past the doorman. But when he stepped outside, there was no one. The traffic on Second Avenue moved briskly. No one took much interest in him except a taxi that slowed to see whether the tall man on the corner might want a ride.

Mel had his eyes on the housekeeper, who stood in front of the Chase Manhattan Bank across the street. He crossed the avenue, took the bag from her, went into the bank, and put it in his safe deposit box.

This small task gave Mel a sense of relief. He left the bank and went to the telephone on the corner. He called Al Albenga at the office.

There was more bad news. At that very moment, the FBI was raiding Resource Capital Group's office. Every paper, folder, and file was going out the door in the arms of an FBI agent. A raid in pre-computer days meant the government impounded everything.

And they weren't just shutting down Resource Capital Group. They raided all the Cooper companies based in the Lake Success office: Cooper Equities, Cooper Commercial, and Etna, the truck leasing business.

"They killed us," says Mel, "They knew that the loans they were after had nothing to do with Cooper Equities or Cooper Commercial, or anything like that. They came in and cleaned out all the file cabinets, put everything in boxes, and just closed everything. We couldn't collect money. It caused complete chaos in the business."

A moment later, as he stood on the corner, two dark sedans pulled up and several men jumped out of the cars. They surrounded Mel. They introduced themselves as FBI agents. He didn't resist, and they ushered Mel into the back seat of the car.

The conversation was brief. "We'd like to search your apartment and your car. Is that alright with you?" said one of the agents.

"If you have a search warrant, you can search whatever the search warrant says," Mel answered.

"We can get one."

"Good, so get one," said Mel.

Mel was charged with loansharking and arraigned in front of a magistrate. Since this was the initial complaint, the charges were not specific, and according to Mel, no particular loans were identified. The case would go to a grand jury. An indictment would follow if the grand jury decided there was probable cause to believe Mel had committed crimes. Mel was free to go after the arraignment.

Back home, Mel called the office again and confirmed the news; the FBI had come in with a warrant, agents, and a truck, and removed everything. All information about loans, accounts, clients, receivables, deposits, and more was gone.

From the day of the raid forward, Resource Capital Group was basically out of business. The Coopers did what they could to reconstruct the loans, but with no records they could do little. "We had a lot of money outstanding in a couple of the companies like Cooper Equities which was our own investment, our own monies. In other words, Resource Capital Group and Cooper Funding before that primarily lent out banks' monies, and made a profit on the spread. But Cooper Equities primarily lent out the company's monies, and that was our own money. We didn't know where anything was because of the paperwork."

They could expect a formal indictment within six months.

Mel tried to make the best of it. "I was spending a lot of time with my kids. We were going to shows, we were going skiing. One of the things we did is we went to psychologists constantly. Those four and a half years they lived with me, we were very close. We did a lot of things together." His son Wayne at the time of the arrest was 14 years old, Avi was 11, and David, 7.

"I was still trying to work because the government just cut everything off and the income stopped. I was just looking to get something going." Mel tried real estate, he contacted old friends, and tried to stay busy.

As for Doc Hyman, though their partnership had ended with the raid, Hyman and Cooper continued to share their troubles. "We talked all the time. Doc Hyman said that we should get some lawyers quick, so the first thing we did when we were arrested was we went to see Jimmy LaRossa, the famous mob lawyer. That was the first lawyer. He told us there was nothing he could do, not until there was an indictment.

The indictment, signed by Rudolph Giuliani, came in August of 1983. Cooper was charged with twenty-three counts of criminal activities, Doc the same. The charges were sobering: unlawful debt collection, racketeering, loansharking, extortion, wire fraud, conspiracy. Still, Mel took it in stride. "I didn't take it that seriously. I was told you could indict a tree for speeding. There's no defense when you have an indictment. So I wasn't shocked that the government was able to present a case to the grand jury and get an indictment."

What did turn out to be a shock for Mel and Doc were the co-conspirators indicted with them. Giuliani, then U.S. Attorney for New York's Southern District, charged seven top Mafiosi, many of whom had been sought by the FBI for years. At the top of the list was Jimmy Rotondo, followed by Michael Franzese, Benny Aloi, Tony Napoli, Carlo Vaccarezza, Lenny Di Maria, and Frank Di Stefano.

Together, they represented four different organized crime families.

Says Mel, "I knew of all of them, but many of them I only met once or twice prior to that. I had met Benny on Carroll Street; he was associate of Vic's. He was involved with Sylvie's. I knew Michael Franzese."

The indictment also charged eight Resource Capital Group employees, associates, and investors with various crimes: Besides Mel, Doc, and Chaim Gerlitz, there were the Albengas, Junior and Senior; Anthony Capo and Joey Lipari; Stanley Gramavot, the go-between in the Sylvie's loan; and Joseph Biasucci, the Yonkers union official of Local 531 who had invested $100,000 in Resource Capital Group's loans to the Cowboy Palace.

In addition to the Mafia and Resource Capital Group contingents, sixteen other individuals were named as unindicted co-conspirators. Among them were "Frankie G" Castagnaro, James Feynman, and Tony "The Gawk" Augello. The government considered them part of the conspiracy, but they were more useful as witnesses against the bigger fish. Many of the co-conspirators agreed to testify for a chance to win a reduced sentence on concurrent cases they faced elsewhere.

Other co-conspirators were simply not worth indicting. They would be required to testify about their role in Mel and Doc's business. These co-conspirators included Mel's "lawyers-at-every-closing," Gil Greenberg and Ed Zujkowski; John Johnson, an ex-Marine who had overseen security for the Cowboy Palace; Mel's uncle Victor Goldfarb, who managed loans for Cooper Equities; Al Albenga's niece, Elaine Haber, who kept track of collections for Resource Capital Group; and Michael Franzese's secretary, Lynn Jacobson.

Rabbi Toledano and his extended family and friends from Great Neck were not indicted. That would only detract from the narrative that the Mafia was behind Resource Capital Group's loans. Chaim Gerlitz was charged with racketeering, advance fee schemes, and loansharking.

The mood at the arraignment was grim, with forty or so people saying little.

"I remember sitting on the bench there, I had one of the few seats, and Doc sat down next to me," recalls Mel. "And then all of a sudden, his wife Arlene comes up, and this is where we realized the problems we're facing. She comes up to me, and she says, in front of a magistrate sitting on a bench up there, 'You no good son of a bitch, you got my Jesse in trouble.' I mean, she was screaming, 'you bastard.' Her innocent little Jesse. So she just raved, she had to be carried out, she was, like, just screaming on the top of her lungs, just really loud and nasty, and accusing me of everything under the sun, that I got her Doc into all this trouble. Like her Doc just came out from the crib and I grabbed him, and then a couple of guys came over and said, 'don't answer her,' and they took her out of the room."

Even without Arlene Hyman's outburst, it was a surreal occasion. The fifteen defendants and their lawyers—in some cases more than one—assembled in a small room at the Federal Courthouse in lower Manhattan where a magistrate read the indictment to the crowd, who sat on benches and folding chairs.

The case was called *United States of America v. Vincent Joseph Rotondo*, even though Mel and Doc had twenty-three charges against them compared to Jimmy's eight. Mel recalls Rudolph Giuliani was there, watching the proceedings.

Doc Hyman appeared sharp and composed as ever, casually joking in spite of his wife's outburst. "He tried to appear cool and collected as he always was, but you could see that something was bothering him, you could see he was actually nervous. He spoke a certain way when he was upset, almost forcing himself to smile and laugh. You could see this was very upsetting, and it was mostly because his wife was hysterical. I don't think it would have been as bad if she wasn't there."

Doc tried to keep the mood light, as did some of the other characters who had been through this before—Michael Franzese and Al Albenga, for example. But no one would be laughing for long. It was at the arraignment they learned they were being charged under the RICO statutes – the Racketeer Influenced and Corrupt Organizations Act, Title 18 of the US Criminal Code.

Originally drafted by G. Robert Blakey in 1970, RICO was designed to target organized crime, and it did so by creating a category of criminal activity that takes place in the context of an "enterprise" or corrupt organization. With the RICO statutes, no longer could the bosses at the top of an organization insulate themselves from the actions of individuals below. To meet standards of RICO, at least two crimes per conspirator must be executed as part of a shared enterprise. These "predicate crimes" represent a range of federal and state crimes including murder, kidnapping, extortion, gambling, robbery, arson, drug dealing, and more. The crimes must be committed within a span of ten years. RICO sentences, often referred to as "draconian", carried significantly greater penalties than ordinary criminal convictions.

Rudolph Giuliani had purposely cast a net over a group of men unconnected to each other, but each traceable to Mel or Doc. By sweeping them into one huge RICO conspiracy, the government was trying to turn the whole association – "Jews and Italians" as they would later be referred to – into a single assembly line of crimes and rackets.

Mel hardly recognized the narrative outlined in the indictment. Everybody sat quietly as the charges were read aloud. It accused Resource Capital Group – "The Enterprise" – of being an outwardly legitimate business that operated as a front for Mafia loansharking. It said the company was backed by members of various New York City organized crime families, and made money for them by "embezzling, stealing, abstracting, and converting" the assets of various labor union pension and welfare funds. It claimed Resource Capital Group invested the money supplied by members and associates of organized crime into "advance fee schemes," in which Mel and Doc allegedly took nonrefundable fees from their clients, promising them bank loans would follow. Later, these victims were denied both the promised financing and the refund of their fees.

The indictment listed ten different loans, including the Cowboy Palace and Wings on Wooster. It claimed Resource Capital had lured borrowers into accepting "emergency" or "interim" money at interest rates of 2 percent a week or more, and the borrowers were threatened with violence if they didn't pay their interest.

Mel wasn't the only one who couldn't make sense of the charges. "When I learned the charges against me, I was amazed," recalls Michael Franzese in his book, Blood Covenant. "I had been hit with seven counts of loansharking and racketeering based upon a Lake Success, Long Island, operation run by Cooper, Hyman, and the rabbi. It almost made me laugh. I was reportedly stealing $100 million a month in gasoline taxes, and here's Rudy Giuliani and his Southern District forces trying to toss me into somebody else's loansharking indictment."

Doc and Mel were released on a bond of $250,000 each.

It took some time for Mel to realize exactly how much trouble he was in. "I'm an eternal optimist. I was convinced this would blow over. We lost a couple of million dollars, and the victims all ended up with cash. Nobody got hurt."

As Mel saw it, the charges were so overstated they would have to be reduced to more realistic proportions if not thrown out altogether. He had a relatively clean record – a minor bribery conviction while serving the trash business and a few misdemeanors. None of them had involved violence. The government planned to let witnesses keep the millions of dollars they collectively owed Mel and Doc. Hadn't everyone come out ahead?

And there was more in Cooper's favor; he was active in the Jewish community and the guardian of three children. Even if he were convicted, leniency certainly seemed the logical outcome.

In reality, he was in an entirely different class of trouble, thanks to the fact that his activities were now tied to the Mafia. The very same things Mel had done to minimize his legal exposure – the lawyers at the closing, the real estate collateralization of the loans, the signed documents – would now be cast as a front for the Mafia.

"It definitely didn't sink in. And I wouldn't let myself get depressed, I just had to figure out a way out." A master of denial or a guru of acceptance, Mel Cooper kept driving forward. With a multi-million-dollar business shut down and an impending trial, Mel didn't have the luxury of flipping out.

"It's never a question of whether life is fair or not. Life is what it is, and you make it work. I wasn't completely distraught about what I'm going to do. I don't get depressed. I felt I have to do what I have to do to alleviate the problem." And so, after Mel heard the indictment, he decided to treat it all like just another project. "I was meeting with the attorneys. This was my next deal, to try to put together a defense. This was an important deal, so this is what I was working on."

In addition to this stress, Naomi Cooper's ALS was progressing quickly. Mel had crisscrossed the country looking for help when his mother was initially diagnosed. The Coopers tried everything, from hiring a nutritionist, to using a serum derived from the venom of the cobra and krait snakes. They even gave her a computer so that, as the ALS took its toll, Naomi Cooper could continue to communicate with her family. But eventually the disease won out. Five months before the trial, Mel's mother passed away.

"It was very difficult," recalls Mel. "That was the closest person to me. My father and somebody else had to help me out of the funeral home. We sat Shiva at my father's house, all my brothers were there. The whole thing was a rough time."

Nonetheless, even in the midst of this upheaval Mel had to make a decision about who would represent him at the trial. "I met with a couple of attorneys. They all had their sales pitches or their cons or whatever, so it was interesting. I ended up hiring Jay Goldberg."

Jay Goldberg was a well-known criminal defense lawyer, famous for representing high-profile clients, from the music business to the Mafia, to political figures like the Kennedys. Later, he would represent Donald Trump in all his divorces.

Recalls Mel, "Goldberg was a guy in his early sixties, and he had a little hairpiece, he always watches his weight, he wears a blue suit. I didn't like him from the beginning or very close to the beginning. I didn't think he was really involved in the case. His main thrust was how much money he's going to get, and when he's going to get it. And that was substantial, probably close to a quarter of a million dollars.

"I remember there was one time when I came back to him, and I said 'Jay, I find you to be a very cold person.' We were in his office. And he says, 'really?' Like he was shocked I said this. And he had no answer, but, like, a week later when I came back to visit him in his office, he was sitting there, making sure his hairpiece was straight, and he turns around and has a picture of him and his wife and his son on the desk. He had his arm around his wife in the picture, and he goes, 'Is this the sign of a cold person?'

"In other words, this was a week later, and he was still so preoccupied with this statement, which indicated to me that this was the prime thing on his mind in between my last visit. And I'm talking about, this is one of the most renowned attorneys around, he's like one of the top five criminal attorneys in the country.

"He represented me at the trial. Every time he got up to speak he made sure his suit was just so. He's a showman. My partner had Dave Breitbart. Out of the fifteen defendants, there were fourteen top-name attorneys. Breitbart, from all of the attorneys at that trial, I happened to like the best. The guy was not only good, talented, and creative, but he had a heart. I saw how he dealt with his client and it was more than just a monetary situation. There was a definite warmth about him. He wasn't my attorney but he was sitting next to me. The complete opposite of Jay Goldberg."

Doc, meanwhile, having settled on David Breitbart, focused on crisis management at home with his wife, Arlene, and their three children. And like Mel, Doc made sure his professional life stayed in motion. He continued to stay on top of his projects with Jimmy Rotondo. This was his most profitable association and, arrest or not, he had no intention of letting it wither. With the Lake Success offices closed, Doc moved into an office in Penn Plaza on Seventh Avenue, subletting space in the law offices of Michael Asen.

Michael Asen was living proof that once a man entered the world inhabited by Mel and Doc with its rivers of cash, he didn't depart easily. Asen had started off as a partner in Wings on Wooster, making him one of Mel and Doc's "victims". He later found himself, at Mel's recommendation, working with James Feynman from the Babylon marina. It was the same Michael Asen who ended up serving as Tom Duke's bankruptcy lawyer. Now he was Doc's new landlord.

Forrest Bedell, owner of Penvest, Doc Hyman's favorite investment firm, was not so lucky; in August of 1984 he appeared in Federal Court to plead guilty to racketeering. It had been illegal for Bedell to accept Teamster pension money from Jesse Hyman, then lend it back out at Hyman's direction. Less than a year after Mel and Doc's arrest, Penvest filed for bankruptcy. The company had violated ERISA – the Employment Retirement Security Act of 1974 – by engaging in risky investments, conflicts of interest, and above all, self-dealing. Penvest and Bedell were also under investigation by the New York Attorney General.

Though Mel had once laughed at Doc and Bedell's imaginative financing deals, those who trusted Bedell lost everything. An in-depth profile of Jesse Hyman called "A Charmed Existence Ends," appeared in Newsday in 1985. Author Kenneth C. Crowe documented Hyman's criminal history, and the lives that were devastated by his partnership with Forrest Bedell. Thirty-six investors had put $5.3 million into Penvest. It was all gone, disappearing into dead-end investments with familiar names: $79,097 to Wings on Wooster Street; $1,111,468 to Resource Capital Group in Lake Success; almost $793,000 to Frank Deutsch, who was by then in prison and convicted of 15 felony charges of fraud; and $61,927 to Jesse Hyman. Millions had gone elsewhere, to businesses that listed Bedell as a board member or principal.

Teamsters Local 808 had invested $1.3 million in Penvest but the loan money had not come from Teamster pension alone; many small business owners had invested with Penvest. The owner of a luncheonette, a man who worked in a paint company, a beauty salon owner, the office manager of a flooring company – all had trusted Bedell with their retirement savings. Some of them even knew him through their church. He ruined their lives.

Said Norman Schmuckler who had put $278,735 into Penvest, "Bedell came to my home. Broke bread with us. Had dinner with us. The son of a bitch... He certainly deserves to be punished for ruining the lives of so many people."

As they awaited trial, everyone Mel knew seemed to circle around the same prospects and associates. Even after their arrests, partnerships continued to form and dissolve among the same group of players.

These connections would be revealed to a jury in Doc and Mel's upcoming trial. The trial would serve as a tribute to the mind-boggling greed of the defendants, witnesses, and co-conspirators involved. The trial would also lay bare the relentless resolve of Rudolph Giuliani and the Federal Government to achieve its ends, no matter what the cost.

11

THE TRIAL

The trial began on January 22, 1985, on a clear day in Lower Manhattan. Judge Leonard B. Sand of the Second Circuit District Court presided. Judge Sand was a highly respected judge who had been on the bench for many years and approached the law with a rigorous standard of precision and intelligence.

Mel recalls how it began. "The trial starts and after spending millions and millions of dollars on the investigation, they prepared for a very elaborate trial. The government is very professional, they have untold funds to bear for a trial. They started by spending a lot of time in showing the jury what makes up the Mafia, which had nothing to do with our case. Giuliani was looking to make this his stepping-stone up, so he wanted a big case. I saw him when they first brought in the jury. Giuliani made the first speech in front of the jury and the most severe speech. He was like an actor. Very effective, very well-spoken. He was dressed in a black suit and a tie. Very sharp."

Cooper's trial was one of Giuliani's first attempts to use the RICO Statutes to go after organized crime. It served as a dry run for the famous "Commission Trial" which followed soon after, in which Giuliani successfully prosecuted the heads of five New York City organized crime families.

The assistant US attorneys prosecuting the case for Giuliani were

Bruce A. Baird and Aaron J. Marcu. Baird, a tall and slender young man in a dark suit, delivered the opening statement. From the moment he began to speak, it was clear the government intended to come down hard on Mel Cooper and Jesse Hyman.

"There was a company," he began, "called Resource Capital Group and it was located on Long Island in Lake Success." He pointed to Mel and Doc, "It was run by Mel Cooper and Jesse Hyman, the two gentlemen seated near the file cabinet. Mr. Hyman has the red tie on and Mr. Cooper is right next to him.

"They claimed to be able to give legitimate loans and financing to people who needed money. But the office was a front, ladies and gentlemen, and Mr. Cooper and Mr. Hyman … were the tip, the small tip of a large ugly iceberg. Visualize that for a minute. That iceberg was 10 percent above water and the rest of it is down below. You might have seen movies about the Titanic or whatever. That is the structure of an iceberg and that is the structure of this business.

"Their money, the money that Hyman and Cooper used to run their business, came from organized crime. Organized crime isn't content with legal profits, ladies and gentlemen. They sucked people in, promising them easy money. And before they knew it, these victims were in the icy grip of these loansharks."

The government was off and running, metaphors blazing.

After introducing its iceberg scenario, the prosecution launched into a history of the mob. The courtroom was decorated with pictures of the known universe of organized crime, from Albert Anastasia, to Carmine Persico, to Aladena Frattiani, AKA "Jimmy the Weasel," who was scheduled to testify at the trial.

"They actually had a picture of an iceberg," says Mel. "They showed the jury pictures of bosses and capos and underbosses and soldiers, and said all the names of the people, and then they took Jimmy Rotondo's picture and put it where it belonged, then Michael Franzese's head and put it where it belonged."

The prosecution drew a genealogy of malfeasance leading right from the birth of the American Mafia to each of the fifteen defendants, hoping to relate the defendants to the most heinous figures in the history of organized crime.

"There's this whole theory of spillover prejudice when you put the bad guys together with the good guys," explains David Breitbart, Jesse Hyman's lawyer. "It spills over on the good guys. If you put a rabbi on trial by himself, where are you going to go? But in order to see the impact of what these guys did, you put them next to these guys who look evil."

This is a common practice in racketeering megatrials. With so many defendants in one trial, the prosecution needs to create an aura of guilt. Racketeering charges and RICO statutes, by definition, require an enterprise in which all conspirators participate. In United States v. Rotondo, the prosecution's mission was to connect that enterprise, Resource Capital Group or "the tip of the iceberg," to the whole amoral heap, known throughout the trial as "the bottom of the iceberg."

Says Mel, "I saw his opening statement as the government's attempt to tie in the Mafia to my business. The only difference is, I knew where the money came from. It came from Great Neck. It came from rabbis. And meanwhile this is what they were attempting to prove to the jury, that it's the Mafia's money. But it wasn't true! So it was like a trial starting from the wrong premise. So where's it going?"

The courtroom was crowded with men dressed in their best suits for the occasion, each powerful, nervous, sweating, wondering if they were showing the right mixture of concern and loyalty given the situation. Mel Cooper went for a corporate look.

"I was wearing a blue pinstripe Armani suit, solid blue tie, Calvin Klein white shirt. I wore something like that almost every day of the trial, mostly with suspenders.

"The jury was mostly white, mostly middle-aged. The seven Italian guys were sitting in a line at a long table, and the eight guys were sitting in a different row at tables, the lawyers behind everyone.

"Doc was quite nervous, from looking at him and speaking with him during the latter part of the trial, for sure. He manages to keep his cool, but I can tell from looking at him and talking to him that he was nervous. He was sitting there turning a little red at times, turning colors. When I spoke to him, there was rigidness or carefulness in reaction to what I was saying or asking. He's very cool and collected, and he has to maintain his cool in the front line for Jimmy Rotondo. He was nervous about what might happen."

Oscar "Al" Albenga was one of the older, more mature members of the group. Says Mel, "He has gray hair, a little balding and a little heavyset. He had a suit on. Neat."

Among the Italians, the mood was light; they hid their concern. "They all knew this could be bad," says Mel. Though they were from different organizations, almost everyone knew each other. "Benny Aloi is near the top, higher than Jimmy. Certainly, higher than Michael. Jimmy Rotondo is close to what Michael is, but from a different family. They definitely spoke to each other.

"Al and I spoke to a number of guys, and a couple of guys spoke to Jimmy. Even Breitbart spoke to a couple of them. Doc also spoke to some of the wiseguys.

"There was concern right from the beginning of the trial, with Giuliani, Baird, and Marcu involved, that this was serious. There was less talking to Jimmy Rotondo than there was to everyone else. Based on what happened, he was starting to be frozen out a little, just in case. That definitely came through as a coldness, because he was the one that led Doc on this trail that brought us all here.

"These people are very conservative, very cautious and if they sense something can happen, they protect themselves. That's their main ethic and concern."

Fifteen defendants get fifteen lawyers. Another feature of racketeering megatrials is that the courtroom is crowded with strategy, ego, and conflicting interests. The lawyers representing the accused were a collection of present and future legal superstars; besides Jay Goldberg and David Breitbart, there was Gerald Shargel, John B. Jacobs, Frank Lopez, Mark Pomerantz, Thomas Casey, and the only female attorney in the group, Susan Kellman. John Jacobs had been a former assistant US attorney in the Eastern District of New York. Gerald Shargel was considered one of New York's top criminal lawyers, and would later gain fame defending John Gotti. David Breitbart would soon defend Nicky Barnes, notorious drug dealer and crime boss in his own right, who partnered with the Mafia in the heroin business. Mark Pomerantz went into criminal law defending a range of organized crime figures, after serving as an assistant U.S. attorney and head of the Criminal Division for the Southern District of New York. Years later, in 2021, he would lead an investigation into Donald J. Trump for Cyrus Vance in the Manhattan District Attorney's office.

"The government's attorneys were extremely official and strict. I was very impressed with Bruce Baird and Aaron Marcu," says Mel. "They were very good at what they did. They didn't waste words. They had good control over what they were working on. They were very stern, very clear, very effective. And harsh at certain points. Baird didn't smile at all, not in front of this group. He was serious."

Jay Goldberg's plan for Mel Cooper was sophisticated, businesslike, and intelligent. He would argue on substance, getting into the inner workings of Resource Capital's loans. Goldberg claimed the financial transactions the government identified as "usurious" were not actually loans at all. Resource Capital was just a broker. The 2 percent a week represented fees spread out over time. He pulled out the paperwork and broke down the numbers to prove the government had willfully mischaracterized the entire operation.

Said Goldberg in his opening statement, "The proof will show that Resource Capital Group was not engaged in the business of lending money. It was not a creditor. It had no funds. It had no accumulation of capital.

"It didn't operate as a front. It doesn't operate illegitimately. It had no business that was unique. It acted as a financial money broker.... Resource Capital Group, for a fee, contacted any number of legitimate lenders in the hope of raising money for, and on behalf of, its clients. For the loans they made, Resource Capital Group was entitled to be paid a fee, a fee from the borrower, which they took, in this case, in the form of weekly payments. Everything was above board... It's the government witnesses who come from the bottom of the iceberg."

Goldberg also planned to make the most of the fact that rabbis were funding Cooper's loans. Though Rabbi Toledano and his party were not indicted – nor would they be called as witnesses – their paperwork certainly made an appearance.

Explained Goldberg, "When the debtors, people like Frank Deutsch and Brindley, failed to pay the creditor ... they had guaranteed repayment to Rabbi Toledano. You will find that a restaurant by the name of Wings had borrowed a considerable amount of money. When it failed to pay as it should have paid, you are going to find that Resource Capital Group had to pay the rabbi monies, because it was the rabbi who was the creditor–not mentioned by the prosecutor."

According to Goldberg, the people who borrowed money from Resource Capital Group were bad people. "To get their loans, they furnished Resource Capital Group with phony financial statements overstating their assets. They pledged certain collateral to Resource Capital Group.

"And when Resource Capital group would go to repossess the boat, it had no engine. When they went to repossess the car, the car had been moved and stolen by the government witnesses; that when the government witnesses had to repay the lawfully incurred debts, they gave bad checks.

"The government came along and said to these borrowers, 'You can have a windfall if you attempt to convince the authorities that the loans were made at higher than the lawful rates, if you yell usury, or you claim that somebody threatened you in an effort to get that money back. You can have it all by leveling those false charges.'" Goldberg rewrote the entire narrative.

Hyman's lawyer, on the other hand, used the strategy of the showman: distract, mock, outrage, confuse, and badger witnesses until their credibility was completely lost. This approach was not to defend Hyman as much as it was to make the government's case look like folly.

"Mr. Baird talked to you about an iceberg, which you only see the tip of," began Breitbart in his opening statement. "I want to talk to you about a volcano, which spews up from the bowels of the earth the worst dregs of humanity, and that's what you are going to see take the witness stand here. Because you have to make two decisions in this case. A witness will take the stand, and he will tell you a story. You don't even have to consider the story, if you determine that the witness is unworthy of belief.

"You will find that many taking this stand have stuck guns in people's faces and taken their money. They have robbed banks. You will find people who they took out of an insane asylum, that's what you are going to find here. . .You will find that the Cowboy Palace borrowed money, and that they snorted the money up their nose, and that put them out of business.

"You have to determine whether or not this case was doomed to success against Jesse David Hyman because the FBI was sucked in by the things that were dredged up from the bowels of the earth."

Fifteen lawyers got to make not only fifteen opening statements, but just as many cross-examinations, motions, closings, and more. The objections and interruptions were endless, and from the start, it was clear the case would be a long and complicated. The prosecution would have to do more than decorate the courtroom with stock photos of old-time mobsters to make their case.

The second week of the trial turned into a criminal version of This is Your Life. Almost everyone Mel knew was there. Don Kulick, James Feynman, Frank Deutsch, and Donald Brindley, who participated in Mel's first experiments in loansharking; FBI agents Walt Stowe and Stanley Nye; Tom Duke, who cheerfully admitted on the stand to blowing thousands of dollars in loan money on drugs and limousines; Peter King, boat-racing cokehead, who admitted on the stand that he had lied to the FBI; Sylvie Goldstien and Doc's friend, Michael Asen; sidekicks of Michael Franzese, relatives of Tom Duke.

But the trial would not be complete without its star witness: the indefatigable Billy Breen who, it turned out, had been peddling not just Rolex watches, but stolen diamonds, and Quaaludes, even as he targeted loansharks at the Cowboy Palace.

If one word summed up the collection of actors in the government's case, it would be "shady." There were con artists, swindlers, frauds, rats, phony check-writers, expert mob-witnesses, hustlers, grifters, and embezzlers, many of whom faced other charges, trials, and investigations. The New York Times reported, "The government presented 39 witnesses, 120 taped conversations and hundreds of documents in the trial, trying to show that the defendants conducted extensive loansharking for organized crime."

But not all the government's witnesses were lowlifes. Among the most powerful to testify were some of Mel's customers: Elaine Reisman of Champion Roofing, and Mikael Nevruzian, the rug merchant. Even Moshe Mendelson, the Mexico City cantor, made an appearance, explaining in broken English how he had taken his hard-earned money, given it to his uncle Chaim, who gave it to Mel Cooper, who made the money disappear.

One witness after another came forward to report how they had been threatened and bullied by Resource Capital Group. Some, like Donald Brindley and Frank Deutsch, were ruthlessly cross-examined by the defense lawyers and revealed as con artists. But it was hard not to be moved by Mikael Nevruzian who, crying on the stand, described how after he diligently repaid all the money he had borrowed, Mel Cooper claimed he lost the man's collateral—a $20,000 Oriental rug.

With so many of Mel's customers ready and willing to testify, the prosecution had plenty of chances to demonstrate Resource Capital Group played fast and loose with interest rates, and threatened customers.

"I was amazed," says Cooper. "The government got all these people to march in and say, 'Sure, we thought they were going to kill us.' Why shouldn't they say that? They wouldn't have to pay back the loan! The government said to them, 'Are you sure you weren't intimidated? He said "happy birthday," weren't you scared?'"

Mel and Doc had helpfully kept ledger books that showed each customer's principal and interest paid. Al Albenga's niece kept track of the collections. Resource Capital Group had accepted checks. They had given receipts. Argued Jay Goldberg, what loanshark in history has ever given receipts?

But no matter how Jay Goldberg spun it, calling them brokers, factors, or middlemen, it was obvious the We-Had-a-Closing-With-a-Lawyer approach was a fraud, and the paperwork, phony. Attorneys Baird and Marcu had enough canceled checks, books, and receipts to show the weekly cash Resource Capital Group took in was beyond any normal commission.

The extortion charges were harder to prove. The only time actual violence had occurred was when Anthony Capo slapped Tom Duke. The defense claimed Duke was not slapped in order to coerce him to pay. He was slapped because he was irritating. David Breitbart argued it was just a schoolyard fight; Mel and Doc were frustrated entrepreneurs who simply wanted to move their project forward.

Unfortunately for Mel and Doc, a charge of extortion doesn't require violence. In legal terms, extortion is "obtaining money or property by threat to a victim's property or loved ones, through intimidation, or by false claim of right." Like robbery or blackmail, you don't have to complete the act implied, you just need to get caught making the threat.

This meant that Resource Capital Group's collection technique—implied threats of violence—was enough to make extortion charges stick. If a victim believes he's going to get roughed up if he doesn't pay, it's extortion. The nuances of the Cooper and Hyman philosophy—use the threat of violence, and when that doesn't work, sue—was lost on the jury. Mel and Doc had forgotten how far they had drifted from a normal way of doing business.

Still, Mel recalls his frustration at the trial. "We didn't meet on the corner and give a guy a bag with $25,000. This was a loan with a lawyer and a closing. We weren't going to meet him with a bat. A lawyer was going to foreclose on his property that he put up. That's why a lawyer was there! But the government was saying 'No, we wanted to go beat them up.' For what? We had a lawyer beat him up with a pencil.

"We even started foreclosure on a couple. The government didn't say that in court. The government tries to drown it all out. They asked each of them on the stand, did you ever get beat up? No. Did you ever get threatened? No.

"Then the prosecutor came up and said, did you *think* that you were going to get hurt, and each of them said yes. I *thought*. And this is a crime. If you make somebody think they could get hurt, there's a crime.

"Every person that came up to the stand was told that they would not have to pay back the principal. The government knows how to tickle their fancy."

But in a high-profile Mafia trial, it isn't especially credible to claim your threats were merely tough guy role-playing. Not when you're having Mafia sit-downs at Brooklyn social clubs, or are caught on audio tape saying to your customers, "We have the biggest un-uniformed army in the world behind us," as Al Albenga said to Donald Brindley. Or as Mel Cooper said to Tom Duke, "There's a lot of wiseguys involved here with money. And that's money, secured, unsecured, and they gotta get their money out." Or as Doc Hyman declared, "We have people behind us who can blow your fucking head off."

The jury heard Tom Duke testify he was told by Al Albenga that he would be thrown through a window, made into a "fly without wings." No matter how Goldberg tried to shape Mel and Doc into young upscale entrepreneurs, witness testimony undermined them.

Mel learned that the problem with dancing on the edge of the law is you don't have the control you think you do. When you write phony contracts and do business with con artists, then leave a trail of paperwork and documents, you don't get to say how it looks to others. Like a foul ball that's close to the line, you're not the one who gets to say when it's out. Hyman and Cooper miscalculated how their activities would look in a courtroom, particularly when the prosecution played the audio tapes.

The jury listened to Mel Cooper's deep voice and heavy Brooklyn accent as he explained to union treasurer, Joe Biasucci, "When I give out any kind of loan like this, whatever it is, I always take a house as collateral and put it on paper. A lawyer closes it, and I have an understanding." The trial was turning into an exercise in unintended consequences.

Image courtesy of University of Virginia Law Library

Above, left to right: Mel Cooper, Oscar "Al" Albenga, Anthony Napoli, Jimmy Rotondo, Leonard Di Maria, Carlo Vaccarezza, Alan Albenga, Jr., unknown.

12

COURTROOM FOLLIES

By the second month of the trial, it was clear that the government was struggling to connect the bottom of the iceberg to the top, and had yet to prove Resource Capital Group was connected to the Mafia, as required by RICO Statutes. They still needed to demonstrate the Cosa Nostra's money and muscle, their savvy and say-so, was behind Cooper and Doc's high-end loansharking.

The Italians were not pleased with the fact that their fate lay partly in the hands of two Jews from Long Island. They were not sure they could be trusted; this was particularly true of Mel, whom they did not know as well as Doc.

Says Mel, "I think their underlying thoughts were, there's a good chance that the Jew is going to do the wrong thing. That if somebody's liable to go bad, I mean if they had to pick everybody out from the trial, they'd pick me out. Little did they know Doc was the first one to flip."

There were several conversations between Mel and his friend Vic Orena. "Vic just wanted to get filled in on what's going on. He was concerned, you know, that nobody else is going to be dragged into this thing.

"You could see there was talk and concern. I was going over to Monte's on Carroll Street in Brooklyn, and I met with a number of them. My meetings were mostly with Little Vic. Carmine Persico would be there sometimes. Allie Boy Persico would join us for a short update about what we were talking about, but mostly I met with Vic.

"There was always a warmth among everybody because Vic knew me for a long time, and we did a couple of things together and they worked out. So he was standing by my side. I didn't have much to say to Carmine or Allie Boy Persico because there was coldness now. There wasn't the warm feeling I felt earlier, and you could sense something was wrong.

"Little Vic took me on the side and said, there was talk and concern about Doc but even more about me, and he was saying it's not on his part, but there is concern.

"I told him, 'Vic, there is nothing to worry about.' And he knows me, here was no reason for him to believe otherwise. They're very cautious, especially at the top level. They don't want to confide anything in me, which they didn't do anyway. It's not like I was part of the circle, but you hear certain things. Vic made things as clear as possible. He said, 'If there's a problem with Doc, there's a problem with Jimmy.' And if Jimmy flips, a lot of them are finished, the big guys. This went right to the top.

"I told him, "No, everything is moving along and we have good lawyers.'"

In spite of being armed with hundreds of hours' worth of wiretaps, videotapes, and conversations, the government's claim that Resource Capital Group was a front for the mob relied on circumstantial evidence. There were suspicious meetings, isolated recorded remarks, FBI theorizing, claims by mob wannabees, and sensational side trips with little bearing on the actual charges. If nothing else, the digressions made for juicy entertainment.

They learned how Jimmy Rotondo had been in a meeting at his Brooklyn social club with the city's most infamous bosses. They learned Michael Franzese met with Don King in Atlantic City. But when all was said and done, Jimmy Rotondo, the top banana in the bunch, hadn't even been caught on tape once. And it didn't matter how many times Doc had been seen handing paper bags of cash to Michael Franzese in a diner off the Long Island Expressway. None of it was linked to any of the loans.

Lawrence Iorizzo, a friend and partner of Michael Franzese, testified that he used to go to the Monday meetings at Casablanca in Huntington, Long Island. The Monday night parties had been going strong in 1983, and Iorizzo testified that he gave large amounts of cash to Jesse Hyman

–from ten to fifty thousand dollars. He also claimed that Jesse arranged for Iorizzo to open a bank account for him in Vienna with half a million dollars.

"The trial was absolutely spellbinding," says Mel. "It's too bad they couldn't videotape that whole thing. Any time that Breitbart was going to cross-examine, they had standing room only, people would hear about it. Every time Breitbart got up there it would give you a feeling of comfort, like you just got six points for your side."

It did not help Giuliani's case that each of the two contingents—the Resource Capital Group crew and the Mafia—were themselves composed of disparate, unconnected elements. The Italians represented four different families who were not particularly engaged in business together except to the degree they bumped into each other at the Cowboy Palace.

"Everyone had a little peripheral involvement, and the government scooped them up in a big net," says Cooper.

Weeks might be spent establishing the mob credentials of Michael Franzese, for example, before they would even bother connecting him to the Cowboy Palace, and when they did the payoff was a snooze. He had invested seven thousand dollars in a cigarette concession.

"Franzese had conversations with Doc, and they were talking about turning the Cowboy Palace into a franchise and opening up a hotel called The Cowboy Palace. Doc was going to let him have the cigarette concession and that was on tape with the FBI. So his involvement in the case was because of the cigarettes."

The Gambino contingent, Lenny Di Maria, Frankie "The Hat", and Carlo Vaccarezza, had loaned money to Tom Duke. Tony Nap of the Genovese family had not only discussed loaning money to Duke but wanted to take over the Cowboy Palace lease. Benny Aloi, Colombo family capo, made his appearance in the loan to Sylvie's.

Of all the wiseguys, only Jimmy Rotondo was genuinely and deeply involved in Doc's financial schemes, but he hovered out of sight like the silent partner he was, remote from day-to-day operations. Nothing connected him directly to any of illegal loans.

Many in the Resource Capital contingent were equally detached from the core business. They were associates and outsiders with temporary and fleeting relationships to Resource Capital Group. Stanley Gramavot had been a go-between on the loan to Sylvie's, put there by Anthony Augello, a Colombo family soldier. Joseph Biasucci, secretary-treasurer of Teamsters Local 531 in Yonkers which represented ambulance drivers and attendants in New York City and Westchester, had sunk $100,000 into the Cowboy Palace. Mel claims Biasucci was just an investor, "a nice guy not looking for trouble."

Which isn't to say these associates were just bystanders when it came to crime. Said the US attorneys, "Stanley Gramavot has spent his entire adult life avoiding any productive employment while 'working' as an associate of the Colombo Family," noting that Gramavot "has an extremely high IQ and was a successful student. Despite this obvious potential for a successful and productive legitimate career, Gramavot deliberately elected life as a professional parasite."

Joe Biasucci ran two illegal numbers operations. His union had a history of involvement with organized crime.

But even Michael Franzese, hardly shy when it comes to crowing about his own mob-related activities, found the government's claims a stretch. "I guessed that the Italians had been swept in at random for their publicity value. Indict four Jews and the media yawns, but salt the proceedings with seven Italian gangsters and the press goes wild."

Mel disagrees. It was all about the Mafia. "If the government wasn't looking to hook in the Mafia, they wouldn't even have been interested in us. I think the government would do anything to get these seven Mafia guys, to get them convicted on something. Once it started coming up that the money didn't come from the Mafia, it came from the rabbi, you could see the desperation from the government. They were sharp enough to understand where this was going, they saw their house of cards collapsing."

Breitbart exploited the tension the government had introduced between Jews and Italians. Said Breitbart, "Whether or not I believe this is an ill-conceived prosecution where several Italians are thrown in with three Jews for window dressing, is not the question. It's the allusions to organized crime when they showed the money is coming from a temple in Great Neck. The prosecutors are acting in a way that is an affront to this court." How could Cooper and Hyman be front men for the mob when Rabbi Lionel and Leah Toledano's names appeared on all the paperwork?

Says Mel, "The government is saying, this is where the money comes from to make these loans, from prostitution, from gambling, and so on. Actually the money came from the rabbi in Great Neck. The three million dollars all came from Great Neck. But the government is saying all the money came from these dirty, murky people."

January turned into February, February into March, as week after week, defendants, lawyers, journalists, friends, family, and curious observers gathered to watch the proceedings. Even the jurors got into the act. The trial was interrupted by a stream of emergencies. A juror's stepson was shot. Anthony Capo's uncle was killed. Chaim Gerlitz was carted off one day to the emergency room at St. Vincent's Hospital, thinking he was having a heart attack. Lenny Di Maria and Frankie The Hat were arrested in a Gambino family sweep.

Among the defendants, the mood was high. Indeed, more and more it seemed that the government had gotten all the right people at the wrong time. They sat at their table and joked, they kibbitzed in the hallways.

Only Chaim Gerlitz saw no humor in the situation.

"He was beside himself," Mel remembers, "He was very nervous, you could see he was sweating. His wife was there, almost sitting there with her hands out to him, telling him to calm down. She was concerned about him."

Gerlitz was the only defendant who chose to testify. On the stand, he described his role at Resource Capital Group, how he sent "little brochures" to potential customers, then followed up by telephone, promoting Resource Capital Group's services. He wrote to construction firms, importers, shipping companies, even to Manhattan Borough President, Percy Sutton, whom Gerlitz referred to as "The President of Manhattan."

Chaim's lawyer, Mark Pomerantz, argued that Gerlitz believed he was engaged in legitimate deals. Pomerantz also unintentionally reinforced for the jury Mel and Doc's habit of getting personally involved in their clients' businesses, bringing in networks of family, friends, and personal associates with a promise of profit. Gerlitz had involved his son and nephew in one of Mel's special loans.

Richard Vasquez planned to open a pinball arcade across the street from Juniors Restaurant on Flatbush Avenue in Brooklyn. Chaim's son and his nephew, Moshe Mendelson, invested in the project, and as part of the deal, they were promised a food concession. They enthusiastically made plans to open a falafel restaurant. Mendelson invested $8,000 in the project. Rabbi Toledano put in $60,000. It was a legitimate proposition backed up by Resource Capital Group's phony loan papers.

Like so many others, this loan fell apart. On the stand Gerlitz told the story of how Cooper and his collection department–Capo, Lipari, and Alan Jr.–met with Mr. Vasquez at Juniors. Sitting in one of the large booths with the orange upholstery, they told Vasquez he owed money and hadn't paid it back so they were going to take his machines. The pinball machines were loaded on a truck and taken away, and Mel Cooper and company left Vasquez crying in the restaurant.

"Honestly, I'm ashamed for Malka. I'm ashamed for myself," Gerlitz said. On the stand he explained how, when the interest payments stopped coming, "there were lots of telephones and shoutings of all kinds. I was battered day and night by my nephew, my wife, by Lionel Toledano about money."

By December of 1982, when the Cowboy Palace closed, Gerlitz acknowledged everything was falling apart at Resource Capital Group. "The office started to become a little out of order. It was very dim. There was no life, and because there was a lot of checks which bounced, people didn't get paid. It was hard." Gerlitz also testified he never engaged in a transaction he knew to be involved with "extortion, violence, intimidation, or organized crime." As far as he was concerned, all his payments were interest, incentive, finder's fees, or commission. And when he was heard to say "juice" on the tapes–slang for illegal interest–he was actually saying "choose." His testimony revealed a hapless man, willfully naive.

Certain themes began to appear among the defense, passed from man to man, like a football down the field, with increasing self-confidence. In particular, three themes established themselves among the defense lawyers, best labeled as "Don't Hate Me Because I'm Italian," "Forgive the Sins of the Fathers," and "Who Are You Going to Believe, My Client or These Criminals?" These themes have become a staple of Mafia trials. But at this early RICO prosecution of the mafia, the claims resonated through the courtroom week after week with a freshness rarely seen since.

The Cowboy Palace was the centerpiece of the prosecution, and

Giuliani's prosecutors presented their two star witnesses: William Clifford Breen and FBI Agent Walter Stowe.

Unfortunately for Giuliani, David Breitbart was proving masterful at turning the government's narrative on its head. He claimed it was the FBI who turned the Cowboy Palace into a crime scene, who filled a legitimate business with instigators and troublemakers. After all, who besides Billy Breen and Walt Stowe was caught on tape using words like "vig" and "juice"?

If there was a compromising fact worth noting about one of the so-called "victims", Breitbart would uncover it, suggest it, or proclaim it. Though his philosophy infuriated the prosecutors, explains Breitbart, "My job is to see that the system works. My job is to make sure that if they get them, they get them right. My job is to prove that the system is more important than any single defendant. My job is to see that the agents don't frame people, my job is to see that the agents don't overreach, my job is to make the system fair and impartial, that's what I perceive my job as."

"So, you are a loanshark?" Breitbart asked Don Kulick, making sure the jury knew Don Kulick had "street money" of his own out.

He called Joey Lipari, Alan Albenga Jr.'s sidekick, a "half-wit." He called Breen a "psycho." He called Donald Brindley a "scheming, planning, con man." He suggested Michael Asen, the lawyer involved in three of the nine loans, was guilty of a felony because he didn't report what he knew to be phony loan papers.

The U.S. attorney complained. "Mr. Breitbart attempts to use cross-examination to abuse witnesses and to put misleading conclusions in the mind of jurors in an outrageous attempt to dirty the record."

A snipe-fest began between attorneys. The prosecutors went after the defense lawyers, calling one attorney a "sleaze," another a "son-of-a-bitch," and "unlearned in the law." After two months, the stress between Breitbart and the assistant U.S. attorneys in particular neared a breaking point.

Judge Sand had had enough. "I don't want any comment to be made by any attorney to any other attorney," he announced one day.

"I thought you people were the cream of the crop," said Judge Sand on another occasion. "I see I was wrong."

Recalls Mel, "The judge was always reprimanding people. It was very chaotic with 15 lawyers. It wasn't easy, but this judge had complete decorum. If this judge says we start at 9 o'clock, it starts at 9 o' clock, it was like the army. This judge had complete control. The one thing that I was always amazed about is the man has to say so many things, and I never found him to say one extra word out of his mouth. In other words, every word had three meanings, it didn't have only one."

In Breitbart's quest for the truth, no cross-examination proved more astonishing than Billy Breen's.

"Were you ever convicted?" Breitbart asked Breen on the stand.

"No. Never," replied Breen.

"What about in Boston, 1971?"

"Right. You got me there, counselor."

It went on like this for days.

"Breen looked like a snake," says Mel, recalling Breen's testimony, "and from what everyone knew of him, he was a snake. He was promised protection, so he was telling what he knew. "I would say he looked sleazy, like a con man, and he talked like a con man. If he told you the sun was out, you have to check to see if it's true. He was dressed in a sports jacket, and a shirt and a tie. He was middle-aged, and nervous. He was a professional at this, but each lawyer tore him apart. I don't know if he was ever confronted with this kind of situation. This is one of the few times when he had to go face to face with everybody, including the FBI. You could tell he was nervous when he was talking. He was like a wreck when they found him lying. He had no credibility."

On the stand, Breitbart elicited the full spectrum of Billy Breen's criminal activity and penchant for lying. Looking squarely at the witness, Breitbart's New York accent signaling confidence in his place in a New York City courtroom, he continued his cross-examination.

"You told us that you have never worked. But you are not a thief. Is that right?" said Breitbart.

"I beg your pardon?"

"You have never been a thief?"

"No, sir."

"You never stole any money?"

"Did I steal any money? I don't think there's anybody alive that hasn't taken something."

"Did you ever steal any money?"

"No, sir."

"Did you ever use a gun to steal money?"

"You're right. You've got me again. Yes, I did. You asked the question, did I rob the restaurant? I did."

"Did you ever defraud people?"

"Have I ever defrauded people? No, sir."

"Mr. Breen, have you ever held a job in your life since you were thrown off the Police Department?" Breen's only job had been a brief stint as a police officer in Massachusetts as a young man.

"No, I haven't."

"Have you ever earned a legitimate dollar in your life since you were thrown off the police department in Somerville, Massachusetts."

"No, I haven't."

Breen admitted he had done bookmaking, served seven years in prison, been convicted three times – twice for robbery and once for bookmaking in Florida in 1984. While out on bail, he committed another robbery. He was stopped with $37,000 in cash and a pile of jewelry in his car. The IRS found that William Breen had engaged in "gambling and illegal narcotics trafficking activities."

But it was Breen's mental illness that became the focus of Breitbart's efforts to discredit the witness. It emerged Breen had been diagnosed as an aggressive, violent personality, that he had uncontrolled, impulsive behavior, was depressed, and had been diagnosed with Munchhausen's syndrome. He was considered generally delusional to the point where it was noteworthy that, while working in the Cowboy Palace, he did not have one of his bouts of amnesia. Said Billy Breen, "That was one of the times I was in reality, one thousand percent."

Under oath, Breen stated he was not a paid or registered informant for the FBI. He had been acting on his own, putting up his own money. In fact, the only reason Breen had gotten involved with Tom Duke to begin with was to get some cash so he could pay off the $49,000 he owed the IRS.

Said Breitbart, digging into Breen's self-declared role as a crime-fighter, "So you don't instigate these investigations; you go into them."

"I said I'm a catalyst. I will not take an active case. I only take my own."

"Do you feel that you are a great law enforcement official?"
"I'm an expert."
"So you feel that you do a good job in rooting out crime in America?"
"That's true."
"And do you feel that you do an important job?"
"That's right."
"So you teach these things to the FBI."
"Yes."
"Do you teach these things to drug enforcement agencies?"
"Not the drug enforcement agencies, but I've taught schools of law enforcement agencies and FBI agents."
"Was there anyone else on the faculty who was a paranoid schizophrenic?"
"Well, your honor, I object to that," said Mr. Baird.
"Sustained," said Judge Sand.

There was much discussion of whether Billy Breen was drunk while at the Cowboy Palace. On the stand he said no, but revised it to "yes," after being reminded of his own words on tape: "I was drunk out of my fucking mind, I don't remember a fucking thing."

Only FBI agent Walt Stowe felt Breen was a reliable witness. Said Stowe, "Breen was trustworthy. But you wouldn't have convicted anyone based on just his testimony."

The Mafia remained elusive. Walter Fagin, Sylvie's boyfriend, was the only witness who could firmly link Jimmy Rotondo to any of the loans. Unfortunately, he had been killed in an accident only weeks before the trial, run over by a tow truck a block from his home. All that remained was his grand jury testimony.

He was not the only co-conspirator dead before the trial; another key player, Anthony Augello, also involved in Sylvie's, had committed suicide some weeks before. According to another witness, after screwing up a deal, Augello had been told by the family it was time to go.

Said Walter Fagin, whose taped grand jury testimony was played in court, "I met Jimmy a couple of times through Stanley and Tony. To my knowledge, he lent them [Mel and Doc] enormous sums of money. This sort of came out in conversations. Jimmy said, 'They are into me for hundreds of thousands of dollars.'"

Fagin claimed Cooper "carried around enormous sums of cash. He carried it in a leather portfolio in his pocket. It was never less than this thick. The transactions in the office, whenever you were there, were frantic. There were people running in and out of the office, bringing him money, him, giving them money.

"We made a deal with them which looked very real for at least a month until we started getting very suspicious... money came forward, expensive money, but money. They showed a great deal of interest." As often happened with Resource Capital, the mortgages Fagin used as collateral to secure the loan were pledged to a rabbi named Lionel Toledano, and the permanent financing never came through.

Tom Duke also took the stand, patiently answering questions and making increasingly outlandish claims. He claimed he owned 11 limousines, and that T. Duke Industries was a $34 million company with projects in North Carolina, South Carolina, and Georgia. He referred to Cooper and Hyman as "his financiers," and stated there were only two people agitating him, frightening and upsetting him: Maury Joseph and Billy Breen.

Recalls Mel, "He was also very nervous because he knew what he was looking at, it was staring at him from seven chairs. He was concerned about that during testimony, so he was trying to save himself. He was scared out of his mind. He dressed with a suit and a tie, he came across to me as not that credible. He was making statements that did not jive with what really happened. 'I built my club, I borrowed money, I didn't feel threatened. I didn't have any fear for my life.' He didn't dare say anything that would hurt these seven guys."

Duke explained how his eviction from the Cowboy Palace unfolded between December 6 and December 20. The landlord wanted $25,000 to satisfy the lease. According to Duke, Mel refused to write the check. Duke defaulted on the money he owed and the marshals evicted him from the premises.

Walter Stowe, the third key witness in the Cowboy Palace affair, was cross-examined at length. Breitbart and Goldberg tried to discredit him any way they could. Breitbart, in particular, made every effort to paint him with the same brush as Billy Breen, accusing Stowe of using cocaine, attaching himself to a psychopath, and playing at being a tough guy.

"He was a good-looking, tall guy, calm," says Mel. "Based on this background, he had no fear. Stowe was trying to tell a story that made some semblance of sense. It was the story that the FBI wanted to hear, and it was more general than Breen or Duke. He was sticking to what he knew. Stowe was trying to bend anything towards the seven guys. But it was 95 percent hearsay."

One of the most amusing moments of the trial was provided by Breitbart's cross-examination of yet another co-conspirator, a man named Lawrence Iorizzo, who was Michael Franzese's partner in his alleged gasoline scam. Iorizzo claimed he had witnessed Franzese hand bags of cash to Doc Hyman in a Long Island diner. As with all the witnesses he cross-examined, Breitbart wanted to cast doubts on Iorizzo's truthfulness, and by extension, his claims concerning Doc.

Asked Breitbart, "What is your wife's name?"
"Rosemary," Iorizzo answered.
"How long are you married to Rosemary?"
"Twenty-seven years."
"Do you have any offspring with her?"
"Five children."
"What about Cheryl, are you married to her?"
"Yes."
"You are married to Rosemary and Cheryl at the same time?"
"Yes."
"For how long were you married to Rosemary and Cheryl at the same time?"
"About twelve years."
"Did Rosemary know about Cheryl?"
"Yes."
"Did Cheryl know about Rosemary?"
"Yes."
"Did you know about the law?"
"Objection," said Mr. Baird.

By April, things had become impenetrably complex. The jury followed scores of players as they appeared and disappeared, shifted positions, and assumed different roles. The borrower of one loan might be the loanshark of the next. Both victim and victimizer took a point here, half-a-point there. The trail of victims led from the pinball machines in Brooklyn, to boats in Babylon, to farmland in Texas.

James Feynman, involved in Peter King's loan, needed total immunity before he could testify, as did Tom Duke and Peter King, who both confessed to using cocaine regularly.

Feynman, who was facing Federal tax charges, had agreed to tape Michael Franzese. On the stand, James Feynman testified he made two cash payments to Franzese for a usurious loan. The grand total involved in the payments was $500.

The witnesses included so many frauds and scoundrels that the prosecution went out of its way to remind jurors that loansharks "attract a certain type of person."

Trying to answer the question of guilt in relation to everyone involved in the loans—associates, lenders, borrowers, co-conspirators, and silent partners—was like trying to unravel a tweed coat. Pull the threads apart and there's nothing, no pattern. The more the government teased apart the whole mess, the more incomprehensible it became. Threads seem to lead nowhere or even worse, to absurd subplots that seemed right out of a bad mob sitcom.

Someone told the judge a body had been found in the trunk of Mel's car. Says Mel, "They neglected to say that I had a car leasing company, and had about 2,300 cars out, and in one of the 2,300 cars there was a guy found dead. It wasn't my personal car.

"He happened to have owned a gas station in the five towns, and I used to gas up my car over there, so I knew the guy, Richard Stone,"–AKA Richard Slomowitz–"and he leased a car from Cooper Leasing, an Eldorado, and there was a time that he was found in the trunk in the El Dorado in Kennedy Airport. And the government chose to put down that."

Some of the borrowers, like Elaine Reisman and Sylvie Goldstien, realized that the entire situation–signing phony loan papers and paying exorbitant interest rates–was illegal, and they sued Resource Capital Group. Rabbi Toledano sued Donald Brindley. Resource Capital Group was foreclosing on Thomas Rajkumar and Billy Breen. Elaine Reisman sued the Toledanos. And Sam Cooper, Mel's father, was suing Jesse Hyman for the balance of the money Doc still owed him for buying into Cooper Funding.

Adding to the confusion, Resource Capital Group's victims often praised the accused. Sylvie Goldstien called Stanley Gramavot an "upstanding gentleman." Rabbi Gerlitz called Mel a "brilliant financier," and said he "wished everyone would have a son like Alan Albenga Jr." Don Kulick, under oath, said no one had ever threatened him. Even Tom Duke said he was never afraid of being hurt by Resource Capital Group's "thugs," though he admitted he didn't like being slapped by Anthony Capo. The prosecution bravely chugged forward like the Little Engine That Could, deconstructing each loan, with narratives going on for days at a time.

For every mobbed-up witness the government produced, Mel's lawyer, Jay Goldberg, waved papers signed by Lionel and Leah Toledano. Chaim Gerlitz testified the loan money indeed came through the Toledanos, who didn't know anything about the Mafia. After three months, the prosecutor conceded the point to the defense, and said, "I stipulate that Rabbi Toledano's money didn't come from organized crime." Never had mobsters and rabbis been on two sides of a tug-of-war like this.

As the trial drew to a close, the fifteen defendants began to seem like character actors with recurring roles, cast in the same part over and over. Mel was always The Greedy One. Doc, The Smooth Operator. Oscar "Al" Albenga was The Enforcer. His son, Al Jr., Joey Lipari, and Anthony Capo were The Muscle. Chaim Gerlitz, The Sap. And Jimmy Rotondo–always in the background but never seen or heard–was The Puppet Master.

Perhaps the government hoped that by overwhelming the jury with such a disparate and breathtaking flood of information, after three or four months–most likely out of sheer exhaustion–they would put away the whole crew.

But they didn't.

At the end of every story, no matter how crazy, there was only Mel and Doc. Their financial interests appeared as the backdrop to each story. And no matter how ambiguous the situation, there were still the cancelled checks, the phony contracts, the audio and videotapes, and the credible witnesses.

Jay Goldberg had mentioned the audio tapes in his opening statement, warning jurors, "Cooper may be heard to say not nice things, not things necessarily meant for a courtroom–not entirely appropriate to an office. What was said in a particular place may be taken out of context when you take it from a room where people are free to rap and say whatever they want." Much like the "locker room" defense years later, Goldberg argued people say things in private they wouldn't say in public. But logically, planning a crime is always done in private, behind closed doors. And it became apparent after three months of testimony, Doc and Mel had done plenty of rapping.

Finally, it was time for closing arguments. Jay Goldberg went first. In language that seemed more elaborate and florid than the other lawyers–perhaps reflective of a man whose couch sports throw pillows embroidered with the word "Harvard," according to the New York Times–Jay Goldberg made his case.

"Now, I tell you, I couldn't ignore throughout the entire case the continual barbs thrown at Mel Cooper throughout the entire case. Mel Cooper did this, Mel Cooper did that. It's so easy, when people come to a money broker, anxious to get the money, they are so pleased when they walk out with that $100,000 or $150,000, but no one wants to pay. Not the ten people I will discuss."

Again, Goldberg argued that many of the loans in question were not loans at all. They were investments. Mel Cooper was merely the middleman. "Resource Capital was a broker, not a lender. Resource Capital was a guarantor. And the 2 percent a week interest? That was mostly fees. The actual interest was just half a point ... a perfectly legal amount of interest.

"Resource Capital was akin to the Bank of England. It wasn't the wholly lawless operation painted for you by the prosecution, operating just above the surface of the iceberg, a wholly lawless entity operated by Mel Cooper.

"Mel Cooper's business had operated in this metropolitan area for more than 35 years. It operated serving hundreds upon hundreds of clients. If you are going to service hundreds and hundreds of people, whether you are a lawyer, a doctor, a money finder, a broker, aren't you going to have disgruntled bad apples make accusations against you?

"I think it's a fair and accurate description to say that when you take the money, half a million dollars, never intending to repay it, you are not a victim, you are a thief.

"People like Lawrence Iorizzo, James Feynman. Jimmy the Weasel Fratianno, Lipari, Breen–these were professional criminals." Moving from the iceberg metaphor, Jay Goldberg called them all "the seasoning" in the recipe to discredit Mel Cooper. The purpose in bringing them forward was to prejudice the jury.

"If this were a case where the Mafia organized crime was involved, you would find the facts to be that the people borrowed one million and had to pay back three million. If the money was not paid, you would find what? Bones would be broken, limbs would be snapped. You wouldn't find, Mr. Baird, lawsuits, concessions of judgment, mortgages, and legal proceedings by Resource Capital in an effort to collect the debts.

"I mean, ladies and gentlemen of the jury, you have read books, you have seen movies, The Godfather. Can you imagine Marlon Brando saying to a debtor, 'You don't pay me that money, I am going to smack you in the face with a summons?' Al Pacino saying, 'You don't give me that money, you are going to be hit over the head with a confession of judgment.' One more, Robert De Niro, 'You don't pay me, you are going to be mauled by a mortgage.'" The jury laughed.

"For three months you lead this jury down a path designed to inflict prejudice on the rights of every one of these defendants, because nobody likes organized crime. Bad. Who likes organized crime? No one. But you don't use that in a case to jeopardize the rights to a fair trial of people who have so much at stake.

"The talk on the tape? It was lawfully done, in someone's private office. The government offered a piece here, they took a bit of what a guy said on Monday afternoon and then put it next to a Tuesday afternoon and they orchestrated the tapes for you.

"The government has not proved beyond a reasonable doubt that Mel Cooper or anyone else 'physically abused, beat, threatened or took property through criminal unlawful means.'"

Goldberg's affected delivery and use of repetition played well with the jury. But where Goldberg had relied on reason, Breitbart unleashed fury, decrying the respective "creatures" that the government had called forth.

Began Breitbart as he addressed the jury, "He talked to you of an iceberg. I talk to you about a volcano. The same shape, but not hidden. But a volcano erupts and brings from the bowels of the earth the worst foul vermin and slime and sludge that you could ever see. This is the analogy I see when I look at what's been put up here; the foulest stench that has corrupted or attempted to corrupt our justice system."

Judge Sand spoke up. "May I interrupt you for a moment and see you at the bench?" Breitbart walked over to the judge. "I just wanted to remind you that there was an explicit request from a juror that the lawyers not shout. You have three hours to go."

Pacing himself, Breitbart reviewed the evidence for the jury and asked them to examine it with care.

"2,500 hours of tape. 47 days of recordings. They did not prove any money came from organized crime. They dress up Frankie the Weasel to look respectable. Others they dress like thugs, they put a psycho lunatic on the stand. What are these men doing here? There has been no evidence against them. What are they doing here?

"I don't know what Breen is. I have never seen a creature like that in my life. Do you know what Billy Breen is? Ladies and gentleman, I talk to you about a poisoned well. I talk to you about a funnel of filth that emanated from one room and one building."

He reminded jurors, Billy Breen "conspired with others, and supplied one James Kearns of Revere, Mass. to shoot to death a United States judge, John Wood, Jr. He introduced the hit man.

"This is the guy who not only conspires to kill judges and gets involved in assassinations and steals money and moves drugs, but robs banks with a gun, he robs bars with a gun, he runs a gambling operation.

"Duke, Stowe, Breen. That jury doesn't need much time, huh? Guilty. Guilty of a half-million-dollar bankruptcy bust-out. Guilty of drugs. Guilty of conspiracy. Guilty. And all of a sudden, the victims are the accused and the accused are the victims. Who is crazy? Billy Breen? He ain't so crazy. He's free. They're facing this. All of a sudden, day after day, week after week, the bad guys are the good guys, and the good guys are the bad guys.

"This man took fifty milligrams of Thorazine a day," proclaimed Breitbart referring to Billy Breen, "and that knocks down hippopotamuses, the most powerful depressant known, but imagine with an acting-out maniac?

"And he did it right on the witness stand. Have you ever seen someone have a breakdown before, besides Duke – do you believe he's got $34 million without putting up a dime? 'I'm a catalyst. The FBI is stupid. The world needs me. I travel here, I travel there. I move drugs. I kill judges.'

"This is the evidence in this case, ladies and gentlemen. You go from Breen to Stowe, because they're one and together. This genius, I'll tell you, he looked like a linebacker for the New York Giants, beautiful, good looking, tall, undercover agent, dignity and respect. This guy talks to Billy Breen, puts his life in his hand. How small is Stowe?

"Ladies and gentlemen… Think and evaluate. Use the loupe of the jeweler. Tear away the outer shell. Use the microscope of the laboratory technician. Turn on the floodlight of reason."

Concluded Breitbart, "I am telling you, the people that we are talking about; we are talking about the volcano that spewed up from the bowels of the earth, that sludge and slime that I talked to you of.

"What are you supposed to do? What are you supposed to do if you think someone is guilty but you have a reasonable doubt? You are supposed to vote not guilty. That's your sworn duty."

But sometimes it's the smallest thing, an overlooked, spur-of-the-moment choice that can topple everything you've built. It was in passing that Mel Cooper "lost" Mikael Nevruzian's $20,000 rug. But that kind of small choice can help a jury, even one receptive to the arguments of Goldberg and Breitbart, see another possibility.

Assistant US Attorney Baird sensed this. He began the prosecution's closing statements acknowledging, "The defense did a spectacular job of discrediting the witnesses, of confounding the order of things.

"I heard all these people referred to as thieves yesterday, all the people that borrowed money from these guys were called thieves. You notice all of the government witnesses fell into some category. They were either thieves or they were crooks or they were lying to you, they were con men.

"Mikael Nevruzian paid every dime back, ladies and gentleman. Where is the thief there? He paid every dime. He paid him interest, he paid him the 2 percent a week, and he paid him every dime of the loans back.

"Thomas Rajkumar, another $30,000 loan, 24 percent a year interest and a so-called management agreement that adds another 38 percent for a total of 62 percent. Another unlawful debt.

"The 'management agreement' is there, just like the 'incentives' and the 'fees' that you have heard about. What do they talk about on the tapes? Do they ever talk about incentives, interest, fees, commissions? No. They talk about the money, cash weekly.

"Then when Mr. Rajkumar couldn't make his payments they just tried to grab his building. Now, you heard some argument, too, about how, well, if they go through the legal process and they foreclose in a legal way, that's not a crime.

"Well, that's not what happened… they just went up to the building. They mailed mailgrams to all the tenants and said, 'Pay us.'

"Now let's talk about Hyman and Cooper. Hyman and Cooper don't even have a defense, ladies and gentleman. They have a fantasy. We [the government] made it all up. Every bit of it. We just made it up. Well, when you are caught on tape like they were, what can you do?

"You heard Cooper talking about his scheme. He and Hyman talk about their mob backers. They talk about Jimmy Rotondo being a captain. They talk about Michael Franzese, about how to deal with the different factions involved in Sylvie's and the Cowboy Palace, the two transactions where the mob guys come to the surface.

"You heard it from half a dozen witnesses, and you see it on the tape. Hyman and Cooper, what are they talking about? They are just puffing? This is just, what do they call it, silly talk, locker room talk? 'Jimmy's a captain. Jimmy's got money here. We have to back up something for Jimmy.'"

"The government is not asking you to do anything to anybody because of their ethnic background or whether or not they are a member of a union or anything like that. That is just an outrageous suggestion. They're here because of this evidence."

Concluded Baird, powerfully capturing the entire karmic drama in a few sentences, "This is the way crime really works. It is not a movie. It is not Al Pacino or Marlon Brando. It's real and you have heard the way they talk, the way they make money, the way they make deals so they can all earn. You have seen that sometimes their plans fail and sometimes they talk to people that they shouldn't have trusted. And you ought to give thanks for that, ladies and gentlemen, because that's the only way we catch them."

The jury took five days to decide the fate of Mel Cooper, Jesse Hyman and their co-defendants.

Mel Cooper was found guilty on seven of twenty-one counts. Doc, the same. All six associates of Resource Capital group including Al Albenga, Chaim Gerlitz, and Anthony Capo were found guilty of various charges.

All seven Mafia associates were found not guilty. The prosecution failed to prove beyond a reasonable doubt that they were involved in this particular set of crimes. The claim that it was Mafia money behind the loans did not stick. Even Baird had admitted in his closing arguments that "it's the tips of the iceberg, Hyman and Cooper, that do most talking. The organized crime members, the hidden mass of this iceberg, talk much less."

Observes Mel, "the Italian guys shouldn't have been there to start with. It's not so confusing that they got off, they shouldn't have been there." They were not the bottom of the iceberg. "What the government said they did, they didn't do.

"At the same time, the people that were convicted were disappointed, especially when they heard the other seven were not convicted. I guess it's a shock. I mean, some of the seven guys *were* involved in some of the loans. Franzese gave us advice. A number of the wiseguys were showing their faces, or letting it be known through Doc, that they were expecting something from the Cowboy Palace. And Rotondo was getting a piece, and he was bringing that piece up to his bosses."

Michael Franzese saw it more in black and white. "When the scorecards were tallied, the result was a split decision. All of the Jewish defendants and their associates were convicted, while all of the alleged mob members were found innocent. For once, I felt, the system had worked perfectly. The jury had somehow managed to wade through the government's misrepresentations and separate the guilty from the innocent."

The government tried to put a happy face on the matter but anyone with a vested interest in the success of RICO prosecutions wasn't pleased. U.S. Attorney Rudolph Giuliani called the verdict "a compromise" by the jurors.

Said Giuliani, as reported in the New York Times after the verdict, "The defendants they convicted were on tape, and they were the defendants against whom the most evidence was admitted. They acquitted those where there was somewhat less evidence. We are, of course, quite pleased with the conviction of the eight who were the day-to-day operators of this illegal enterprise."

Some of the defense lawyers didn't buy it. Said one, anonymously, "I'm sure the U.S. Attorneys office is going to call it a victory, but given the amount of money they spent [on a two-year investigation and a three-month trial], they weren't looking to convict a rabbi or a Jewish dentist. They would have been much happier if everyone who was acquitted had been convicted and vice versa."

Said Jay Goldberg, "They lost the thing that they were trying to gain in this case, the conviction of the seven that they were really interested in."

Chaim Gerlitz and Anthony Capo were released on bail. Mel was remanded in custody and sent to MCC–New York's Metropolitan Correction Center–where he would remain until sentencing.

13

THE WORLD FADES AWAY

"We were remanded after the conviction," recalls Mel, "and we were brought into the marshal's office and put in the holding pen. This is the part of the whole system that's the most suffocating, the most frustrating. An entire day can go by, just to get from the holding pen to your cell.

"At MCC, your cell is, like, a regular room, it's about eight feet by five feet, and generally it's for two people. So you have a toilet, and a sink on top of it, made out of aluminum or stainless steel, then you have a steel desk attached to the wall, with a metal seat. You have one lamp and a double-decker bed. And there's a window, but it's thin and it's got bars on it.

"There's only a little recreation area with maybe a pool table or a ping pong table, there's some tables where you'll eat your lunch when they bring it up. Everything is in an elevated building, because it's Manhattan. So you're limited to a very small area, there might be 100 people in your unit, 50 rooms, and every room is filled to capacity."

At least it was clean, according to Mel. "One thing about the Feds is they keep it clean. It may be old but it's clean."

The sentencing took place on June 3rd, 1985.

More than anything else, the sentencing symbolized the disconnected nature of this trial. "After the Italians got off, the thing had a life of its own and it just kept going. The whole time they're telling how this bottom of the iceberg is behind the scenes, and then there's no bottom of the iceberg! There's just the pure white top."

But it was too late. Call it the government's own brand of bait and switch; although the Mafia half of the enterprise was gone, RICO sentencing would still be applied. And RICO sentencing guidelines are brutal, to put it mildly. A charge that would carry a five-year sentence under normal Federal guidelines might garner a twenty-year sentence under a RICO prosecution.

Until the very end, Mel expected to do time, four or five years at the most. "I remember talking to Jay Goldberg who said that if you're found guilty, you might get, like, seven years. I said 'What are you talking about? This is the first-time offense, there's been no violence, the victims all made hundreds of thousands of dollars, who's the victims?' He says 'maybe you're right. Maybe four years.' I said, 'Is there any reason why we shouldn't get probation?'"

Having settled on probation in his own mind with the outside possibility that he might have to do a few years of time, Mel was ready for sentencing.

On Monday, June 3, Mel, Jesse, and their guilty associates were back in Judge Sand's courtroom. Both the criminal defense attorneys and Federal prosecutors had submitted sentencing memorandums to Judge Sand in which each argued for a particular sentence.

The prosecutor's sentencing memorandum was a no-holds-barred affair in which Assistant US Attorneys Baird and Marcu argued for the maximum penalty. Their memorandum started off with an expansive and grandiose view of the crimes at hand: "What the proof showed is that loansharking, and the fear and societal corruption that flow from it, has grown in New York City from a crime involving low-level loans to individuals, into a multi-million-dollar enterprise infecting the fabric of our lives…. Enterprises like this one threaten the foundations of civilized society. They mock our puny efforts on behalf of the rule of law."

The memorandum included a section dedicated to the criminal conduct of each defendant. Here, anything was permitted including unproven allegations, gossip, and flimsy circumstantial evidence. Mel Cooper's profile was more or less a list of his relationships with Mafia-run carting and trucking companies. It reviewed the Cooper family's network of companies, stating that Resource Capital Group, Cooper Funding, and Mel Cooper engaged in a variety of criminal activities, from loansharking to money laundering to fraud regarding loan and leasing arrangements based on nonexistent or overvalued equipment.

Curiously, it concluded by paraphrasing an observation made by Frankie G and Al Albenga, originally intended as praise: "These two criminals agree that it is Mel Cooper who has taught organized crime in New York City the sophisticated brand of loansharking characterized by fake documents and security interests."

By contrast, the tone of Jesse Hyman's memorandum was dripping with venom. The prosecutors seemed indignant at Hyman's willful amorality. After five pages of a criminal resume extending from East Coast to West, they summed up his criminal activity as "loansharking, advance fee schemes, bank frauds, ERISA frauds, and embezzlements, Taft-Hartley Act violations, money laundering, narcotics conspiracy, petty larcenies, grand larcenies, arson," and more, concluding, "The evidence gathered in this investigation demonstrates that Hyman is utterly without moral scruples. His personal brand of depravity is best illustrated by a fraud he perpetrated on Joseph Podnos and Podnos' daughter, Rona Shukovsky." The prosecutors recounted how Hyman promised to invest the money of family friends—Shukovsky was the godmother of one of Jesse's children—then proceeded to steal the money, mock his friends, and tell them "if he was caught, he would only get a few years in 'Allentown' where he would play tennis and be out in a short time for good behavior." If Mel was all about the money, Hyman seemed to enjoy the pain.

Indeed, the Newsday profile of Hyman that had appeared earlier in the year revealed that, far from being a successful entrepreneur, "Hyman has a history, documented in the civil court records of New Jersey and New York, of not paying his debts. Judgments totaling more than $400,000 in unpaid debts and loans have been filed against him in Nassau County alone." He left a trail of aggrieved partners, and several incidents in which arson and burglary factored in. Said one of his partners, "He thought he was a miniature Wall Street executive. He came off knowing everything about high financing... Here is a son of a bitch talking about millions here and there, and taking money from the company."

In the face of narratives like this, the defense lawyers had to make their argument for leniency.

During the trial, the defense lawyers had agreed to present a coordinated front. No one did anything to directly implicate any of the other defendants. But at the sentencing hearing, the gloves came off.

Jesse Hyman went first before Judge Sand. David Breitbart launched his final argument with unabated passion. First, he objected to the suggestion that "anybody who was a Teamster was in the Mafia, and that anybody that is involved in unions is improper. Dr. Hyman is tainted by these suggestions.

"Dr. Hyman did financing over this period of time, over these 10 years basically by word of mouth. As a barber cuts the hair of somebody who comes to him, a financier who arranges financing gets a reputation in the community. If some of the people who Dr. Hyman arranged financing for were involved in other activities – I know there were allusions during the course of this trial…that Michael Franzese was a capo in the Colombo Family…the point is that Dr. Hyman supplied his particular expertise.

"He did meet people. He does know people. He perhaps might be considered, in his terms, a buff with regard to people who have unsavory reputations. He has read all the literature."

After painting Hyman as a Mafia hobbyist, he went on to address Doc's role in Resource Capital Group, telling the story of a junior partner who only wanted to help.

"Dr. Hyman's involvement in the Resource Capital Group situation lasted over a period of approximately nine months, as the evidence indicated. Dr. Hyman told you in his letter to you that, in fact, he was not aware of any improprieties when he entered into the organization. The evidence was clear, as far as I am concerned," continued Breitbart, "that Dr. Hyman was a peacemaker, that he was an ameliorator, that he was a negotiator.

"Judge, what we have is the perception of a lawyer and the perception of the court. I see Jesse Hyman as a warm, caring father, as a loving husband, as a concerned member of the community, both civil and religious. I draw from the experiences, from talking to the people, from reading the letters, that he would be the one to be called at 2 o'clock in the morning when there was a health problem, and he would show up with the bagels and the coffee... He is a salvageable human being. What I am trying to do is save a life, not destroy one."

Judge Sand was having none of it.

Said Judge Sand, "I have rarely encountered a situation in which there was the disparity of perception that exists in the memoranda which have been submitted to me by the government and by you on behalf of Dr. Hyman.

"It is frequently the case that although there are somewhat different perceptions as to what the court's exact sentence would be, there is some general acceptance or recognition of the seriousness or the magnitude of the crime. I find here that there is a total lack of perception to this moment on the part of Dr. Hyman, as reflected in the submissions that I have received, that this was anything other than commercial irregularities, and that is very distressing."

Continued Judge Sand, "I would suggest to you that this is the type of case where there is not the sudden yielding to temptation, where there is not the hungry family or crime of passion; that this is the type of case in which an intelligent, professional man makes a calculated judgment, whether, as one would say in the vernacular, crime pays."

Judge Sand asked the assistant US Attorney to comment. Bruce Baird had little to add except to say, "As to whether Hyman is salvageable, the overwhelming answer is simply that he hasn't cooperated. He knows a lot, your honor. He knows it from the tapes and he hasn't cooperated."

The judge turned to Jesse Hyman. "Dr. Hyman, you stand before the court convicted of the counts I have just indicated. Is there anything that you wish to say before sentence is imposed?"

Recalls Mel, "Doc was very calm. Not loud. Very exact in his choice of words. Basically telling them it's all been understood incorrectly. He was sorry this whole thing happened. Not arrogant in any way, he spoke nicely. He's good with words and sentences, he's respectful.

"At sentencing he was impeccably dressed. I think it was a dark double-breasted suit. His red hair was neatly combed, he looked neat."

Jesse Hyman stood up and began by revisiting some of the claims made by the prosecution, reminding the judge that his involvement with Sylvie's was to seek credit for the store and resolve disputes. Said Jesse, "I undertook the role to meet with Sylvie and at that time, Walter Fagin, to try to ameliorate everybody's position and try to resolve it." He continued in this vein until Judge Sand cut him off.

Said Judge Sand, "I am familiar with all of that.... But I spent 15 weeks listening to the evidence and listening to you, Dr. Hyman, listening to you on those tapes, and you still have not grasped the fact that this jury has not accepted the flimflam and the window dressing and the 'I was the peacemaker and the good guy,' and you still have not accepted the fact that you were one of the two masterminds that went from them, down to the Capos and the Liparis. They exist and they acted the way they did because of you and because of Melvin Cooper."

Defendant Hyman began again. "All I can say is that the feelings I am about to express to you are very real and honest. I am not in the terms of a shylock. The errors of judgment that I made in this case are my own and I stand before you guilty of the crimes committed.

"First of all, I am angry at myself, believe me. I am angry for allowing my greed and my ego to take precedent over my wife and my family. Secondly, your honor, I am also embarrassed, embarrassed in front of my community, my dear friends, and again, my devoted family. Thirdly I am frightened. Frightened for what the future holds for my wife, both physically and emotionally, my children, and our survival as a family unit."

Jesse continued, elaborating the future of his children, though he could not stop himself from echoing Breitbart, reminding the judge that the links in the chain of conspiracy were basically broken, with only eight of the fifteen convicted. He concluded by quoting Milton, stating, "'Lucifer, because of his overzealous prosecution of man, was cast out of heaven.' I stand here full of sorrow, and hopeful that my family and I aren't damned for the error that I have committed over the past 42 years, and that I am given the opportunity to return to them and resume my obligations and duties as a husband and father."

If Jesse thought a quote from Milton could charm the intellect of Judge Sand, one of the most distinguished and rigorous American Federal judges, he was mistaken. The harsh observations of the judge were in sharp contrast to the platitudes expressed by Hyman. Having spent over a decade dabbling in criminal activity, Doc had forgotten what it meant to face consequences.

Jesse Hyman had been recorded in Resource Capital Group's office saying, "I can never get into trouble. I'm always the guy on the outside. I don't want to be on the inside." At the sentencing, only Jesse didn't seem to realize, he was now the guy on the inside.

Said Judge Sand, "The concerns which you have expressed with respect to your family, which move me, and the letters that they write, which move me, are regrettably concerns which are expressed at the time of sentencing and not during the time of the commission of these crimes.

"I regard this crime as being of a very high magnitude because it was the professional, the legitimate front, the masterminding of a complex, large criminal activity. It is the type of conduct which our society simply cannot countenance.

"It is the judgment of the court that you be sentenced to a term of 30 years and a fine of $160,000."

As the judge explained how the sentence was allocated, Arlene Hyman screamed. "How can you do this? No, I don't care. I have three children. He never did anything wrong. No." She was standing now.

But the judge just continued, "Count 1 and 6, a term of 20 years to run concurrently with each other..."

Recalls Mel, "When we got sentenced, she was yelling so much the marshals actually carried her out of the courtroom. She was screaming, 'murderers' to the judge, 'murderer, you murdered my family.'"

Says Mel, "Based on the way she was taking it, you could almost second guess that Doc is going to look to do something if there's a chance, depending on his allegiance to his wife. He's going to look to do something to get back together with her. And when Doc got 30 years, right away the lights went on Jimmy. They don't know if it's going to be hours or days before he flips, but there was no question that Doc was going to flip.

"I was sitting there with my lawyer who was telling me we shouldn't be looking at more than four years. The judge starts saying to Doc, 'I'm giving you ten years for this count, and 20 years for this count, and another 10 running concurrently.' I listened to this, and I turned white.

"My whole world went in front of me. I knew I would get a duplicate of what Doc got, it was like I saw my whole life, I was white as a ghost, everything was passing through my head at those few moments. I remember like it was yesterday, how shocked I was. You would not believe how many things can go through someone's mind in a couple of minutes while this was taking place. It's all disappearing, my whole life."

When Jay Goldberg addressed the judge, it was with the knowledge that Mel's sentence had to be the same as Doc Hyman's. He began by finally saying out loud something hinted at throughout the trial: Jesse Hyman was operating on an entirely different level than Mel when it came to a life of crime.

Said Goldberg, "Cooper manifested no independent awareness comparable to that of the codefendant," said Goldberg. Mel was suddenly a follower with none of the grand ambitions of his partner.

Goldberg reminded the judge, Doc Hyman's relationship with Teamsters and Longshoreman went all the way from New York City to his days in Buffalo and Cincinnati. He had been involved in a continuing relationship with organized crime and the misuse of union pension funds since 1975. His pension-fund operation dwarfed Mel's opportunistic loansharking; Cooper's sentence should be "drastically, substantially" less than what had been imposed on codefendant Jesse Hyman.

Goldberg continued, his normal tone of detachment tinged with stunned advocacy, "I have had people sentenced to thirty years, fifty years." Goldberg's voice filled the silent courtroom. "I have been through all of that.

"I don't collapse when somebody has dedicated his lifetime to crime, who has been guilty of acts of violence and murder, narcotics peddling, importation of heroin, I have had those cases. I don't think this case warrants the kind of sentence that obviously has to be in your Honor's mind with respect to this defendant because, as the government points out, he and Hyman are on parallel tracks, and I sit here having heard what your Honor said in the sentence that was imposed upon Hyman, and I am arguing against that sentence.

"It may offend Cooper that I don't argue for a suspended sentence or community service because I don't think he is entitled to it for the very, very serious crime that he has committed. But how long? Judge, he has been here 38 years on this earth, and he did terrible things in 1981 and 1982.

"The defendant was in the finance company business since 1970, we will say. One company after another. Is that agreed? CBS Leasing; M.

Cooper Leasing; a host of finance companies. Was there ever a complaint in all those years against him? What did the FBI agent Lang tell us through the testimony of Breen? As of August 1982, they never heard of Mel Cooper.... This wasn't some notorious person who for the period of fifteen years lived outside the law, and it took the combined efforts of the government and cooperating witnesses to bring him to court.

"But from 1969, when he started working for his father, until 1981, is there one act of greed? Is there one act of usury claimed against him? Is there one bank that was defrauded by him, of the forty banks dealt with by Cooper Funding and Resource Capital? Is there? …. Is the crime that he committed so very great that it causes your honor to impose the kind of sentence that a state judge would impose for a murderer?"

"It isn't a technical crime. It is a crime that hurts people," replied Judge Sand.

"It is true," said Goldberg.

"And, again, this isn't a low-level role. This is a mastermind."

"Very bad."

"And this is somebody who exhibited, with respect to a number of people, a viciousness."

"Should he get a life sentence?"

"You take the rug dealer and the rug and the man who paid back everything, but they took his Oriental rug and Cooper put it in his apartment and then when the man said, 'I paid you everything. Give me my rug back,' and they said, 'Oh, the maid lost it…'"

"He should get a very strong sentence. But should he get a life sentence? Because make no mistake about it, when you sentence somebody to thirty years, in effect, that is twenty years. The state law is what? Fifteen to twenty-five if you murder one person or twenty people… I think there is a severe sentence that fits the crime that he committed. But I don't think that it is thirty years, twenty years in prison, for a crime that the jury found, with all due respect, was not funded by organized crime. They found that."

Having a brief window of time in which to engage the judge, Goldberg tried every angle. There were traumas in Cooper's life, he said. Mel was influenced by "severe emotional disturbance." There was his mother's ALS, the daily hospital visits, his three small children at home.

"These combined factors in 1981 and 1982 caused him to go off the deep end and commit these terrible acts," said Goldberg.

He pointed out that even the jury agreed the government overreached, as demonstrated by the fact that they wouldn't convict the mobsters; that Cooper had loaned out millions and had only been repaid $500,000 – punishment in itself. Goldberg reminded the judge that violence was indicated in only one count. Said Goldberg, "thirty years is a sentence doled out to someone who has dedicated his life to criminal behavior."

Though Goldberg's argument was compelling and significantly more reality-based than Breitbart's, even he sensed it would have little impact on the judge.

"Give him a strong sentence," concluded Goldberg, "Give him a message…[but] as you sit there, if you are going to give him that kind of a sentence that was meted out to Hyman, then nothing I say will have any impact if you come to it with that mind-set."

The government had little to add. Said Marcu, "Mel Cooper brought to the criminal world, and to organized crime in particular in this area, according to the conversations recorded, a new brand of loansharking that apparently hadn't been thought of before. He was a mastermind of sorts and he dealt with enormous sums of money." Marcu stood by his request for a sentence of 140 years – seven consecutively served terms, just as he had requested for Jesse Hyman.

Echoing Baird, Marcu added, "if there is any question that he had serious remorse for what he had done, or that he seriously hoped to change his ways, he had the opportunity to show that by offering to tell the government what he knew, and it is clear from his own statements that that is an enormous amount about the criminal element in this community, and he has rejected that opportunity."

Before the sentence was handed down, Judge Sand gave Mel a chance to speak.

By then, Mel could hardly think clearly. It all felt like a dream. Luckily, he had written down his comments in large, neat print on a yellow legal pad. He read from his notes. "In the spring of 1981," Mel began, "our family became aware that our mother and grandmother had been diagnosed with ALS. The more time I spent to try to find a cure for my mother, the greater my other problems seemed to become. My marriage was dangling and I just couldn't cope. I lost all interest in the businesses that I worked so hard to build up, the fundamental theories that guided the businesses I had forsaken.... I never knowingly intended to hurt anyone. I am not a loanshark. The crimes I have committed were an error in judgment."

Replied the judge, "When you say you are not a loanshark and when you say you never intentionally intended to hurt anyone, I have to hear those remarks in the context of what else I know about you, the words that came out of your own lips, the evidence of the role that you played, and of your greed, and of the various activities in which you were engaged, all of which hurt people." Judge Sand returned to the magnitude of the sums involved, and Mel's complicity with Jesse Hyman, concluding, "But in everyone's life there are tragedies. There are parents that are lost. There are bad marriages. There is not anyone who does not have some area of personal suffering. But that hardly explains, hardly justifies, indeed, hardly mitigates the Melvin Cooper reflected in the evidence received in this case."

Judge Sand gave Mel his thirty-year sentence.

Says Mel, "No one gets thirty years. There were murderers in the place that I went to who were doing a lot less time. I asked, 'Can I at least arrange for my kids to live someplace?' And the judge said, 'You should have thought of that before you committed these crimes.'"

What no one knew at the time was that the government was preparing an elaborate case against Jesse Hyman's Teamster associates. Within a few years, various union officials and Mafiosi would be charged with conspiracy and racketeering. Hyman would become the key witness in the RICO prosecution of John Long and John Mahoney of Teamsters Locals 804 and 808, respectively. He would publicly confess to paying kickbacks so the unions would steer their investments to Penvest.

The government was also preparing charges against DeCavalcante family boss, John Riggi; Gambino capo, Nino Gaggi; and acting boss of the Cleveland Mafia, Anthony Liberatore. Most people involved in Mel and Doc's case would later agree, the harsh sentence was designed to get Doc to flip. The Government had plans for Jesse Hyman.

Mel and Jesse were each fined $160,000 on top of their sentences. A few days later Mel was on his way to Federal Penitentiary in Terre Haute, Indiana.

14

TERRE HAUTE

Terre Haute is a high-security penitentiary in southern Indiana. There are five gun towers, a razor-wire fence, and a road around its perimeter where two armed trucks circle constantly in opposite directions.

When Mel was there, Terre Haute housed over 1,000 prisoners, divided into seven units. Each unit had its own manager and guards, its own doors, and of course, its own cells. When Terre Haute opened in 1940, sprawling across 1,100 acres of farmland, it was considered a model of a therapeutic approach to incarceration. A 1953 brochure about Terre Haute from the Bureau of Prisons observed "beauty is itself therapeutic and a prison need not be grim, forbidding, and repellent to be custodially secure."

Mel arrived in Terre Haute in mid-July, in the middle of a heat wave. His first vision of Terre Haute was on an overcast, steaming day, and it was as grim, forbidding and repellent as anything he had ever seen.

"There were three gates, and I went in with about twenty guys after arriving by bus. After the first set of gates, they took off the shackles but they left on the handcuffs. Then they brought us over to our unit." After registration, Mel was shown to his cell in what is known as an "Honor Unit" of Terre Haute Penitentiary.

Getting assigned to an Honor Unit was Mel's first break. An Honor Unit is all about doors and bathrooms. Because of the prison's age, there existed several units where bathrooms were separate from the cells. There's no traditional "lock down" in these units. Prisoners would ordinarily be kept in their cell from 11 pm to about 6:30 am. In Honor Units, cell doors aren't locked so prisoners may leave their cells to use the bathroom.

Mel's cell was approximately six feet by nine feet with bunk beds for him and a cellmate. "There was a bed, a table, and one or two metal shelves on the wall. The fact that you have the ability not to have to stay in this tiny room, to be able to walk out—not that you do it—but just the idea that it's available to you, is a tremendous relief. Just not to have it locked is almost like you have half your freedom." As he would find out later when he was less lucky, "one of the biggest shocks is when every day you hear the keys going in the door, and the keys turn, and it's like a knife that just goes in, another knife every day, and you just imagine how many days you have to listen to that."

The thing about finding yourself in a high-security prison at age thirty-eight is, it doesn't sink in all at once what you're going to go through, what your life will be like. Little by little, as you learn the system and observe your surroundings in this new world, you begin to understand the society within a society to which you've been assigned.

"I remember walking in, and it was July, and I came into the place, into the unit I was assigned to, and immediately to the right there's like a TV room, and I went in and sat down for a few minutes. I remember it was about 98 degrees and there was no air conditioning, and this was one of my biggest fears in life. In general, I'm the type of person that can't tolerate the heat, and I was sitting there and the sweat is just dripping and I'm thinking, wow, I can't even take it now, much less thirty years. It was something that I had to try to get accustomed to little by little. But this was the first realization, the fact that it's so hot, and no matter what, there's nothing I can do about it. During the summer I'm going to have to suffer the heat and in the winter, I guess it'll be the cold. This was like another level of understanding."

Air conditioning was the least of his problems.

"My second night, I was sitting there playing cards with the Italians in this Honor Unit. We're sitting there, and all of a sudden I see this guy buck-naked running through the door behind us. There was a big door that goes to the corridor and he runs over and he's banging on the door screaming, and he had at least seven stab wounds in his back, because he was gushing blood from all different areas of his back. The one guard came and saw him right away, one of the guards from the hallway, but he wouldn't open the door until he got all the guards dressed in their riot gear just in case there's a riot. It took them at least a few minutes to do that, and they came and took this guy on a stretcher to the hospital, and I never saw him again. Typically, what would happen with someone like this is either he died or they shipped him off to some other place so it doesn't happen again. But this was the first day or the second day in the place."

The card game didn't stop and no one got up. Immediately Mel realized he was going to have to figure out how to make this system work for him, just like he had always done on the outside.

"The first thing I did when I got there was, I went to the weight shack and I started working out six days a week." Mel is blunt about what was at stake. "So there's one thing when you come in when you're 130 pounds, and you have to face everybody else who's there for life or fifty years or ninety years, and are just looking to take a woman on. So as far as that goes, if anybody approaches, you just have to fight. And I've never been approached on that basis."

Inmates self-organized into groups. "You had black Muslims, you had Spanish, you had some American Indians. Any time an Indian is arrested, it's a Federal offense. The Jews had cliques in all the places. We had services once a week, or the rabbi came in." The Jewish population at Terre Haute was small, only thirteen or fourteen out of a thousand.

Mel also made sure he had protection. His first roommate was a young guy from the Bronx named Ralphie, in for dealing drugs. "Ralphie had started in State prison and had been transferred to Federal prison because they couldn't handle him.

"There are certain protocols that you have to learn about, which is why Ralphie, who had already been there for a bunch of years, became my bodyguard. He would tell me about different things – what you could do, what you shouldn't do. I mean, I didn't come born knowing all the amenities of prison, or what you have to do. So he tells you about different things and his perspective on things, and once you learn it, you have your own common sense, and you judge it for yourself. Like, when we walked in the hallway, he'd walk on the outside, and he'd say 'you walk over here, on the inside.' Because if you walked on the outside, that's where somebody would get shanked."

Ralphie took an interest in Mel for two reasons. "Ralphie started a 'store' where you could get cigarettes, potato chips, different non-perishables they would usually have in the commissary. In other words, when the commissary is closed, you can get what you need from Ralphie, and then you have to pay him back. So I financed him. And second, he liked me. We got along. He was okay. His mentality, the way he thought, was when he was leaving, he said 'Can I help you with anything when I get out?' He said, 'You have a sister in Westchester, right?' I said, 'Yes.' He said, 'Listen, if you want, I can help her out, walk her to the store.' He offered to go to the store with her. His mentality is, everyone is going to the bodega. So he legitimately wanted to help."

Prison has its own laws, and very quickly Mel learned to follow them to the letter. If you cut in line, if you changed the TV channel without asking—that's a reason to get stabbed. Mel also learned that in prison, it's a big deal just to accumulate a few things, a few comforts. "For instance, if you see a little rug on the floor, it's like, wow, when did you get something like that?

"You go into a guy's room, like Fat Gigi"—Fat Gigi Inglese was a tough guy associated with the Lucchese family, in prison for selling heroin—"He was down for like twenty years, and he had his room, his private room in Terre Haute. You go into his room, and you see a big radio, and because he's down so long he has this big radio, he has curtains, he has a rug on the floor. You can see he has the amenities. They're very little things, you wouldn't think anything of it. But when you're in prison, you notice one guy has a bare concrete floor and a concrete wall and a sink, and this other guy has a cover for his toilet—all of which, when the guards come and they search the room, they just rip apart, so everything that you might build up and make nice, they'll have in a pile within ten minutes."

The game between guards and inmates is another lesson to be learned when it comes to surviving prison life. "Certain times they'll let the guy keep his stuff, sometimes they'll take two of the things that he's been collecting for a long time and now instead of twelve things he has only ten and then hopefully the next guy who does the shakedown is not going to take three more of the things, so eventually it circulates, it all comes back out. Maybe there's a nice guard who won't take anything, so if you're there a long time, you know the guards."

Mel's first months in Terre Haute were filled with "new levels of understanding."

Race: people basically stuck with their own kind.

Food: it was your only pleasure as well as valuable currency. It bought you favors like clean linen and pressed clothes.

Guards: don't mess with them and they won't mess with you.

Within his first few months at Terre Haute, Mel learned he had lost his appeal to overturn his sentence. The eight defendants who had been found guilty had asserted their right to an appeal and claimed their sentences should not stand because they had been illegally videotaped. That evidence should have been suppressed. They claimed the consecutive sentences imposed by Judge Sand violated the double jeopardy clause of the Fifth Amendment, and furthermore, there had been prosecutorial misconduct. Specifically, the appellants did not like the iceberg metaphor.

The appeal had been filed while the group was still in New York City. "When I was at MCC, I had a certain amount of days to file a piece of paper to say I was going to file an appeal. So I had time while I was in MCC to interview a couple of attorneys." Mel hired Thomas Puccio and Joel Cohen, two of New York's pre-eminent young criminal lawyers. "Tom was a former US Attorney, and his claim to fame was winning the notorious Claus Von Bulow murder trial with Alan Dershowitz. That's where he got his stars."

But Judge Roger Jeffrey Miner put an end to Mel's hope that his sentence would be overturned. Concluded the judge, "We have considered all of appellants' arguments and find that none of them requires reversal. Accordingly, the judgments of conviction are affirmed."

Mel remained focused on finding a way out. Even after he lost his appeal, it was impossible for him to believe his thirty-year sentence would stand. "My energies were constantly on the legal system, trying to figure out how I'm going to get out. I always had things that I was working on, thinking, I'm going to get it thrown out, thirty years is insane. That's what allowed me the sanity of continuing to do the time–thinking that hopefully I'll come up with something that's going to work."

Without a legal remedy, Mel could still see his sentence reduced by ten to as much as twenty years, thanks to "statutory good time." This was time off a sentence awarded under what was known as the "Old Law"—the pre-1987 sentencing guidelines. Congress changed the law when it passed the Sentencing Reform Act of 1984, in order to better standardize the time prisoners served, among other things. They wanted a closer match between the sentence awarded an offender and the time he actually served.

Under the Old Law, prisoners automatically received one-third off federal sentences simply for being there and following the rules. From there, you earned points that either added to your sentence or reduced it further by up to another third. A "shot" or a mark on your record took away your statutory good time. On the other hand, you can earn "Extra Good Time," an additional third off your sentence, by just laying low and doing your job. On a thirty-year sentence with parole for good behavior, ten years in prison was the best Mel could hope for. Of course, a warden or a vengeful guard could easily see Mel did every minute of his thirty years.

Besides working on his case, Mel distracted himself in other ways. By law, he had to work.

"My first job was feeding the fish. There were two fish tanks and that was my job. And to remove any fish that dies. And then from there, I became an orderly in the hall. You would go into the hallway where everybody walks—there were three eight-hour shifts, and I think I was on the ten o'clock shift—and you would have to run down the hall with about six guys with a mop or a dry mop, or whatever, and you'd do the whole area with six guys. It would take about two minutes.

"And also, I was very strong in Kosher. Much of the time I was there, I ate quite well, where most people would get whatever slop they served. Many times, in Terre Haute we'd get our own kitchen, and a guy named Marshall Shrager was in the kitchen with me. He was a good cook and he would prepare duck and chicken, and then the Italians got jealous and they wanted to have the Jewish food, but the rabbi wouldn't put them on the Jewish line. 'You're not Jewish.'"

"Marshall was an interesting guy that was doing, I think, twenty-five years. This was, like, his third time in prison for armed bank robbery. He robbed about thirty banks. He was really a nice guy, and a guy that's been down a long time, and he had a prison mentality. Pretty pessimistic."

The law permits inmates to follow the dietary rules of their religion; it's considered a First Amendment right. Recalls Mel, "During that time in Terre Haute there was an actual kosher kitchen, which was supposed to be manned by Jews, and at a certain point, we had complete freedom over the menu. We would make pasta dishes with really good sauce. Marshall was very close with the Italians and he used to make food for them in the kitchen and he figured out how to get them the food. Eventually the Italians would come and pick up their dishes. They would get their food one at a time off the kosher line.

"The Italians had some old-timers there. There was Anthony 'Bruno' Indelicato. He developed, like, a little epilepsy. He was a sharp looking guy." Indelicato was in for the murder of Carmine Galante, and had also gained a reputation as one of the men who brought FBI undercover agent, Joseph Pistone or "Donnie Brasco" into the Bonanno organization, which meant he was always watching his back.

Mel's strict following of the laws of *Kashrut*–he had kept kosher all his life–meant that whatever facility he was in, Mel ended up in the kitchen. This put him in a perfect position to buy favors from other prisoners, like clean laundry and cigarettes. "Food or cigarettes or stamps would get your bed made, it would get you new linens, you get your sweatsuits washed and ironed."

Like many people in prison, Mel became more religious. "I had a lot of time, so in the morning I'd do my prayers, and because of not having a regular job, my day was pretty free to work out and read and do different things. On holidays, like Passover, we made the best of it, in the sense that we got special food for the holiday. Again, we made special food when we had our own kitchen.

"I worked out at least six times a week, from an hour and a half to two hours. It was a way to get your frustrations out. I was lifting weights I never thought I could lift. The longer you're doing it, the more you can lift."

Mel learned very quickly that in prison, the rules are designed to humiliate and control, and never let you forget that you are no longer deserving or worthy of the liberties accorded people on the outside.

First there is the noise, the loudspeakers constantly barking orders and summoning prisoners. Then there are the random raids on your cell, and the strip searches every time someone visits you. There is the schedule, the "hourly move," with pressured rushing alternating with endless waiting. And there is the fact that you are no longer a name with a history. You are just a number.

Should you prove to be a danger to yourself or other prisoners, or refuse to follow the rules of order, you go in "the Hole," or administrative segregation. The hole is designed to separate certain prisoners from the general population. You're left alone in a concrete cell, usually for 22 or 23 hours a day. It's not just for those who break the rules; prisoners who are weak or vulnerable sometimes need to be separated from the population for their own safety.

Says Mel, "Terre Haute was a real rough place. Terre Haute was a place where it would not be unusual for someone to get stabbed for either disrespecting someone or for a gambling debt, drugs, or being queer. For any number of things, people would get stabbed. You could be stabbed for fooling around with someone's 'wife.'"

Mel associated with the right people, and was helped by his connections to the Italians, who quickly learned Mel had been on trial with friends, and had done right by them.

"Everybody finds out about everybody. I knew Italians outside, I was in the garbage business, certain people were on trial with me, and in prison their friends are all there. All the Italians were associated with somebody in the five families. They looked at me as the guy on the case with their friend Michael Franzese or Tony Napoli. It got around that the Italians were my friends, and you don't screw around with friends of theirs."

Mafiosi enjoy a comfortable position in the prison hierarchy. "They have power up to a point. It doesn't stop them from getting smashed in the face in the yard. They have to respect people too. But typically, people would stay away from them. Some of the Italians were in there for drugs, but there were a bunch of them with organized crime. In different places, the top guys would surface, the capos, the underbosses, if they were in prison. They were very well-respected in the prison by the other Italians."

At Terre Haute, a maximum security prison, inmates tended to have long sentences. "You wouldn't get someone there for just three years. You don't need that kind of high security for three years. So typically the person is in for things like bank robbery, big drug cases. You had people doing big time in this penitentiary."

The only way to bend the rules in prison is the same way you do it on the outside: with influence, money, or power. Sometimes all you need are the right friends. The Jews and Italians basically got along well, and with his influence in the kitchen, Mel could get them some of the things they needed. Mel saw what happened to those who didn't know how to make it work. It could be terrifying.

"I had to help one Jewish guy that got raped," says Cooper. As usual, his view is strictly practical; there is no mystery as to why some make it and some don't. "The ones who don't make it in prison are the same people that can't make it work out in the street. There's not much difference. You use your head, you have common sense. You know what you can do, what you shouldn't do. If you can make it on the outside, you can make it on the inside."

Mel's maxim served him well. Within six months he had his own powerbase in the kitchen. He accumulated a few comforts that made life easier, a small fan for the heat, a few sweatsuits, a little radio with speakers, and a paint set he bought through the commissary.

One day the case manager told Mel somebody had come to see him. The visitor was waiting for Mel in a room above the library, a special area Mel had never been to. Immediately Mel knew something was up; they had even given him a pass.

In prison, everything happens on a schedule, and inmates are only allowed to change locations at a designated time known as the "hourly move." With a pass, you could travel anytime, even between moves. "I went down the hall, by the library and upstairs. No one is lounging around at this time, so nobody sees me go upstairs."

Mel entered the room. A man dressed in a suit and tie sat at the table. He looked like he was in his early forties. He seemed relaxed, not like someone who worked in the prison.

"Can I help you?" said Mel.

"Agent Dietrich," said the man, standing up for a moment and reaching out to shake Mel's hand. He sat back down. Mel sat down at the table, across from him. "So Mel, how do you like it here?" asked the agent.

"It's not as bad as I thought," Mel answered.

A look of disappointment flashed across Agent Dietrich's face. This was not what he hoped to hear. He persevered. "Things could be made a lot better, if you want to talk to us."

"There's nothing to talk about."

"You sure? This is not a good place for you. We can arrange something different."

"I have to go, because things could get a lot worse if I don't get going." Mel knew this conversation better be short and sweet.

"Okay, Mel, thanks for your time. Maybe some other time."

"Or maybe not. Thank you."

Recalls Mel, "I was not interested in talking to him, it wasn't going to do me any good to be seen talking to an FBI agent. Just the fact that he showed up there wasn't good for me. I went downstairs and I went into the unit and met with some guys and told them what just happened.

I also told my lawyer what happened, and he called up the U.S. Attorney and said he'd appreciate it if agents don't come to speak to me without going through my lawyer, especially since they know I have an attorney. They're not supposed to do that. If someone has an attorney, it's illegal to go directly to the person.

"I mean, I expected to finish the papers I was working on, get them into court, win an appeal, get a motion, get a this, get a that, *habeas corpus*, whatever. But getting out this way, this was not one of my options."

Mel settled into a routine that included daily workouts in the weight shack. In this way, he turned his previously soft six-foot frame into solid muscle.

The weight shack was a large room just off the yard. "They had a lot of different dumbbells and barbells. It was a dark room, not too bright, gray walls. Myself and four or five guys would meet there every day.

"You're free to work out, but guards are walking by. I was addicted to it. I looked forward to working out, it took a lot of anxiety away. And I saw progress. I was bench-pressing close to 300 pounds. After that, I would walk around the yard, talking to different guys.

"The prison wants you to work out, it's a way to use the energy so you don't use it in fights or other negative ways. They have it as a way to keep the prisoners calm. They learned it's a good way to keep energy going to the right place so it's for the benefit of the BOP, the Bureau of Prisons."

At the same time, Mel revived an old high-school football injury in order to get out of the mandatory work required by the Bureau of Prisons. "I went to the doctor and complained about my knee, and told him I have a bad knee from an injury, and they gave me a cane to walk with, and from that time on they were scheduling me to go to a hospital facility. So when I got the cane, I requested a job that didn't require much standing."

After almost a year in prison Mel got some news: Suffolk County in Long Island was charging him with four counts of loansharking. New York State wanted its piece of justice. The good news was he would be shipped back to Long Island for the trial, near family and friends.

15

HAVE A NICE FLIGHT, MR. PARISI

Travel in the prison system is painstakingly slow. If it takes three weeks to cover what would normally be an hour-long plane ride, that's okay with the Bureau of Prisons. But unlike his long trip from Manhattan to Terre Haute, this time Mel was put on a commercial airliner.

"I remember going to the local airport in cuffs, and they were not allowed to keep the cuffs on when I went on the plane. But when we were walking through the airport they put a coat over my cuffs so people don't see them. The guys who took me were nice, one of them said, 'If we take your cuffs off will you run? Because if you run I could shoot you in the back before you get twenty feet.' I said, 'No, I'm not going no place.' So he took the cuffs off."

Once in Suffolk County, Mel did everything he could to make sure he stayed there. The food was better, the security looser, and he was closer to home. He could see his kids more often. He had only seen them once while in Indiana.

This didn't mean life was particularly comfortable. Under any circumstances, life in prison is not pleasant. "It's a torment to have to go to talk to the DA; they shackle you, they bring you over to the courthouse, they put you down in the bullpen, and you have to stay there for six hours. You talk to the DA for three minutes, then you have to stay there for another couple of hours before you have to go back to your cell, shackled legs and arms."

Mel was kept in the Suffolk County Correctional Facility. "Once again, I asked for kosher food, and they had to bend over backwards. Since I was a federal prisoner they had to accommodate me, so they had a guy come up and question me about what I can eat. So I told him what kind of omelets I could eat, and the fruit juice. It was really funny there, they used to bring me a big can of juice, and three-egg omelets with mushrooms and cheese and bread, and everything would be covered up, and the cook would bring it up with two guards. Most of the time I had too much, and I'd give it away to the other guys. The cook was a friend of Little Vic Orena and Vic had been there. So aside from the guy being willing to cook kosher, he knew I was a friend of Vic's."

In Suffolk County, visits from his children were more frequent. "The visits took place in, like, booths in a diner. The kids knew everything already. They were reading as much as they could on it. They were finding out a lot by themselves. I liked to get visits, but I didn't like what you had to go through before and after the visits. The kids were living with different people at that time, their mother sometimes, their aunt sometimes. They resented most of my family for not helping out more."

Mel had other visitors while he was in Suffolk County. Time passed, and word got around that Mel was back East. He saw his father, even a few old friends.

One of the people who found out Mel was in jail on Long Island was an old acquaintance who used to work for Mel's finance company. "His name was Patrick Bradley and he started writing me letters in Suffolk County. Nobody told him I was in Terre Haute before. So he wrote me three letters in Suffolk County and I responded, and he wrote I should call him collect, so I called him from the jail, and he said 'Mel, how are you doing? I can't believe what they did to you, thirty years,' he says, 'it's insane. Me and my girlfriend, she's an undergraduate in law at Yale, tell us anything we can do for you. We'll both fly into New York, whatever we can do, tell us.'

"I said, 'there's nothing I can think of, thanks for your offer and we'll be in touch.' I spoke to him a couple of times after that."

The trip to the courthouse included one of the most humiliating aspects of prison life—a strip search each time Mel left and reentered the prison. If a court appearance was scheduled, Mel would be awakened at 5:30 in the morning, and after breakfast, he was handcuffed and shackled. The leg and arm shackles came off only once Mel was in the holding pen beneath the courthouse. Sitting there for hours at a time in the holding pen, there was not much to do except bullshit with the other prisoners. This was usually when the self-pity kicked in.

"You start to feel sorry for yourself a bit, but it's something you can't change. It's a very desperate situation, you can't control your destiny anymore. Sometimes I would actually be moving like I was in a cloud. It's like you're not really there, you're just moving with the group. So you're not really functioning in your own capacity."

Suffolk County had charged Mel with usury and extortion. Since he had already been convicted of these same crimes in Federal court, his attorneys, Thomas Puccio and Joel Cohen, filed a motion to dismiss the charges as double jeopardy. Mel should not be tried for the same crimes twice.

Rather than go to trial, the State offered Mel an option: plead guilty to one year with a felony charge, and time would be served concurrently with his Federal sentence. Mel said no. Two weeks later he was back in court. This time, the offer was six months and a felony. Again, Mel said no. Why should he plead guilty a second time?

Rejecting the Suffolk County District Attorney's offers was also a way of remaining on the East Coast. It would be weeks between offers.

"After about five visits—about ten weeks—they finally offered me something similar to a traffic violation, a misdemeanor." He would be let off with time served. Mel agreed. For the actual court appearance, says Mel, "I was using a court-appointed lawyer. Because how much should I spend on this bullshit?"

"I was brought in May 5, 1986. They took about fifteen guys to the county jail at seven in the morning, and I got there, something like eight o'clock and they put me in one of the cells. There were about eight cells." At 8:30, the court officer called Mel's name, cuffed him, and brought him upstairs to the courthouse. A surprise was waiting for him.

"I met my attorney there who told me that the DA wants to dismiss the case. I sat down in the jury box for a moment, and then the judge was ready. They put me in front of the judge and the judge started by saying because of my Federal attorney's motion for double jeopardy, she's dismissing the case. She said she's now going to turn me over to the custody of the US Marshals to continue my Federal sentence, and that was pretty much the end of her speech. I then said goodbye to my attorney, congratulated him on getting this case dismissed and went downstairs."

"About fifteen minutes later, I'm sitting in the bullpen again, and they call my name. I go to the door and the cop says 'Follow me.' So I noticed he didn't put cuffs on me this time. He opens the door, we go into the next room, and there's a little cubicle with a kid sitting there. He says, 'wait here.'

"A couple of minutes after that, they called me out into the next room and there was a sergeant sitting at a desk up there, and he asks me what's my birthday. I give him my birth date, he walks down, and comes down next to me and gives me a three-by-five card for a thumbprint, which I give to him. He looks at the two cards. He comes around me, and opens the door and says, 'Have a nice day.' I say 'you too.'"

Which brings us to the May morning Mel Cooper was left standing alone in the Hauppauge breeze.

Mel considered whether he should go back inside and tell them they had made a mistake. But before he could even blink, his practical side vetoed that plan.

Then time stopped. Mel looked at the sky. There was stillness. No loudspeakers, no grinding shackles. Just the sound of cars passing on a nearby road. He could move in any direction, he was completely alone. It seemed simple enough, but it was a feeling Mel Cooper hadn't known for over a year.

There was no time for timelessness. Any second the door would burst open, someone would yell "freeze," point a gun at Cooper, and order him back inside. He had to move. He headed toward the Motor Vehicles Department across the street.

"It was thirteen months to the day, the fifth of May, and I had been ten months in Terre Haute, three months in county jail. Suddenly, it was like, you have to think very quickly, and the only thing going through my head was to make distance between myself and this courthouse as fast as possible. And this all went through my head in a few seconds. It was very exciting, but I knew this could all end if I don't get away from this courthouse."

After his first attempt to get a ride to the airport failed, Mel tried again.

"I got all the way across the parking lot and I see these two guys walking towards their car, and I went over to them, and I asked them if they were going either past the Long Island Railroad Station or if they were going into the city, and they said, yeah, we can drop you off at a Long Island Railroad station. So I got in the car, a four-door medium-size car, and I got into the back seat, and they started to drive. They drove about three to four miles to this Long Island Railroad station and I thanked them. I think I told them if they wanted to lease a car or something to call my brother in the leasing business, and he would try to do something for them." Mel Cooper may have been on the lam, but he always had time for a business opportunity.

The Long Island Railroad station was closed. A bus waited in front of the station to shuttle passengers to the nearest working railroad station. With the assurance of a morning commuter, Mel climbed on the bus, found a seat, and sat down. Almost immediately, the doors closed and the bus took off.

"I was becoming more and more relieved as I was making more distance. My personality is such that I can't have too much insurance. In other words, if I was a thousand miles away already, I would look to get a thousand and ten miles. So I was breathing more and more easier.

"The bus drove probably eleven or twelve miles until it got to the next station, at which time I was thinking that I should make some calls to line up some money."

After being dropped off at an elevated station, Cooper looked for a pay phone—it was 1986 and no one had a mobile phone in their pocket—and made some collect calls. Unable to reach his son or a friend, on the third try, he reached his ex-wife, Miriam, who still lived in their old Lawrence, Long Island home. They were back on speaking terms after an ugly divorce.

"I told her that I needed her to bring five thousand dollars over to Ninth Avenue and 37th Street as soon as she can, and I would explain everything when I see her. She said she would meet me.

"Then I spoke to the porter on the station and I told him that I had lost my wallet and I didn't have any money, and I'd like to be able to mail it in to the station if I can ride on the train, and he said just get on the train and explain it to the conductor, I'm sure you'll have no problem.

"So I walked up a long flight of stairs to the platform, and the train was just sitting there, it had just pulled in, and I got on the train and the doors close, and the train pulls out. Within 60 seconds I hear the conductor say 'tickets, tickets.' He's coming over to my seat, and he approaches me and I'm sitting there with my khaki pants and my sneakers and manila envelope, and I said, 'Listen, I'm not a bum, I just want you to know. I lost my wallet, it's a long story, but if it's okay, if you give me an address I can have the money sent in, or I can have someone meet us at the last station in the city and I'll pay you over there.' He said 'no, I'm sorry, you have to get off the train at the next stop.'

"I said okay. I wasn't going to fight with anybody, and it's not my style anyway. As he starts walking away, I called him back and I ask, 'by the way, what's the next station?' and he says 'Jamaica station.' So I was relieved because here we're getting into Queens. Maybe this is an express train, I don't know, but again, we're talking about a quarter to ten in the morning. Probably close to ten o' clock by now.

"I get off at Jamaica station, I go downstairs to the street, and I walk about four blocks, to the corner intersection of Jamaica and Sutphin, and I get on the phone and call collect to my brother Jeffrey's office, the car leasing business, which they hadn't closed down, and the secretary answers and connects me to my brother.

"'How long would it take you to get to Jamaica and Sutphin?' I said. He says, 'Seven or eight minutes.' So I said 'Come on over and bring whatever you have on you and whatever you could put together, and don't go out of your way, just come over as soon as you can.' Less than ten minutes later, he pulls up in his car on Sutphin Boulevard, he sees me on the corner and I signal him that I'm going into the bar, and he went and parked the car. He comes into the bar and sits down at the table, gives me a hug, and I tell him what happened, and he gives me $850."

Jeffrey was shocked to see his brother. Says Mel, "I mean, he knew that I was away for 30 years, and here we are one year later. He was shocked. He listened very intently to every word of the story. When I finished, I told him to go back to his office. He asked me where he could drop me. He wanted to know if he could take me someplace.

"I said 'No, go back to your office, and when they come to see you, just tell them that you haven't seen me at all.' So I got up and started walking out of the bar, and he calls me, 'Hey, Mel.' I turn around and he says, 'Mel, tuck your shirt in. Your number is showing.'"

The subway is right under the elevated Long Island Railroad tracks by Jamaica station. Once again, timing worked in Mel's favor; as soon as he got to the platform, the Manhattan-bound train pulled in. He got on, and half an hour later, he was in the city.

Cooper had been up since 5:30 in the morning. Still, he felt no fatigue. He felt nothing. There was no thirst, no hunger. Says Cooper, "it was like I was just gliding on air. Oh, I was oblivious to everything that was happening. I just wanted to get to the city, take care of my business, and start heading further away. I didn't know where I'm going to go or what I'm going to do, but I got to 37th and 9th, and my ex-wife was sitting in an Alfa-Romeo. I walked up to the car, got in, and told her what had happened, and she handed me an envelope with five thousand dollars in it."

It wasn't just a favor; when Mel went away, he had put a large amount of BW Energy stock in her name, and had given her money to help her care for the kids.

"I told her the story, and I also told her that in the next few hours I'm going to be leaving the country. I told her that because I wanted her to believe it was part of the truth, as I told her everything else. And I also told her when the FBI comes to see her that night, she should be honest with them, and tell them that I called her and that she met me with the money, that she should be truthful with them about everything that happened. I was expecting her to tell them that I'm leaving the country. Which she did. Which is why they were looking for me in Brazil and Israel most of the time. Then she asked me, can she drop me anyplace, and I said, no, you go home, and just don't forget to tell the FBI the truth." Mel kissed her goodbye and left.

"I started walking towards the Port Authority Building. And right now I had like, $5,800 and change in my pocket, so I was okay. And I got to the Port Authority, walked up to the cashier window and asked if I could get a ticket to Newark Airport. And it was about $4.75. I said, 'When is the next bus out?' and she says, 'if you hurry and take the elevator up, they're boarding one now.' So I remember getting the ticket and I went over to the elevator, and when I got out, there was the bus loading up. As soon as I got on, the door closed and the bus pulled out towards Newark Airport. Again, maybe a half hour later, we pulled up in front of Continental Airways."

At Newark Airport, Mel was greeted by the liberating whirl of life in motion. In 1986, there were few demands made when it came to security. You didn't need identification to board a plane and enjoy the freedom of flight. Getting on an airplane required about as much security as getting on a city bus.

There was room to move now, through the long white hallways of the terminal, past huge glass windows. Mel moved in one direction only: away from New York City. He walked quickly to the board showing flight departures. Los Angeles was the furthest destination.

He went to the counter and asked the agent for a ticket to Los Angeles.

"Name, sir?" asked the ticket agent. Though you didn't need ID, you still needed a name. Any name would do.

Cooper looked at a pile of tickets on the counter. On the right was one that said "Parisi." On another was the first name, "Tony."

"Anthony Parisi," said Mel.

As spontaneous as it was, there was logic to his reasoning. Explains Cooper, "I was thinking that the government or the FBI normally looks for people who change their names to something very similar to their old names, that's what most people do. I was consciously looking for something that would differentiate from that formula. So I took the name of Anthony Parisi which was a non-Jewish name and Italian, so it was much different. And I gave her an address, somewhere on West 55th Street, and she gave me a ticket for Los Angeles."

Mel walked over to a bank of phone booths and was about to make a call when he scanned the departures board again. He noticed for the first time that the plane to LA didn't leave until 4:40 pm. It was only 11:30 am. Sitting in an airport for five hours waiting for the U.S. Marshals to collect him was not part of Mel's plan. The next flight out, boarding at that moment, was to Logan Airport in Boston. He walked back to the ticket agent.

"Excuse me," said Mel, once again calling on his powers of invention, "I just spoke to my office and they want me to go to a meeting in Boston before California. Can I switch my ticket?"

"That's no problem, Mr. Parisi," said the agent, taking Mel's ticket. She made the exchange, handed Mel a ticket to Boston, along with his change. The whole transaction had been in cash. She added, "You'd better hurry. They're boarding right now."

Mel ran to the gate. His shirt was tucked in and no one seemed to notice the number on his pants. Mel attributes this to the fact that he didn't look like a prisoner in his clean sneakers and pressed pants. Or to put it differently, perhaps it's a matter of prejudice and privilege; people just don't assume that the well-groomed, good-looking white guy hurrying to his departure gate is an escaped convict.

Mel got to the gate, boarded the plane, and sat down. "I was further relieved that I'm getting into a compartment now that's going to fly to another state.

"So I'm sitting on the plane, and within minutes, they close the door and it starts to taxi, and I'm really getting relieved. We're moving, and there's no turning back. I was sitting next to the window, trying to be invisible. Again, I wasn't looking to make any friends. And the plane is driving, and all of a sudden it stops. And I'm waiting for the takeoff and it's five minutes, ten minutes, and I'm starting to think, what the hell is this? Then it's fifteen minutes, and now I'm starting to sweat and think, 'wow, what's going on? I wonder if the marshals have this place surrounded, and they're coming onto the plane and they're going to get me, and it's twenty-nine years, and damn.'

"And twenty-five minutes passes, I'm really nervous and sweating. This was a very difficult time. And I'm thinking. 'Why did I take a plane, why didn't I take a train or a bus or even a bicycle,' I mean if you get caught – I would rather walk to Boston. All of these things are going through my head, and all of a sudden the plane starts to leave and gets onto the runway and takes off. So I gasp for air, and I was on the way to Logan airport."

16

BOSTON ALIVE

Boston was euphoria. With every breath Mel felt as if gravity didn't apply to him anymore. He was in an altered state of aliveness, removed from all constraints and obligation. "I was just released from twenty-nine years. Everything had color to it. When I was walking on the street, I looked at the cracks in the ground, and the cars and the trees, and I looked in the windows, like this was all new to me. I had been looking at fences for thirteen months and one day and I'm out in Boston walking in the streets.

"I didn't feel safe until I got to Boston, but then the feeling of euphoria hit me, because until then, I was preoccupied with what I'm doing and getting where I'm going. But when I finally arrived at Boston, it seemed to overtake me.

"I got off the plane saying, 'I'm going to get myself a nice hotel room with a big bath and a shower.' So I get into a cab and I say, 'Take me to a nice hotel in Downtown Boston.' The driver pulls up in front of a hotel, I don't remember the name, it was a very ritzy, opulent lobby, and I walk up to the counter in my khaki pants, and ask for a room, and they were very courteous. The woman at the desk asked me for information, and I gave her all the information, and I said I was going to be leaving a cash deposit. She said we need to have a major credit card or a driver's license, and I told them I don't have that." Having taken in the sparkling chandeliers, the thick rugs, and fancy furniture, Cooper knew it was time to go. They wouldn't give him a room. "I said thank you and I left."

Cooper tried the next nearest hotel. But one hotel after another refused to give Mel Cooper–now Anthony Parisi–a room, without identification. Eight hotels later, Mel stepped into a Victorian boarding house on Brookline Avenue ready to take anything they had to offer.

Meanwhile, back in Long Island, it had taken fifteen minutes for someone at the courthouse to realize they had made a big mistake. As planned, the US Marshals came to pick Mel up.

When they found out he was gone, a public war of recrimination ensued between the Suffolk County District Attorney's office and the Sheriff's Department. Newspapers learned about Suffolk County's mistake, and turned it into a colorful, ongoing saga. "Shark Set Free" announced the New York Daily News, adding "Prisoner Off Hook after Error in Tank."

"Error Lets Prisoner Walk Free," said another, referring to Mel Cooper as the "brains behind a Long Island-based loanshark ring."

The sheriff, whose deputy let Cooper out, claimed the District Attorney's office never told them about Mel's federal sentence. Said Sheriff Eugene Dooley, "The court papers we got had no indication that he was a federal detainee."

The District Attorney Patrick Henry replied, "there was no problem with the paperwork...I can't possibly see any slip up on the district attorney's part." A judge at the courthouse pointed out, Mel's federal sentence for the same crime was the whole reason the charges were dismissed to begin with. How could the sheriff not know? Said County Court Judge Kenneth Rohl, "there is no question that sheriff's deputies were to blame."

According to Sheriff Dooley, when the deputy told Mel Cooper he was getting out, Cooper "had a funny look on his face but didn't say anything. Our guys picked it up and called the records department, but they said there was nothing on him. So they let him go."

Meanwhile, that same evening, the FBI visited Cooper's ex-wife. As per Mel's instructions, Miriam told them the truth as she knew it: he was on his way to Israel.

In Boston, Mel's escape progressed methodically. "I took a room for thirty-nine dollars a day, and then I went downstairs and got a cab and went over to Faneuil Hall and went shopping for clothes.

"The first day I was actually so excited, I couldn't go to sleep. I finally went up to the room, it was ten o' clock. I lay down on the bed, then I jumped up like a jack-in-the-box and I had to go downstairs, and it was four flights. I had to take a walk in the street because I just couldn't sleep."

After hitting a local bar accompanied by a disabled vet he met in the TV room at the boarding house, Mel went to sleep. The next morning Mel went to see Professor Alan Dershowitz at Harvard.

Mel remembered Dershowitz had been one of the partners of Mel's appeals lawyer in the Claus Von Bulow case. "I felt I could call, because I couldn't call my appeal attorney, because I believed they would have his phones bugged. They were looking for me." He hoped the professor could give him some insight into the precedence for a situation like his. Like the notorious Pearlman who was accidentally released in 1926, perhaps all Mel had to do was stay out of jail for five years.

"At about 11 o' clock in the morning – and this was the first morning – I got up, and I found out how to get over to Harvard Square, and I went over to the Law Library in Harvard. I was really fascinated by the campus, it was a beautiful campus, and then I ended up going to Professor Dershowitz's office, and he was not there, so I told his receptionist I would come back the next day, which I did."

"I couldn't leave my name because I was all over the TV. They were announcing on the news that they had released me by mistake. They were saying things like, 'Hey, you forgot your luggage at the jail,' because when they let me out, I didn't take my property. They made a joke out of it."

After coming back for four days in a row, Mel left a sealed envelope with his name in it and the name of his attorney. When he came back on the fifth day, the receptionist said, "The professor wants you to call him between 8 and 9 pm tonight."

She gave Mel a phone number.

"I ended up calling him at home about 8 o'clock at night, and I went over the whole story about how I was released in error, and who my attorney was – Thomas Puccio – and how I'm concerned to call my attorney because of the fact that they might have my phones tapped, and after he listened to the whole story, the first thing he told me is that I should talk to my attorney because he's very good, and I shouldn't be concerned about the phones being tapped because the government would never tap a huge law firm's phone like that. They have, like, a hundred lawyers, and if the government would ever tap their phones and it was found out, this would be enough to knock out every case in the courtroom for the last year and the next two years, and the government would never take a chance in doing something like that, so he assured me I could make a phone call without concern. So I thanked him for his time."

The next day, with a mix of anticipation and fear, he called his appeal lawyer.

"Where are you?" was the first thing Tom said. He quickly reconsidered his request. "No, don't tell me where you are. What are you doing?"

Cooper told him the story: the accidental release, the trip out of New York City.

"You have to turn yourself in," declared Puccio.

"What do you mean?" said Mel, incredulous. "Didn't you hear what happened? They let me go by accident."

"Of course. But you have to turn yourself in."

This was not what Mel wanted to hear.

"That's what I'll do," said Mel, "I just need I just need a couple of days to think things through. I'll get back to you."

Recalls Cooper, "This was, like, the worst thing that I could have heard. I could hear that he wasn't receptive towards the books that I read, and the Pearlman case, and everything. And that's when I took a nosedive into a state of depression—listening to my attorney say, 'Yeah, turn yourself in for another twenty-nine years.' That didn't sound too inviting."

It wasn't simply a matter of being depressed. "It's like when I was in Boston I felt like I was free, but I could have just as well been put on Mars and set free. How does someone feel if they're on a planet all by themselves? That's the way I felt in Boston. I didn't know anybody."

He barely knew himself—after all, he was not even Mel Cooper anymore. To everyone he met, he was Anthony Parisi.

"I'm not very good at being another person. There are people that can live a lie, and it's natural. It didn't suit me. And there's a strange feeling about not knowing anybody. You're completely on your own. It's like you're on the outside looking in. There's a difference between people that know your past, know your family, know you from before, compared to meeting a whole bunch of new people for the first time. So there's a certain tie-in that you get when you're talking about people from your past. There's a warmth that comes out of it, which is what I needed after this depressing conversation with the lawyers. So I said to myself, 'I have to speak to someone from my past, from my past life, from my pre-incarceration.'

"So I'm thinking, I can't talk to anybody in New York because the government is watching everybody I know. Then I thought about Patrick Bradley, who had been writing letters to me in Suffolk County. He's in Miami. Nobody's suspecting that. I have money in my pocket, so I call him."

Patrick picked up the phone. It was the first time Mel was not calling him collect.

"My God, where are you?" said Patrick.

"It's not important," said Mel. "I'll explain to you later. But basically, I'm out."

"Mel, you've got to come to Miami. I'll put you up, I'll take care of you. We'll go to the beach, we'll go boating, fishing, skiing, whatever you want to do."

Mel considered the offer. On the one hand, he had his attorney advising him to turn himself in and do another twenty-nine years. If he did well, and behaved himself, it might be only another ten. And on the other hand, Patrick Bradley was urging Mel to come down to Miami, and go fishing, sailing, skiing, and have a great time.

"So I said, 'I'm going to Miami.'"

17

WELCOME TO FORT LAUDERDALE

Anthony Parisi woke up every day at 9:30am. He went down to the beach, walked for half a mile, then stopped for coffee. After a stroll home, Parisi spent the rest of the day on the beach talking to friendly northerners and locals. Sometimes he went sailing or waterskiing with Pat Bradley, but almost every day at 3:30, he headed over to the Oceanside gym where the Miami Dolphins trained, to work out a few hours before heading upstairs to get ready for dinner.

Parisi—formerly Mel Cooper—had made his way to Fort Lauderdale after a brief stay in Miami with Patrick Bradley. Miami had been too crowded for Mel's taste. It turned out some of Pat's friends were ex-convicts who had parole officers watching them. The last thing Mel wanted to do was attract attention. He and Patrick took a drive up Highway A1A to Fort Lauderdale to look for other options.

They found a motel called The Riviera on "The Strip," across from the Atlantic Ocean. Anthony Parisi checked in. He told the front desk he would be around for at least four or five nights.

"The first night I got to Fort Lauderdale, Patrick came to pick me up and take me over to a club, and after a few hours, I said 'I'm tired.' He took me back about 11 o' clock."

Overwhelmed by the simple joy of being free, Mel had no intention of sleeping. He went to the small bar by the pool at the back of the motel.

There were about 15 barstools, most of them occupied, and Mel took seat next to a pretty girl with dirty blonde hair. She had just gotten off work at a car rental company.

"Hi," he said, with a smile, his delight almost unexplainable to anyone who didn't know he had just escaped from prison.

"Hello" she replied.

"I'm Anthony."

"I'm Pam," she said.

"Nice to meet you, Pam."

"Anthony, why do you look so happy?"

"I just had a great night, and it's not over." With that, Mel turned to the bartender and said, "I'd like to buy Pam a drink, and you too." Mel ordered a whiskey sour.

"So Pam, what do you do?" There was something sparkly about her. She was put together in that uniquely Florida way, with pink, blue, and rose shades of eye makeup, frosted pink lips, and a white blouse. She glowed under the lights of the bar.

"I work for Hertz," she replied. "I just got done with my shift."

"Fantastic," Said Mel.

"I guess so," she laughed. What do you do?"

"Me? I'm in finance. I just got down here."

Recalls Mel, "We were enjoying our time together, and I did my best to convince Pam to join me upstairs. I found out having sex was like riding a bike, you don't forget how to do it."

They began to see each other once or twice a week, though with her short blond hair and cheerful Midwestern style, says Mel, "she wasn't exactly my type."

When he wasn't seeing Pam, Mel would circulate among the clubs on the Strip with Patrick. They would go to dinner, and afterwards to the noisy bars with beachy themes and names like "The Candy Store." They were the kind of places you would expect in a town that caters to tourists and college students all year.

Mel kept his circle of friends small. It was too much work to maintain the fictional story of who he was and where he came from, though most people in Fort Lauderdale, a town of transplants and people just passing through, didn't ask a lot of questions. "Call me Tony," was as much as Mel wanted to say, and most of the time, that was enough.

When someone persisted in asking questions about what he was doing in Fort Lauderdale, Mel had a story ready. "My rationale to whoever I met as to why I'm 'undercover,' so to speak, was I told them I had a bad divorce and that my lawyer told me to stay away for a while. Typically, everyone in Fort Lauderdale is hiding from something. There's a lot of characters there, it's a known place for hiding out." In Mel's fictional backstory reality had been flipped, and it was his lawyer who told him to get out of town.

Meanwhile up north, Federal Marshals and the FBI were still looking for him. Federal Marshal Charles Healy admitted publicly they had no clue where Mel Cooper might be, but they were sure he had "access to a lot of money," and could "travel anywhere." He claimed 100 deputies statewide were looking for Mel Cooper.

By June of 1989, officials at least had an idea of the errors that led to Mel being set free. It seemed Mel's federal "detainer papers" had been sent to the wrong judge. Mel's paperwork turned up a month after his escape. "How…[the papers] got to my chambers is a big mystery," said State Supreme Court Judge George F. X. McInerney.

Various probes and investigations determined that three different errors led to Mel's accidental release. A local legislator, Joseph Rizzo, summed it up nicely for a local newspaper: "It was a Rube Goldberg situation where one thing just rolled into another… it could only happen again if everyone was as stupid as they were the first time."

After six weeks of motel life, Cooper felt it was time for Tony Parisi to settle down and get a place of his own. "I couldn't take the one-room motel anymore. I got claustrophobic. I guess it reminded me of a cell." Using the money he had brought with him, he rented a posh one-bedroom apartment with a balcony overlooking the ocean in a building about five blocks away from where he had been living. The building was called The Seasons.

Mel's social circle expanded when he befriended a young man in his building named Caspar. "He was from up North, and he had a ski boat. And he had an SUV which came in very handy for transportation."

Caspar's purpose in life seemed to be to have a good time. He was an out-of-work bartender, and he often took Mel waterskiing in the afternoon.

Sometimes they would sail down to the keys with Patrick Bradley, then go out to the clubs at night. Pam, Caspar, Patrick, and Patrick's girlfriend, Monica, formed the core of Mel's social circle.

"It was nice, especially when you compare it to where I was. Just being on the beach and going in the water and being able to walk around. I had never taken a vacation that long, and now I'm there on the beach month after month, like a beach bum. You start to forget things you were doing, the things you know. Like math. It starts to fade away."

Long walks on the beach, weightlifting, waterskiing, dinner. Cooper, not yet forty years old, was not ready for a life of retirement. "As months went on, I shook my head, and it felt like my head was getting full of sand. I used to take a vacation for a week, sometimes two weeks, but this was six months of walking down the beach. I said to myself, my mind is becoming like mush, I can hardly count to ten anymore, never mind going into the finance business, so I was thinking, I have to do something, to become active. So I got hold of Caspar and I said, 'Caspar, we're going to start making some money now.'"

Mel decided to go back into finance. Caspar knew nothing about the money business and Mel instructed him to follow along as they pitched potential customers and banks.

Caspar, who still calls Mel Cooper "Tony" remembers, "He was teaching me something I never knew – the finance business. I was a carpenter by trade even though I had been working in bars. I didn't know how to do algebra and fractions and geometry. I was never book smart, so when Tony was teaching me this stuff, I wanted to learn. He called it 'creative financing.'

"In the beginning he was going to teach me the equipment financing business and how to do financing. I didn't know anything, he was training me. I thought he was all legit."

Mel told Caspar to start talking to people at the bar and see if there were any business people in the market for money. He explained the basics: the borrower would have to have some kind of property for security – a house, a car, a boat. Mel would do the rest, as long as he could secure the loan with some property. And he taught Caspar one of his prime lending principles: "When they need money, they'll do anything for it."

It only took a week for Caspar to come back with a few leads; one man had a house and needed a second mortgage, another wanted a first mortgage. Mel took the information to a mortgage company in Fort Lauderdale.

After 15 years of packaging loans for banks at Cooper Funding, Mel knew just what it took to get a bank to say yes. "You walk into a company and say 'I'm going to bring you deals,' and nobody says anything. They're happy to get the deals. I met the manager of the bank, her name was Kathy, and I worked out a deal where we would get a commission on anything I brought her." It didn't take long before Mel was back in business and making money. Legitimate money.

As his new life continued to take shape, Mel began to venture out of Fort Lauderdale. He wanted to see his kids, which meant he would have to travel to New York City and risk being captured. He approached that challenge as if it were espionage, arranging transportation, planning discreet meetings, and wearing disguises for the encounters with his children.

Cooper assumed he was on FBI and police wanted lists, but suspected the authorities were not looking for him on a train from Florida. The first trip went well and after that, every six weeks, Mel would head up north. He eventually gathered the courage to go by plane to Newark airport rather than travel north by train. He and his children would usually meet in a movie theater in Manhattan in the evening. Afterwards they would go out to a restaurant.

On one visit, Mel was leaving a restaurant with his kids, when he noticed a well-dressed man in a suit staring at him.

"Don't I know you?" the man said.

Mel froze. Without thinking, he answered, "No."

"What do you do?" the man asked, looking at him with uncomfortable familiarity. He looked like a businessman, perhaps one of Mel's former clients.

"I have a chain of fruit stores," said Mel. "What do you do?"

"I'm an attorney."

Suddenly, Mel recognized him. He was one of the appeal attorneys who worked with Thomas Puccio. He had interviewed Mel, and reviewed his case. There was no point in letting the man know who he really was.

"Okay, then, have a nice night," said Mel, hurrying off with his kids.

The trips north reminded Mel of one of the most painful aspects of his incarceration; he was slowly vanishing from the lives of his family. He had become remote to them, as if he were a relative from a far-off time and place, another century. He was forgotten.

And his things were disappearing. No one could ever tell him why or how, or to whom his personal belongings had been sold, but almost all of it was gone—his artwork, furniture, leather couches, silverware, wristwatches, Mercedes, even his chandelier. This infuriated Cooper. He had left everything in the hands of his family, and they showed almost no interest in preserving his belongings. Whenever Mel asked someone in the family what happened to his things, he got vague answers.

"I compare it to my family having a dollar of theirs," says Mel, "and a hundred dollars of mine, and it's all blowing in the wind, and they run after the dollar that's theirs. They just didn't safeguard the other hundred dollars at all. They let it go.

"It was very frustrating," recalls Mel. "At the beginning it was much more frustrating. As time went by, I became used to it, and I realized there's nothing I can do. I would hear things about what happened to this, to that, to the other thing. I tried not to think about it. It would have been too traumatic to hold on." He looked at it as another cost exacted by his conviction. At least he was dealing with indifference and not dishonesty, he told himself.

There was one loss, however, that seemed to be more than indifference. Since Mel's conviction, his father Sam had been prodding Mel to shed his more valuable possessions. Specifically, Sam had been pushing Mel to sell the condo he owned on the beach in Westhampton. He told Mel there was no one to take care of the place and he was unable to rent it. It would be better to get rid of it and use the money to pay for legal fees and fines.

Recalls Mel, "So one time, I came in to New York with Pam, and we drove out to the Hamptons. I went out to the apartment, to the condo. I open the door, I go in, and I see somebody's clothes there. There were clothes in the closet, like it was being used. And all this time, I was saying to my father, "Can't you rent it? Can you at least rent the place out so the money will come in? It will take care of the expenses.'

"'Oh no,' he'd say, 'there's no market.' This is right on the beach in Westhampton! You can spit on the beach, before I went away I spent two years fixing it up. If you talk to my father, it's like a sore thumb, nobody would want to rent this! This is what he's telling me, but I go there and I see clothes in the closets, so of course he couldn't rent it. Because someone's using the place."

Later, Sam sold the condo outright.

"I put it in his name," says Mel. "But it was mine. He couldn't even tell me who he sold it to when I asked him."

Back in Fort Lauderdale, Cooper freelanced at finance just long enough to assure himself he still had the touch. After independently arranging a few loans with leads from Caspar, he decided to leverage the enterprise into a more formal organization.

Mel had made the acquaintance of a Cuban doctor named Angel Giraldez. He immediately made an impression on Mel. "He was easily, like, 320 pounds, mustache, big head, six foot one. Big guy. He was doing so well, he thought he'd branch out into investment, and had his eye on a supermarket in Miami, which is how we met him. He wanted to borrow $450,000."

Mel and Casper drove down to Miami in Caspar's Chevy Blazer, and met Dr. Giraldez in his suite of offices on *Caille Ocho*, or Southwest 8th Street in Little Havana. The offices were impressive; the doctor had a receptionist, a bookkeeper, and all the equipment it took to run a growing practice. Dr. Giraldez also worked for a nearby hospital in the neurology department.

Mel liked associating with entrepreneurial professionals, and everything about Dr. Giraldez indicated he would make a fine business partner. He was smart and ambitious, and unlike Doc Hyman, Giraldez didn't have mobsters among his associates–just a network of successful Hispanic businessmen and professionals like himself. As soon as they finished discussing the supermarket deal, Mel made the doctor an offer; how would he like to go into the finance business? Mel explained to Dr. Giraldez he was interested in opening a branch office in the area. He would use the doctor's offices as his headquarters and give him a commission for deals he brought in. The supermarket deal closed three weeks later. Five weeks later Dr.

Giraldez called Mel. He was willing to give it a try.

Mel needed staff, starting with someone who could manage the business full time. He called Kathy, the woman he had met at the bank in Fort Lauderdale. "I figured she could work with us in this company." If Mel Cooper likes someone, his way of showing it is to make money for them.

Kathy was interested and she joined Mel in Miami where they met with Dr. Giraldez. The group clicked and soon afterwards, they launched their new venture: First Professional Leasing Company, Inc.

Mel and Dr. Giraldez took an equal percentage with Kathy getting a cut as well. Using the doctor's offices as their headquarters, the plan was Kathy would manage the company. Dr. Giraldez would bring in the clients, and Mel would structure and set up the deals. Caspar would come on board as a salesman, and visit banks and potential lenders with Mel. The arrangement worked from the moment they opened their doors.

"We decided that since we're sitting in the heart of Miami and most of the population speaks Spanish, we can start by going after the Spanish businessmen and professionals. I said to them, the banks are not really servicing these companies. Let's focus on that.

"Dr. Giraldez brought in twelve or thirteen guys, all from different countries. From Cuba, from Honduras, from all over South America, who could start off as salespeople." Mel put in several hours training them, teaching them how to sell the financing of income-producing equipment. Many of them had been car salesmen before joining Mel and Dr. Giraldez. They were already comfortable talking big-ticket items like trucks and automobiles. In comparison to the car business, finance was a breeze.

In the first week, one of the salesmen went to his brother who sold construction equipment. Recalls Mel, "All of sudden everybody starts bringing in doctors and dentists and medical equipment and construction equipment. Kathy didn't know what to do, she couldn't believe it. The money is pouring in, she's making thousands a week, the doctor is making more than he's making as a doctor, and we're really moving along."

As with the finance businesses he had built in a past life, Mel leveraged one opportunity into the next and expanded into different types of lending. They started doing larger deals, stretching outside of the Miami area. Mel had a cousin in New York who referred him to deals up north.

As the business flourished, the arrangement offered Mel's alter ego,

Tony Parisi, unexpected benefits. One of the banks First Professional Leasing did business with invited Parisi to open a personal bank account. That opened the door to other benefits, like credit cards and lines of credit, which helped his new identity take root.

And Mel began dating Kathy. "She was pretty, smart, and understood the business. She also had blonde hair, she was short, very nice. Easygoing. And helpful—she worked hard. She was in her early 30s. My life had taken on a certain stability, and was moving ahead nicely."

Caspar's admiration for Tony Parisi only grew. "I loved him, I thought he was a great guy. Girls liked him, everybody liked him. There was a sense of class with Tony. He dressed really well. But he kept his mouth shut about his clothes. I remember he had a $1,000 white suit with pin stripes, Bally shoes. He carried himself with class. He didn't put people down, he treated them pretty well, and the only one he really yelled at was Kathy but that's because he was training her. She's sitting at a desk, he's sitting next to her whispering, telling her what to say."

Still, the fragile nature of his situation was ever-present. Mel remembers, "One night, a cop stopped me for making a bad turn." He was driving Dr. Giraldez' Porsche back from Miami with no driver's license. "I'm sitting there, and the cop takes the car registration, then he goes back to his car, behind me. I'm thinking if this cop sees a warrant, and finds out who I am, that's the end of it. I was concerned that he was going to take me into the precinct with no license, because I told him I left my license home. So I'm thinking, should I just open the door and run, and forget about Fort Lauderdale? I'm thinking about running with just what I had in my pocket, that's what going through my mind in the one minute I'm sitting there. Finally, he gave me a summons to show up with the license.

"So what I did was, I searched out a law firm that's right next to the court house, and typically they have good connections with the judges and clerks. It cost me $200 or $300 to give to the lawyer, and he got the case thrown out. It always works like that, if you have a moving violation. There are lawyers that have their office near the court, and they know the clerks."

On another occasion, Mel and Caspar went to a concert on the beach. Recalls Caspar, "We went to see the Beach Boys, and he was wearing sunglasses. And I said 'Tony, why are you wearing sunglasses?' We're, like, right in the front. And he said, 'I don't want my wife to see me on TV.'

"He kept bringing up the wife thing, and I remember him saying that he wanted to get out of town, but he doesn't have ID. He was trying to figure out how to get ID. I said, 'I have a connection, I can get some birth certificates,' and he said, 'do it.' He was going to go to Australia."

Mel had been in Fort Lauderdale for almost eight months when he launched First Professional Leasing. After all that time, only two people in Fort Lauderdale knew Mel's true identity. One of them was Pam. She had figured it out on her own.

Their romantic relationship had faded but Mel and Pam had stayed friends. It's difficult maintaining an intimate relationship when almost everything about your life is a lie. Recalls Mel, "She used to come up to the apartment, and she would go to the refrigerator and see Jewish food in the refrigerator, things that would be strange for an Italian to have. There were kosher hot dogs and salami, horseradish, half sour pickles." It turns out you can change your name but it's harder to change the food you eat.

"Then Sunday we would go sometimes for bagels and lox, and I guess from the outside looking in, it looked odd, and you could start to question things if you're rational. After listening and seeing and questioning for a number of months, like ten months, she ended up with a book, Poison for Profit, which said who I was. I never found out how she got the book. I think she spoke to her uncle, and she ended up finding out who I was, but she never caused me any problems." Mel felt safe with Pam knowing his secret.

Others only suspected something was off. Recalls Mel's friend, Caspar, "We were doing our day to day thing and going to Jewish restaurants, and eating matzo balls and I'm thinking, 'why are we eating Jewish food, this guy's Italian.'"

The other person who knew his true identity was Patrick Bradley, and with him, Mel felt anything but safe.

Patrick had ceased to be a part of Mel's day-to-day circle in Fort Lauderdale. Mel was busy in Miami with his new business, and Patrick came around less and less. When he was around, Mel didn't like what he saw. Pat was jumpy, strange, and aggressive. He looked like he hadn't slept. Mel suspected he was involved with drugs though Pat never admitted it. But every time he and Mel got together, Patrick would borrow two or three hundred dollars. This went on for months until one encounter changed their relationship.

Recalls Mel, "My cousin's husband brought me a big deal up north, from these two guys from Muncie, New York, who were interested in buying the Wedtech plant in the Bronx. They needed a half a million dollars as a down payment. I said I would try to get it for them."

The Wedtech Corporation had been a defense contractor with a huge government contract. The company had recently been at the center of a massive criminal and political scandal, and the plant was now abandoned in the wake of an investigation that had taken down top officials in the Reagan Administration. The property had millions of dollars' worth of valuable equipment still on site in over eighty offices and warehouses. It was all being liquidated.

"We ended up arranging for a loan to them. I told Patrick, 'I'm putting you in as part of the profit because you're a good buddy.' He was going to get $25,000 for himself. He didn't invest or anything, he was just given a gift."

One night at about 8:30 there was a knock on Mel's door. It was Patrick Bradley. As soon as Mel opened the door, Patrick hustled in, eyes bulging, and he started walking through the apartment, checking closets, opening doors, looking in the bathroom, and finally, crawling on his hands and knees to check under the couch.

"Don't worry," he said, "I parked my car ten blocks away, no one's following me."

"Why should someone be following you?" said Mel, taking the time to study Patrick; it was clear to Mel he was on drugs.

Patrick tilted his head and didn't speak, raising his eyebrows as if to say, you know. His eyes were sunken, his skin pale.

"Can I have a beer?" said Patrick.

"Yeah, sure." Mel got him a bottle from the fridge. "So what do you need?" he asked, hoping to get Patrick out as quickly as possible. He was expecting company.

"What, is there a problem?" Patrick answered.

"Yeah, you look like you're having problems."

"Do you want me to go?"

"Yeah," said Mel.

"Look, Mel, I'm sorry. Can you loan me a couple of hundred. I appreciate it, I'll pay you back."

"Sure," said Mel. Patrick took the money and left soon after.

Mel quickly forgot about the encounter. A week after this visit, Mel was on the phone with Howard, his cousin's husband, who was arranging the loan for the Wedtech deal. As they reviewed the details of the loan, Howard mentioned Patrick had been coming around.

"Really?" said Mel. It was the first time he heard about Patrick being up in New York City.

"Yeah, he's been asking for an advance on his money from the deal." The loan had been approved, but the money wouldn't be in for a few months. "Should I give him something?" asked Howard.

"Don't give him anything because he's only going to put it right up his nose," Mel replied. Mel did not know Patrick was in the office, standing right next to Howard. He heard everything.

Howard refused to give him any money.

"Patrick called me every name in the book," says Mel. He believes this was the event that turned Patrick Bradley from friend to dangerous foe.

New Year's Eve of 1988 promised to be the beginning of a fabulous year. Mel spent it at Disney World with Dr. Giraldez and two Canadian women Mel had met in Fort Lauderdale. He returned to his apartment with the two women who were staying on as Mel's guests for another week. Dr. Giraldez went home to Miami.

About six in the morning on January 8, the phone rang. Mel had only been in bed a few hours. He got up to answer the phone. He heard an unfamiliar voice.

"Tony Parisi?"

"Yeah," said Mel.

"Mel Cooper?"

Mel thought for a second about how to reply and decided to play it straight.

"What is it?"

"This is the FBI. We want you to step out the door right now. We have you surrounded."

Mel's first reaction was to look at the balcony. He was on the 17th floor. There was a pool directly below. He calculated his chances of success, should he try to make a dive. He quickly decided they weren't good.

"Let me just get dressed, and I'll come to the door."

"No, come the way you are."

"Let me just tell this girl who's here." Mel wanted to prepare his houseguests for what was about to happen but the man on the other end of the phone was not worried about Mel's guests.

"Come right now," he said.

Wearing just his underwear, Mel went to the door. As soon as he opened it, he was greeted with the early-morning enthusiasm of at least twenty agents with handguns and rifles pointed at him. They were not just the FBI. There were US Marshals, police—whatever authorities were around to assist. Mel put his hands against the wall. They took him back into the apartment.

The two girls looked on wide-eyed, as if a space shuttle had just landed in the apartment

"Get him clothes," the agents told the girls.

Mel recalled how only the night before, they were watching a video, some action flick with plenty of gunplay, chases, and thrills, and one of the girls had remarked how she really liked a lot of excitement.

That same woman brought Mel his shorts and sneakers.

Looking at her stunned expression, Mel couldn't resist.

"Is this exciting enough for you?" he said.

They left the building before 7 am, passing the building manager in the lobby who was shocked to see a tenant being taken away in cuffs. She asked what the problem was. Mel told her it was nothing serious. Insistent, she offered to help.

"Can't I write a letter for the judge?" she asked.

"Thank you," Cooper replied, still surrounded by a pack of marshals. "But I don't think it's going to help, writing a letter saying I was a good tenant."

He was taken away and deposited in the Broward County Jail in Fort Lauderdale. He called Thomas Puccio who was out of the office, and left a message.

"Tell him to call me. I'm in jail in Fort Lauderdale."

18

CLUB MIAMI

Dr. Giraldez and Kathy arrived at the county jail within a few hours of Mel's arrest. They listened to Mel in disbelief, finding it difficult to absorb the story he told them. Not only had their business partner just been arrested—he wasn't even Tony Parisi.

"If you had only told me, I would have put you in another country. I could have done so much," said Dr. Giraldez.

Recalls Mel, "He was genuinely sorry I didn't tell him. He was a nice guy. Kathy was crying. They both said, 'if there's anything we could do just let us know. Take the number, call us.'" Mel didn't have his address book with him, and they wanted to make sure he could reach them. They were distraught over what had happened to their partner.

As for Mel, "there was a combination of things running through my head. I was upset. I was relieved. I was glad to get this thing behind me in a way because living as a fugitive is not my cup of tea. So I was thinking if this whole thing could be finished, it would be nice. But on the other hand, when you're in there, you'd give away anything you own to have freedom."

Doctor Giraldez and Kathy were not the only ones who had an identity crisis when faced with Mel Cooper/Tony Parisi. The government could not take any action like reassignment, extradition, or anything else, until they determined exactly who this man was. While his fingerprints said Mel Cooper, his bank statements, business papers, credit cards, leases, and bills all said Tony Parisi.

Cooper stayed in Fort Lauderdale for four days, and after complaining about the kosher food – or lack of it – he was transferred to the Federal Correctional Institution in Miami.

FCI Miami is a low-security facility with 1,500 prisoners and a Florida vibe. At the time, the facility had a lake in the middle of the grounds with tennis and racquetball courts in the outside yard.

"There was a lot of security but it was not a penitentiary. It was like MCC in New York. People are waiting to be sent somewhere else."

The first question the Justice Department needed to resolve was whether Mel planned to fight extradition back to Terre Haute. Would he willingly resume his identity and the prison term that went with it? He had laid enough groundwork as Anthony Parisi to seriously delay the proceedings.

They brought Mel to court to see if he would sign off on being Mel Cooper. He did. But as usual, the justice system moved at a crawl with weeks between court visits, hearings, and reviews. Besides the question of identity, Mel's case was fraught with unusual issues that slowed a sluggish system even more. "It was a whole procedure, they don't just accept me raising my hand and saying 'I'm Mel Cooper'. They're very careful to make sure they don't have the wrong person."

"Also, the FBI was positive that I paid some officer at the courtroom up north to let me out – that it was a preplanned thing – and they only wanted to know the name of the guy I paid off. They wanted a corrupt cop at the courthouse. That was in Miami. Finally, the facts came in that I did not escape, and that they released me in error. They confirmed it up north."

Meanwhile, Mel readjusted to prison life, this time with good weather. "I was able to spend a lot of time outside there, they had a lot of people who were not permanently staying there, so you didn't have to work. I was weightlifting, playing handball, playing miniature golf, bocce. Bocce was big. Terre Haute was also big on bocce.

"When I got to Miami," recalls Mel, "one of the guys there was saying, 'Oh, you're the guy who walked away in Hauppauge Court, I was in court that day.'"

He filled Mel in on what he had missed. "He said, 'I couldn't believe it. All of a sudden someone came to the judge and said, somebody let Mel Cooper out fifteen minutes before the US Marshal came to pick him up, and everybody's pointing at everybody else in the court.'"

Kathy and Dr. Giraldez visited Mel often in Miami. They continued to run First Professional Leasing Company. They had developed a solid business, and Mel tried to help them run it from jail. The Feds didn't feel the need to shut down his business this time. Kathy and Doctor Giraldez were not happy that their partner, Tony Parisi, was basically fictional, but that fiction had made them both a lot of money.

"I tried to tell them what to do but it was difficult. I was the one who coordinated the whole business." By the time he left Florida seven months later, First Professional Leasing was almost closed. Still, they remained on good terms.

Says Caspar, "Everybody was shocked when Mel was arrested. It was incredible. They surrounded the whole building. There were 30 cops there, and he's gone. When he got arrested, I lost my best friend."

Pondering what might have been, says Caspar, "If he didn't get arrested, he would have built South Beach. That was all his. We were going to all these different banks to get loans for funding equipment, and meeting with bank presidents, and I would just sit there, and he would talk to the bank president and he would give me a look, and I would nod yes or no. Like I was the one in charge. Mel told me exactly what to do. And we did it with every bank president. We financed a drugstore on the beach. And the only other thing remodeled on the whole beach was the Carlyle Hotel. And we're talking to the bank presidents who were saying, 'we're going rebuild this whole area'. Back then South Beach was all ruins, it was a wreck."

How was it all going to work? According to Caspar, "The drug dealers were going to finance it and Mel was going to launder it."

After Mel was arrested, the counterfeit birth certificates arrived. "They were sealed and signed. You only needed to type in a name at the top."

As far as Mel's other acquaintances and associates in Fort Lauderdale knew, Tony Parisi simply disappeared, unless they happened to read about his arrest in the newspapers. In New York City, the Daily News announced,

"Loose 'Shark' Hooked." Then, adding a dash of glamour to the encounter, they reported Mel was arrested in "a luxurious one-bedroom condo as he slept with two shapely Canadian women." Said another, "Mel Cooper was captured by gun-toting US marshals in a $300,000 oceanfront apartment in Fort Lauderdale."

Mel's recapture was not the only news.

Mel learned Jimmy Rotondo had been killed. He had been shot in the face sitting in his Lincoln right in front of his house in Brooklyn. The fish he had been bringing home for dinner was still on the seat beside him.

Jimmy had been killed only days before Mel's recapture. Rotondo, 58 years old, was the highest-ranking mobster to be murdered since Gambino boss Paul Castellano was killed at a Manhattan steakhouse in 1985. It was big news in New York City, and the murder was linked directly to Mel Cooper's case.

Said the New York Daily News headline on January 6th, "Feds think victim let a fink into the mob." That fink was none other than Jesse Hyman, now 44 years old.

Hyman had agreed to cooperate with the government six months earlier. He was scheduled to serve as a witness in the upcoming racketeering trial of Anthony "Nino" Gaggi and nine other Gambino family associates. Surely the DeCavalcante family would be the next target, thanks to Hyman's cooperation. And up in Buffalo, anyone with mob ties to Hyman's dental clinic was worried. A headline in the Buffalo News proclaimed, "Crime Families Fear Testimony of Man Who Operated Buffalo Clinic."

Jimmy Rotondo's funeral had taken place in Bensonhurst, Brooklyn, attended by Mafia bosses from John Riggi to John Gotti to Sammy Gravano. No one had taken credit for the hit. "Investigators said Rotondo may have been killed as punishment for giving Hyman mob entree. Lawyers for Hyman refused to comment."

Says Mel, "One hundred per cent, it was because of Doc. When I was released, not long before, Doc had already had meetings with the US Attorney's office. It came back to me through people who told me what happened.

"This is something they were listening for. They knew Doc is going to talk about Jimmy, and they were afraid Jimmy was going to turn on them."

Jesse Hyman's decision to flip became public only a few days after Rotondo's murder on January 4, 1988. But his Mafia associates already knew Jesse was scheduled to testify.

The fact that Rotondo's murder occurred only four days before Mel was recaptured in Florida, led to speculation that there was a connection between the various events. Well-known mob-watcher Jerry Capeci wrote in the Daily News, "A Rotondo front man, Melvin Cooper, was convicted and sentenced to 30 years but escaped in 1986. He was captured Friday in Florida after news reports of Rotondo's killing generated new leads from informers and anonymous tipsters." This was confirmed by US Marshal Mike Hollander, who said, "I got a flurry of tips from informants, and when I verified it, I sent the information down to Florida."

The exact relationship between Rotondo's murder, Mel's recapture, and the announcement of Jesse Hyman's decision to cooperate is unclear, but their execution only a few days apart suggests the government had a role in the timing of events.

After seven months in FCI Miami, all questions were resolved. Mel's escape was deemed accidental release. Mel requested credit for the time he was out. He was told he would have to pursue that later, once he was returned to the Bureau of Prisons. But he would not be punished, sentence-wise. Soon, Mel Cooper was on his way back to Terre Haute.

For long-distance transport, the Bureau of Prisons sometimes uses a prison plane run by the US Marshals. "They used old 727s or more like 707s—whatever planes they could get hold of. The planes are not set up with the prisoners' comfort in mind. They had three seats on each side, and you're shackled or cuffed."

The long trip back to Terre Haute started eventfully. The departure point was a private landing strip somewhere in Miami. Shackled both hand and foot, Mel was escorted onto the plane along with other prisoners. As he began to walk down the aisle, he saw a familiar face. It was Patrick Bradley.

"You walk on from the back, and he was sitting in the second seat from the rear, in the middle. So I passed his seat, and I kept turning around. Everybody else is in a Federal Prison uniform, and he's sitting there with a black suit. Now I already knew that he's the one that turned me in," Mel explains. "I found out that he had been arrested for something and quickly made a deal to give me up. But he wasn't sure whether I knew it, so as I'm walking, I'm turning around and I see the marshal is right behind me. Then I look at Patrick, and he's six foot four and he's starting to crouch down in his seat, getting lower and lower as I'm looking at him, and then he yells, 'aiding and abetting.' So he's trying to explain to me why he's locked up—for aiding and abetting me, which is baloney."

Mel figured he would talk to Patrick when he got off the plane. They were on their way to Talladega, Alabama, a holdover for prisoners in transit. "We got to Talladega, and everybody gets off the plane. And I'm looking for him and he's nowhere to be found. He must have gone over to the marshal and told him, 'Get me the hell away from this guy,' and they scooped him away and I never saw him again."

Mel never found exactly why Bradley was on the plane. He may have been on his way to a hearing or to testify. The BOP doesn't usually transport people in suits. "I found out later he was picked up for selling drugs. He probably traded information about me for his freedom."

From Talladega, Mel went to El Reno in Oklahoma, and from there to Terre Haute. Finally, after two weeks of traveling, he was—to use the word loosely—home.

19

IN AGAIN

Back in Terre Haute, they actually cheered for him. When the grueling registration process was complete, Mel found himself walking down the hall to the shouts and whistles of fellow inmates. In Federal Penitentiary, the us-versus-them mentality takes hold quickly, and one of the greatest acts a prison inmate can perform is the supreme "fuck you" of escaping–thus the applause. He recognized a lot of faces: Fat Gigi, Marshall Schrager, his Bronx pal, Ralphie. They were all just where he had left them.

Mel's security clearance was raised to the maximum designation. He was now considered high risk even though Federal Court in Miami had ruled he had not escaped. They called it 'unauthorized release.' He was not supposed to be punished for it. But as Mel is fond of saying, "They can write whatever they want. If someone down the line wants to call it an escape, then it's an escape."

Mel's security level was now a "five," indicating the highest likelihood of escape. The paperwork that accompanies a prisoner throughout his stay in the federal prison system reflects the point of view of whoever is keeping track, and soon "escape" was a glaring note on his record.

Says Cooper, "The unit managers and team managers all said to me, 'you escaped.' I said 'I didn't escape, I wasn't charged with escape.' They said, 'Come on, you escaped.' If the court doesn't get their pound of flesh, the system will get the rest of it.

"The guards themselves don't care—they're not looking for personal vendettas. But the team managers or unit managers know all about your record, and they position you in their system accordingly." This has consequences.

"Now, what happens is, you go to the parole board, or you go to the unit manager for a reduction of your security level so that you can get transferred to a lower security facility. They look at your record and start off, 'okay, you escaped.'"

But if the court says you didn't escape? Mel's answer is typically matter-of-fact. "Go argue with them."

Mel returned to the same work he had been doing before in order to earn extra good time. He worked in the kosher kitchen. His free hours were still devoted to reading law books in the library and looking for clues on how to appeal his sentence. He played baseball in the yard, lifted weights, and took up drawing, writing, and painting to pass the time. His kids even came to visit him once or twice.

Life at Terre Haute hadn't gotten any better in his year away, and the place still deserved its nickname, "Terror Hut." There were gangs warring night and day, and virtually no safe corner in the compound—not in the shower or the dining hall, not in the TV room or the yard. Once again, Mel's friendships with the Italians protected him, and he continued to associate himself with the Mafia inmates who incurred some measure of respect and security.

With his Fort Lauderdale dream over, Mel's main goal was to get closer to New York City. In the logic of the Federal prison system, men and women are placed thousands of miles from home, often in rural, hard-to-reach areas. The challenge is to get your security level reduced so you can be transferred. After an uneventful six months Mel's security level dropped. In early 1989, after seven more months in Terre Haute, he got good news: he was being transferred to FCI Ray Brook in Upstate New York.

Ray Brook is in the Adirondack Mountains near Lake Placid, just a five hour trip from New York City. Constructed in 1980 for the Lake Placid

Winter Olympics, Ray Brook has separate buildings, including a dining hall, a commissary, and a library. Mel would live in a converted dorm that had once housed ice skaters or bobsledders.

Ray Brook still had the razor-wire fences and guards circling the compound 24 hours a day, but unlike Terre Haute, it had no guard towers and there were fewer restrictions. Like most prisons, they had an "hourly move" during which prisoners had ten minutes to change locations. At Ray Brook, that meant inmates could walk between buildings in the fresh air. Of course, once the move was over you had better be somewhere for the next fifty minutes. Anyone caught between buildings after the hourly move got a "shot" on their record or went to the Hole.

It snows in the Adirondacks six months a year, which meant that rather than the punishment of stifling heat, Mel now had to contend with the cold. Mel didn't mind. He enjoyed being outdoors.

"I spent a lot of time going outside the unit, sitting and looking at the trees. At the back of our unit in Ray Brook there was a small fenced-in area, and you could sit there, and the only thing that's out there is the forest or a couple of birds that are flying around, and I would sit there and think. I did that a lot."

The amount of freedom and the view of the mountains made life easier at Ray Brook. But not everything was an improvement. As Mel puts it, "the class of people was worse."

Gone were the dons and capos, the professional thieves and world-class swindlers. As Mel learned in prison, the lower the security, the less "professional" the inmates. Ray Brook didn't get Mafia powerhouses like Anthony Indelicato or Fat Gigi Inglese. It got the losers, petty criminals, mules, order-takers, hustlers, amateurs, and low-level offenders; they were an overall mediocre class of lawbreakers.

At lower-security prisons, you saw first-hand what the crackdown on drugs had done for the prison business. "Ray Brook was filled with guys doing time for drug possession and most of them were immigrants, Africans and South Americans, who had been picked up at an airport carrying in drugs for someone else. The government would catch a courier bringing in a pound of heroin and cut him a deal. The D.A. would sit him down and say, 'If you get somebody else to come in, to carry drugs, you'll get less time.' Instead of fifteen years, he'll get nine years. So he would call up his friend, and set him up, and catch him, and then the friend would do the same thing. And they had untold amounts of people doing time this way."

These drug offenders filled Ray Brook and other medium-security prisons to capacity. According to Mel, many of these prisoners made more money in prison than they would in their own country, depending on the pay scale. They worked in Unicor or, more officially, "Federal Prison Industries," the Bureau of Prison's work system. They would work for prison wages, including overtime, and send the money they made back home.

Working for Unicor might have been fine for guys supporting a family on another continent, but Mel Cooper did not plan to work for 18 cents an hour. Mel decided it was time for his high school football injury to flare up again. He told the prison doctor he couldn't walk. Mel was excused from most of the physical labor. "Since I didn't have to work, I would stay up from the time they locked the door at eleven, eleven-thirty until five o'clock in the morning. I managed to do reading, I managed to do painting–I would not be able to sleep. So I would sit there with my pencils and canvas, and I would draw.

"Everybody else had to be up by 6:30 and have their beds made. I had to have my bed made, but then I'd then lay down on top of the bed and go back to sleep."

In spite of the freedoms and outdoor scenery, Mel didn't like Ray Brook and Ray Brook didn't like him. He made a stink over the kosher food, called his lawyer every chance he got, and refused to work. He hobbled around with a cane. Mel demanded Ray Brook meet their legal obligation to provide Jewish prisoners with food that respected their dietary customs. This grew into a constant source of friction between him and the prison administration.

When Ray Brook decided to get rid of their kosher kitchen, it was war. "There was a kosher kitchen up until a certain time, and then they made what they called 'common fare.'"

Common fare is a diet designed to meet the lowest common denominator of dietary restrictions. It's made of foods that anyone on almost any special diet could eat. Says Cooper, "it's to discourage people from joining anything special. It's more like a starvation diet. It was good for anybody, Jews, Muslims. You might get a few sticks of celery, some carrots, a little thing of peanut butter, a couple of slices of tomato and that was your lunch. You would get very little breakfast, and you would get three hot entrees a week. One of them was fish, like three ounces, and one is a hamburger, and the other one is chicken, so this is how they went from kosher to common fare."

"It bothered me that they were feeding us like this." Mel reminded the food services department they still were required to keep a kosher kitchen, even with common fare. "In other words, you still can't mix dairy and meat. They didn't expect this. But this is the law, you can't violate somebody's religious rights. It may not violate the Muslims' rights, but you're violating the Jews.'"

Ray Brook refused to comply. "They felt they would have less aggravation if they just did whatever they wanted, and they were committing all kinds of violations. They feel that they are above their own policies, the warden, the unit manager, the food service administrator. Certain wardens believe it's their own fiefdom and they don't have to listen to anybody. Nobody's going to tell them what they have to feed people. Some of them are nice and some of them are, like, lunatics."

Mel began the process of filing complaints, working his way slowly through the system. "First, you have to file what they call a BP-8, which is an informal remedy, and if you don't get a resolution on that, you file a BAP-9, which goes to the warden, and you wait for a response. You have to get an answer on that within fifteen or twenty days. So again, when there's a problem, the warden is made aware of it. If he doesn't want to resolve it, he'll write you back some kind of answer."

If the answer is unsatisfactory, the next step is a BP-10. "The BP-10 goes to the region and if you have an obvious violation, the region can't overlook it. They come and say, 'hey, fix this.' Or if the region doesn't respond, then Washington gets it. The Washington BP, that's the BP-11. After that you go to court."

Sometimes they don't fix things just because they want to prove a point; they don't have to do anything different just for you. "They have a lot of animosity for your special needs."

After one year in Ray Brook, the Administration decided they had enough of Cooper. Soon Mel was on his way to The Bureau of Prisons' Medical Facility in Rochester, Minnesota, for surgery to correct his chronic, if fictional, knee problems.

There are benefits to a system that moves at glacial speed. While it can take four weeks to take a trip from New York to Minnesota, this pace worked in Mel's favor when it came to hospital care. Cooper would spend a full year in Rochester, waiting to see a specialist, waiting for surgery, and finally, waiting for reassignment. "The people they send there are doing a lot of time. Why rush?" It's as if Mel spent all of 1990 visiting an orthopedic surgeon.

The place was the Waldorf compared to Ray Brook. The food was delicious, the view, magnificent. Televangelist and convicted fraud James Bakker was an inmate in Rochester at the time. And, like every place else in the prison system, organized crime had a presence. Since it was a prison hospital, they tended to be old-timers. "You get some old organized crime guys in the hospital who still managed to carry weight wherever they are. So they get certain benefits from their station in life. Some were barely even sick and got to the hospital as a kind of vacation. They ate better, they relaxed."

It was also one of the few co-ed facilities in the United States prison system. By the time Mel got to Rochester, the hospital had only three female inmates left. "One was there to have a kidney removed, another was about seventy."

People were sick in Rochester, really sick. There was a unit with just AIDS patients. There were people with heart failure, people who needed transplants. The city of Rochester is the site of the famed Mayo clinic, and certain surgical procedures were performed there. At Rochester, the prison system showed a measure of compassion, a loosening of the rules in order to humanely accommodate all levels of prisoners, in spite of its classification as a maximum-security facility. When Mel arrived, he was put in a hospital room instead of a cell, with a real bed.

His first mistake at Rochester was flirting with a nurse. Mel had forgotten his days of limousines and fine dining were over, and that here, he was just another number. Recalls Mel, "They diagnose you, and I think what happened with me is I made some overtures to the nurse, I made some statements to her, something about piña coladas. I think she was bringing me some medication, and I said I'd rather have a piña colada, I don't know, something like that. But I think I got my point across because the next morning they announced my name, that I should move my stuff to Building A. This was a more confined wing of the hospital, with tighter security and a smaller room. They didn't like what could come from a nurse and a patient getting friendly."

Again, after years without freedom or members of the opposite sex, food becomes your top pleasure in life. "That place was like a five-star hotel. I mean, they used to make pancakes, French toast, assortments of lunch and cakes and strawberry shortcake. Because it was a hospital facility, now we had a special kosher kitchen and I had a little input there."

The more Mel traveled through the prison system, the more quickly he learned to adapt and benefit from his knowledge and connections. "Each time it's easier. You get to a new place. You mention the names of people from the last place, from a different place, certain people they might know, and so they ask about them. It's like you just came from a different country, 'How's my family back there?' A lot of people have friends in different prisons that are waiting for word. You can't just write to them because you're not allowed to correspond or befriend other prisoners while you're on parole or probation. So people traveling around will pass word from one guy to another. 'You're going there? Bring a message to this guy.' There are people moving around all the time. People know a lot about you from where you were.

"You don't just talk to everybody, but as you develop relations with people, you talk to them. You talk about different things, about your case. Some people don't want to talk about their case, they're embarrassed about it. Some people say they're in for murder even though they're in for drugs. So you don't necessarily believe everything you hear."

On July 5, 1990, Mel learned his sentence had been reduced from thirty years to twelve years. His attorneys had been trying everything to get his sentence reduced or thrown out, including filing for what's known as a Rule 35 motion.

A Rule 35 motion allows a judge to correct or reduce a sentence.

Usually, a Rule 35 is a request for leniency in recognition of an offender's cooperation with the government. It means the defendant has provided substantial help or useful information in an investigation. Mel claims he never helped the government or informed. But Doc did. By that time, he had already testified at numerous trials of Mafia bosses and union officials. "He gave them what they wanted, and this is the same judge, Judge Sand, and he knew that. The judge looked at this and felt he didn't need to keep me."

A Rule 35 motion is usually only applied within a year of sentencing. "I have to thank Puccio for requesting the Rule 35 when I was out. He sent a motion to Judge Sand requesting that he leave the time for a Rule 35 open until such time as I'm back in custody. Because if he hadn't done that, I wouldn't be able to get my sentence reduced."

It also helped matters that one of the people now fighting for Mel was a respected rabbi, the internationally known activist and Jewish leader, Rabbi Arthur Schneier. A champion of human rights around the world, the senior rabbi at the Park East Synagogue in Manhattan did what he could for Mel. "I used to send my kids to his school, and I used to go to his Shul. I knew him very well.

"He was, at the time, the alternate Ambassador to the United Nations. He was one of the people who helped me. He wrote a very strong letter. Rabbi Schneier did whatever he did, and the judge came down to twelve years. I was ecstatic," recalls Mel, "That was a good day.

"They get the word right away when your sentence changes, because your security level changes. You have less time. So what happened was, because my security level changed, from Minnesota they ended up sending me to Danbury, Connecticut, instead of back to Ray Brook.

"I had been in six years, and now, with a twelve-year sentence, I'm entitled to parole after four years. So I could immediately request parole, the next time they meet, and maybe they'll give me a break. They could let me right out. So when Puccio told me about the reduction, what was going through my mind is, if I meet the parole board tomorrow, they could let me out."

Mel could actually start counting the days without feeling sick to his stomach. He could see the end. He had gone in in the summer of 1985. At the very worst, with statutory good time Mel calculated he could get out by 1994, factoring in the year and a half in Florida. With parole he could be out within days.

Back at the prison hospital in Rochester, they were ready for Mel's surgery. He told them he didn't want it. He told them he would be out soon, and he wanted to get the surgery on the outside. He no longer needed to occupy himself with schemes to make prison life bearable. He would be out soon enough.

20

DOWN IN THE HOLE

"They sent me from Rochester to Danbury in a private plane, a six-seater. They dropped me off, and I got into Danbury, and I was sent to the dorm unit. I was walking into the dorm and I went to the bunk bed I was assigned to, and there was a guy laying there on the bottom bed, and he sees me and says 'oh shit,' because he saw me walking with a cane, and he knew he would be ordered to move to the top bunk. And he introduces himself as Kevin Trudeau."

Kevin Trudeau was a youthful, good-looking peddler of natural cures and self-improvement programs doing two years in jail for larceny and fraud, having used the credit cards of customers who bought his "Mega-memory" program to charge an extra $120,000. He made a career selling a variety of natural cures, including coral calcium, weight-loss schemes, and more. His business was characterized by frequent run-ins with the FTC. Later, Trudeau would return to selling miracle cures, weight-loss programs, and conspiracy theory-packed books until 2014, when he got a ten-year prison sentence for criminal contempt. The judge who sentenced Trudeau called him "deceitful to the very core." Observed the judge, "Since his 20s, he has steadfastly attempted to cheat others for his own gain."

Kevin and Mel hit it off right away. They shared personal history and grievances like longtime friends. "Right away, he told me his story about

Above, right, below: Mel Cooper and friends at Terre Haute Penitentiary in Indiana

Above: The Candy Store in Fort Lauderdale

Left: Mel's friend, Caspar

Mel's friends from Canada at Disneyworld

Above: Christmas in Fort Lauderdale

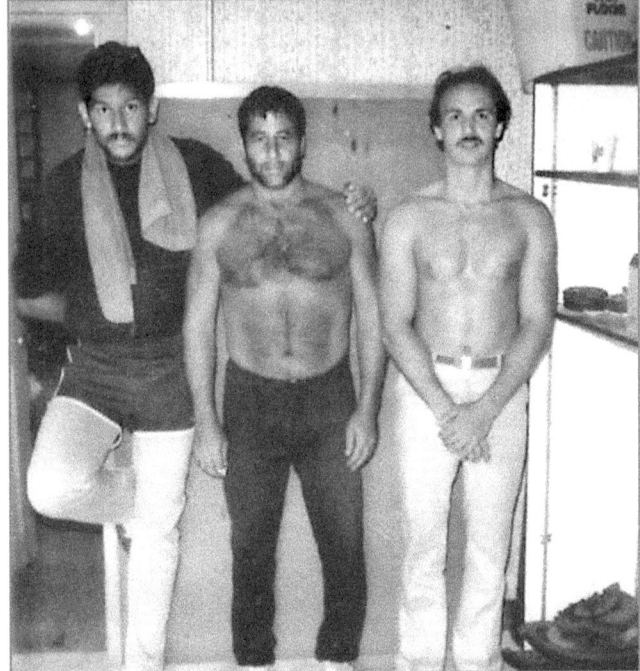

Left: Mel with Ralphie from the Bronx (left) in Terre Haute Penitentiary

Below: Mel and buddies in the yard, Terre Haute Penitentiary

Cooper's father and wife visiting him at Danbury Federal Prison

Mel with sons visiting him at Danbury Federal Prison

Mel visiting his sons in New York while living as Tony Parisi

Left: Mel and son in the telecom business, New York City, early 2000s.

Below: Portrait of Mel in his Trump Tower apartment

Torah dedication in honor of brother, David Cooper and mother Naomi Cooper

Below: Mel with son in the Caribbean

Left: Mel Cooper with daughter, 2006

Above: Postcard of old Diplomat Hotel

Mel Cooper in 2022

being adopted, and recently finding his real mother in Boston, and she's Jewish," Mel explains. At a singularly inconvenient time and place—in jail—Kevin decided to become kosher.

"He became, like, the most hard-campaigning guy for kosher food, and the smartest. He had attorneys on the outside, and he was a good writer himself. I mean, when he wrote a PB-8 or a BP-9, he made them sit back and read. I tell you, when we walked into the dining room, the food administrator didn't know what to do first to get our food ready. We would walk up to the counter and our meals were just decked out, and you could see they were biting a bullet to control themselves, because they hate when a prisoner tells them what to do. So it was almost comical."

But as in Ray Brook, Danbury only offered a common fare menu. He and Kevin turned their campaign into a full-out war, complaining that the common fare program in Danbury was a travesty, with ham sandwiches appearing on their trays, and no observance of kosher laws. They started two lawsuits, one in Connecticut and another in New York.

The prison administration in Danbury seemed to take the accusations made by Trudeau and Cooper personally. Soon after he began to complain, Mel noticed he was sent to the hole with increasing frequency. "They would come into my room and say, 'you left a pair of socks on the floor, you're going into the hole.'"

The hole or "administrative segregation" removes a prisoner from all comforts. Inmates are placed alone in a cell and remain there all day with one hour a day for exercise; there is no company, no books, no window, and the lights are on twenty-four hours a day. If you can imagine punishment that makes you look forward to getting back to your normal cell, that's the hole.

The hole also means the loss of the statutory good time automatically assigned to each prisoner, so getting sent to the hole can have long-term consequences.

Trudeau seemed to relish the fight against the prison administration. Mel remembers, "There were days that we went without food. And that was what the BP-9 said, that went first to the warden then to the region. 'We're starving.' Kevin used to write some of these things, he would be very colorful.

"What would happen is, they would end up throwing me in the hole for some stupid infraction, but it was basically because of the filing. Before I reached the hole, Kevin would have an attorney from outside calling the warden. So this was a short-lived hole visit. Because when someone on the outside knows what's going on in there, once outside legal people are looking over your shoulder, they pull you right out.

"They have people in the hole almost indefinitely. But even there, you have to figure it out, because they don't let you have anything. With no glasses you can't read. So what would happen is, wherever there was a common fare kitchen or kosher kitchen, I knew who the chefs were, and when I was in the hole they would send me an enormous amount of food. They wrap up the food, the whole tray, so it's not open until it gets to you. So I would use this food to give to the guards, so I could get my glasses, and I can get some books."

It was all handled discreetly. "The guard is giving me a huge tray of food which can't come through the opening in the door, so I would tell him, 'Listen, that's too much for me, I'm going to take off a sandwich or whatever, why don't you take it with you, to the rest of the guys and have something. You know, I don't want all this food.' He says, 'Ok, sure.' Right away you get your glasses."

Mel lasted four months in Danbury. "They raised my security. My security was low, I was already getting ready to go home, at that time I was a year and half from the maximum time they could keep me. I think it was a build-up of a few events, mostly related to the food services."

They sent him back to Ray Brook. Mel had hoped he'd never see Ray Brook again, and the feeling was mutual. When he left Ray Brook a year and a half earlier, his unit manager's parting words to Mel were, "Have a nice trip. Don't come back."

In the short time he'd been away, the population of Ray Brook had begun to change. Now, besides the swarms of low-level drug dealers, there were powerful Cosa Nostra associates and bosses who'd been swept up in the other RICO prosecutions of the late 1980s. Mel and Jesse's trial had been just the warm-up.

The Commission Trial was the crowning accomplishment of Rudolph Giuliani and the Justice Department's campaign against the Mafia. It had taken place towards the end of 1986, right after Cooper's trial. In a novel approach to organized crime, the Justice Department claimed that the five disparate crime families acted as one criminal enterprise, from price-fixing in the waste industry, to labor corruption, to murder. It resulted in the conviction of eight powerful bosses and underbosses, including Carmine Persico, "Fat Tony" Salerno, and "Tony Ducks" Corallo. It devastated the Mafia. More prosecutions followed.

When Mel got back to Ray Brook, he recalls running into Benny Aloi and Tony Napoli. The government had managed to get them after all. Ray Brook was often used as a stopover point for inmates designated to other Federal penitentiaries, and Mel ran into other old acquaintances there who were passing through. He saw Fat Tony Salerno again, and got to know Raymond Patriarca, Jr., son of the famous New England Mafia boss.

Mel was now scheduled to serve two-thirds of his twelve-year sentence, or eight years. This was the maximum he had to serve under the Old Laws. Adding in Mel's uncredited time in Fort Lauderdale brought the grand total to ten years. The parole board had refused to give him any additional time off his sentence. Repeatedly in Ray Brook and Danbury, he was told to "continue to expiration."

"The facts were there, including the fact that they released me in error. Everyone believed me but the parole board. They kept saying, 'You got your break with your escape.'"

As always, your history follows you through the system, and besides his escape, Mel's original 30-year sentence accompanied him. "They felt the judge gave me a break by reducing the sentence, and they didn't think that they should let me out early.

"I remember one completely devastating moment. I was always working on trying to get out through different legal means, and I found a notice, through a religious organization, about an alternative program for people that are incarcerated. I reached out to them. They knew my case and agreed to bring my whole thing before the federal judge. I only had about two years left. So they wrote a proposal, and sent it to my attorney. He sent it to the prosecutor and the judge.

"The proposal was, I would do a combination of studying in a school in New Jersey, and do programs for the city, for the government. I was prepared to do that for the next two years. I said, 'this, they're going to give to me, I'm sure.' I lost out on a lot of things prior to that. So when I got the call from my attorney, I remember he just said, very nonchalantly,

'We just lost, the judge turned it down,' and I felt like I fell off a four-story building, that's exactly how I felt like, and I went into a state of depression. That was, like, a devastating blow."

21

NOTHING LEFT

Manhattan MCC	2 months
Terre Haute, IN	10 months
Suffolk County, NY	3 months
Fort Lauderdale, FL	18 months
Miami FCI	7 months
Terre Haute, IN	1 year, 6 months
Ray Brook, NY	1 year
Rochester, MN	1 year
Danbury, CT	4 months
Ray Brook, NY	1 year, 6 months
Travel and Transit	1 year

Everything changes when you go away for ten years. When you come back your friends aren't friends anymore. Most of them are acquaintances now, if that. They've moved on. Lovers are gone, and if they're not gone, they're ten years older. They've lived without you for a long time.

About nine months before he got out, the letters started coming. "I find that nine months before I was released, all of a sudden people are notifying me, they're writing me, there's family, friends. Suddenly, I'm getting remembered by everybody. It was like everybody had on the calendar, after 111 months, call this guy up or send him a letter.

"Certain people meant it, like my friend in Chicago, Kevin Trudeau. He was already out and back in Chicago. He was sincere. But otherwise, I think a lot of it was . . . I don't know, maybe it's the way people are. Somebody gets thirty years, it's like they died."

The places you used to go are often not there anymore. New York City doesn't stand still for anyone. When Mel went away in 1985, Ed Koch was mayor, the Yankees were losers, money flowed among the rich, and crack cocaine was about to wash over whole sections of New York, turning them into pointlessly violent gray zones. In the '80s it was all right to be "flashy." New York was a city of gold teetering on an abyss.

When Mel came out it was 1994 and Giuliani was about to become mayor. The city would soon be his New York, with more policing and less tolerance for crime, no matter how petty. Things were looking up after an early '90s slump, though the good times were more low-key, more discreet, more tempered. The city was experiencing a retail boom. Crime was down, the cops were bold – some say a little too bold – and the down-and-out were still around but now out-of-sight, locked up, or run out of town so as not to interfere with anyone's shopping. And Giuliani had launched a full-scale assault on organized crime. The Fulton Fish Market, the Javits Convention Center, the sanitation business – all were unrecognizable in comparison with what they had once been.

Even if an old haunt is still there after ten years, whether it's a restaurant, a grocery store, or a dry cleaner, in New York the chances are small that the same people work there. They move away, they die, they retire. After ten years, it's as if you just moved here. Only your family is still your family. In Mel's case this was a mixed blessing.

Mel's family was there to welcome him when he returned from jail, ready to pick up where they had left off being brothers, sister, father. And at the same time, according to Mel, they had let him down. They had not looked after him or his interests.

When Mel went to prison at age thirty-eight, he had accumulated homes, cars, and property. He had stocks, bonds, bank accounts, an apartment full of expensive furnishings, a collection of Lalique pottery, the condo on the beach in Westhampton, a red convertible Mercedes 450 SL.

When Mel returned from Ray Brook, there was nothing.

Everyone seemed to have an excuse as to why Mel's material possessions were all gone. The remaining income from Cooper Funding, whatever could be pieced together from the documents the FBI had bothered to return, had been used to pay debts. A building he bought with his uncle Victor on West 168th Street was gone. It had been a huge property with 85 units. The story was, Victor didn't have the spine to be a New York landlord and he lost it.

Mel's personal possessions, his paintings, the pottery, even the track lighting, were supposedly sold to pay for various costs and fees, though some of the pieces had a way of turning up in family members' living rooms.

According to Mel, it couldn't have been for legal fees, because he paid those himself. "When I asked what happened, it was always, 'We took care of payments, we took care of this and that, there were problems, there was nothing left. It was so long ago, who remembers, and anyway, aren't you glad to be out?'"

Even the belongings Mel had managed to hold on to had a way of dissolving, if not materially, then in terms of significance. The papers he kept in his safe deposit box—the books that seemed so important when the FBI was closing in—were about as meaningful as old newspapers lining the drawers of an antique dresser. They meant nothing now, not even to Mel.

There were no big fights or showdowns. Mel didn't confront his family on the question of why his belongings were all gone. And they did not confront Mel over the fact that his actions decimated the family businesses and damaged their reputations.

"I think they were angry because of the disruption of their lives, psychologically, even a little physically. Most of all, I think they didn't appreciate the publicity, the negative publicity. This is stuff that they were angry and embarrassed over. There may have been a few family speeches."

In typical form, Mel remembers what he wants to and leaves the rest in a fog of family history. He chooses to believe his family was not all that put out by his arrest, trial, and conviction. After all, his father and uncle Jack had been bought out of Cooper Funding by Doc, and they still had a thriving steel business. His brother David worked in his father's manufacturing company. His sister was not involved with the companies shut down by the government. Only his brothers Barry and Jeffrey had been directly involved. They immediately started their own leasing company with the same banks they had been dealing with before. "I don't think they missed a beat."

Mel was particularly hurt by his father. He had helped Sam earn a fortune and tripled his steel business as a young salesman in Cooper Tanks and Welding. Mel had set up tax shelters, given his family hundreds of thousands of dollars' worth of stock in BW Energy Systems. BW had gone public with its Pyrolysis system. His father wouldn't even buy Mel's kids tickets to Florida.

The pattern that had started in childhood, of looking to his father for support only to find himself ignored, seemed to be never-ending. Mel gave his trust, sought approval, got burned, and returned to outdo his father, aspiring to ever-higher heights to break the cycle. According to Mel, his father never acknowledged his achievements, even as he profited by them. Trust, reject, outdo, crash.

But after ten years your family is still your family. Mel's father picked him up from Ray Brook the day he was released.

Ray Brook releases prisoners at 9:30 in the morning, just in time to catch the bus out of town. No one wants a recently released convict hanging around, and most former prisoners want to get away as fast as possible.

If someone agrees to pick up a freed inmate, the prison will discharge him as early as 7:30 in the morning. "This shows you something about prison, that you want to get out so badly, you'll do anything for that extra two hours. I mean, that's how much you want to get away."

Kevin Trudeau wanted to send a limousine with champagne and an escort, which sounded good to Mel. Instead, he got a limousine and his father. There was a right way and a wrong way of doing things, even when it came to leaving prison, and letting your aging father pick you up felt more right than a call girl.

Mel Cooper's life may have been on hold for ten years, but not so his father's. While Mel was away, his father had met a woman, and in 1986 they married. Mel did not know Florence, but he had heard about her.

Still, being picked up at Ray Brook seemed like an inauspicious time to make her acquaintance. His father needed company for the six-hour ride from Long Island to Lake Placid, and Florence came with him.

Mel remembers the day. "Oh, it was very exciting. To get out two hours earlier, my father had to pick me up. It was like a countdown, though you try not to think about it. It's the most exciting thing that can happen.

"I remember they let me out, I think it was eight o'clock. And the first thing I did was, I walked out with my cane, and I took the cane and I threw it over the prison fence. I was thinking, I don't need this cane, I don't want this cane, here's your cane back. And I was just looking around for a few minutes, and then I saw my father pulling up into the parking lot. We hugged for a while, and then we got into the car.

"It was a different feeling than before. Before it was a euphoric feeling. This was the second time I left prison. This was more of a feeling of finality, of peace. Tranquility. The other one, the accidental release, was anything but tranquil. It was exciting."

But the feelings were also mixed. On the one hand, this time he was out for good. But on the other, he had nothing but the handful of things he had accumulated in prison. He had no home of his own, nowhere to go. Mel had been 38 when his prison term began. Now he was 47. He went to live in his father's house.

Sam Cooper still lived in Lawrence, Long Island, where he moved with his family in the late '70s, and where he now lived with Florence. The homecoming was a low-key affair.

"There was no party," remembers Mel. "I was certainly not looking to have a big party from prison. It's not in our circle that you have a big prison-coming-home-party, so that was one party I didn't have.

"It took me time to get used to things, it was all different when I got out. You have to picture being in a vacuum for nine years, having not been in the streets. It was almost eight years since Fort Lauderdale. The cars, the people, the way they dress, every single thing you see—there's a lot of new things that happen over ten years. The stores I knew, it was like everything was different than I remembered. I had the feeling things had passed me by."

The first thing Mel did when he got back to New York was see his kids. They were living with their mother at that time. On his second day, as required, he called his parole officer.

Jerome Taub was a Jewish New Yorker and a career parole officer. He had been with the parole board for over twenty-five years by the time Mel Cooper showed up. Mel was required to report to Taub within forty-eight hours of his release. Thereafter, he and Jerome would meet twice a month at 500 Pearl Street, and later, once a month.

Mel was scheduled to remain under the auspices of the Bureau of Prisons until the expiration of his full twelve-year sentence in 1998. He would spend four years on parole. As a parolee, Mel Cooper was expected to stay in New York State, shun any friend or acquaintance with a criminal record, find a new profession, notify his parole officer of all trips and moves, and, of course, not violate the law. He had to "reply promptly, fully and truthfully to any inquiry or communication by his parole officer or other representative of the Division of Parole." In other words, as long as he was under the auspices of the United States Parole Commission, he was not totally free.

Mel's performance vis à vis these rules would be judged by a single individual who had the sole discretion to toss Mel back in prison at a moment's notice. Jerome Taub disliked Mel right from the start.

From the moment they met there was tension, recalls Mel. "He was very cool and calculating, almost like Colombo from the TV show. Everything is very carefully thought out. He's got three reasons behind every question, and your answer is important. He was very tricky and would always remember something else to ask you. He was in his middle fifties, graying hair. Not overweight, probably about six feet tall. Very experienced."

Immediately, Jerome wanted to know what Mel planned to do to earn a living. "What do you think you're going to do?" he asked.

"I'm probably going to go back into the finance business. That's what I know," Mel answered.

"No, you can't do that. You can't do anything related to financing."

"What am I supposed to do?"

"I don't care, but you can't do finance." Jerome Taub had spoken.

"I walked away from this scratching my head, thinking what am I going to do now? It's pretty much the only thing I've been doing for a long time, and I just got out after ten years and he says I can't do that."

Mel desperately wanted to get back to work. After finding himself banished from finance, his first thought was to go back into his father's manufacturing operation.

It never even occurred to Mel his family might not want him—the Cooper brother who had decimated a hundred-million-dollar enterprise. He approached his younger brother David, certain there would be a place for him. The two had always been close.

David now ran Sam and Jack Cooper's steel container business. He had taken on the task of modernizing the business. He offered to give Mel a tour of the place.

"He showed me his whole setup, with all of his video cameras in his office, then he took me around the plant. I thought that this was like an invitation to come in, this is what was going through my mind. As it turned out, there was nothing like this going through his mind. It was very disappointing. I forget exactly what he said, something like 'they couldn't afford to have me in the business.' It was clear that the reason for taking me around was not for an introduction to help become a partner. He set this up because he was very proud of what he did with the company. So when he spent hours to take me around, to show me details, I didn't realize that he just wanted to show me what he's done. I was proud of him. I didn't say anything. I really could have used the help at that time, I had nothing."

When it became clear he was not going back into the family business, Mel looked around for something else. "My brothers were doing something with phones, and it was something I thought I could make some money with."

The telecommunications industry had been transformed by the breakup of the Bell System in 1982. With continued deregulation of the telecommunications industry in the 1990s, telecom had broken open and become highly competitive, particularly in long-distance services. There were more options for consumers, and opportunity for anyone who wanted to sell telecom services.

Two of Mel's brothers had gotten into retail telecommunications and were doing well working as independent agents. They were snapping up customers who wanted to switch their long-distance service.

Mel liked the idea. The concept was not unfamiliar. As in financing, he would be brokering services, connecting a customer and a carrier the way he had once connected borrowers and banks. There was little overhead or equipment needed. And Mel's deal-making skills could be put to work negotiating costs, fees, and commissions. "It wasn't that complex. I knew what my brothers were doing. It was just a matter of finding a different carrier from them.

"I contacted a place called Frontier Telecom and became an agent, and I started doing retail sales for Frontier, who was in Pennsylvania. A friend of mine had a travel agency on East 38th Street. I made a deal where I would use one desk and pay him rent.

"I made arrangements with Frontier to sell long-distance calls to India for seventy-two cents a minute. So what I did was, I advertised in a number of Indian magazines and newspapers, and I had people calling an 800 number which I installed in the office. I had them fill out an application and I would call in the orders to Frontier. I would get a percentage of their monthly usage." Mel stuck to a simple principle: Sell the minutes for more than it cost to buy them.

After four months of this, Mel met a man named Dr. Vishwananth, who owned a TV station in Queens catering to the Indian community. Dr. Vishwananth purchased time each day on a Spanish TV network and broadcast Indian news and stories of interest. "I told him we would advertise this India long-distance rate on his India TV station, and he would get a commission on each application. Instead of him putting this ad on a few times a day, he started running it every fifteen minutes because he was making a commission. The phones didn't stop ringing."

Though he made only a few cents a call, the income added up, and before long, Mel could afford his own apartment. He had been living with his father for five weeks. His sister-in-law helped him find a studio apartment on East 46th Street. His youngest son was now in college so there would be no children at home. Mel settled into his new apartment and focused on rebuilding his life, trying to make up for lost time any way he could.

Jerome Taub looked on Mel's transformation from paroled criminal to entrepreneur with disbelief. That Mel Cooper thought he could go into business and work for himself—this was highly unusual for someone who just left prison. Taub could not fathom why Cooper didn't get a job with a paycheck, and work somewhere normal, like McDonald's or a grocery store. Mel remembers Taub asking him, over and over, "What's going on, what is it you're doing exactly?"

Meanwhile, the mistrust and resentment between Mel and his family slowly melted, and they rebuilt the bonds of better days. They began to embrace their prodigal brother at the same time he began to forgive them for letting him down.

"What could I do?" says Mel, "Do I walk out and hate everybody? Or do I say, listen, I know what I know, and this is my family and these are my friends. I'll deal with people how I have to deal, but there's no sense in being cold and calculating to everybody. What are you going to do, spend the next ten years fighting?"

He still felt anger. But he kept it to himself, knowing the feelings would dissolve on their own. Prison was behind them. Mistakenly, Mel told himself that neither he nor his family would ever be in this situation again.

22

THE NOT-SO-MERRY-GO-ROUND

Jerome Taub was becoming a problem. Mel realized this when the doorman buzzed Mel at six-thirty one weekday morning and told him he had a visitor.

"I was just in the neighborhood. I thought I'd drop by," said Jerome.

Mel told him he could come up, though he was not happy about Taub's appearance. "Six-thirty in the morning, he just happened to be in the neighborhood? He comes barging in, figuring who has the time to straighten out anything? He figures he'll find drugs on the table, 'cause, you know it's a good time to try to catch somebody. But I had nothing to hide."

He may not have had drugs to hide, but on parole, something as simple as being caught with the wrong person's phone number can be a problem. Mel was not allowed to associate with anyone who had been convicted of a felony.

"You have to understand, I had phone numbers of people from prison. Over the years, you take numbers, you meet certain people, and you have them in your book. So I had my phone book on the desk and, as a matter of fact, this is what happened when he came in. He walks around, he sees the book. He didn't turn the pages, but he was looking, and it's open and he sees some name which he wasn't sure of, so he marks down the name. After he left, I saw the page the stinking book was open to." Mel had been talking to Kevin Trudeau. "We had been speaking and were looking to do something together."

"Anyway, the next day he calls up and he says, 'I want you to bring that book in, that address book that you have on the desk.' And there was no way that I was going to bring that book in. I said, 'Jerome, you're not going to believe this but my housekeeper ended up putting it in the garbage and it's gone.' He didn't like hearing that but I think that the other consequence could have been a lot worse. Despite the fact that I wasn't doing anything, he'll figure out how to get me on something. I knew that if I bring him the book, he's not going to see just that name, he's going to see other names, so I figured, let me just erase this thing.

"He's a guy that wouldn't miss anything, and if you have seven names in your phone book, he'll remember all seven. He said 'I saw that name in your phone book, and one of the guys was on parole and it would be a violation to talk to him.' But there's nothing he can do. That's all he can say. But now he hates me.

"He was clearly angry, and he said, 'Come in Thursday.' From that point on he carried an additional grudge."

After this, Mel adhered to the rules of parole to the letter. He reported to Taub on schedule and gave him a thorough breakdown of where he was spending his time. Mel avoided seeing old acquaintances. Since he was not allowed to call or speak to anybody with a criminal record, it ruled out almost everyone he knew in the sanitation business.

"You don't only worry about if they're watching you. If you're going to meet someone that's an ex-convict, it's possible they're watching him. And his parole guy is watching him. He sees you meeting with him, and he writes it down and takes your picture meeting with him. So if they followed him and caught me, now all of a sudden, I'm violated. So you just stay away from everybody."

There were some attempts on the part of old friends to get in touch with Mel. Someone from Little Vic Orena's crew tried to contact him and wanted to meet with Mel.

Vic was already away for life, having risen through the ranks of the Colombo family to the very top, where he participated in what became known as "The Colombo Wars." Vic had replaced Carmine Persico as acting boss in 1991. He wanted to make his role as acting boss permanent, which led to a violent battle for power. The war ended with the deaths of more than ten people and a life sentence for Vic Orena. Mel wanted to stay as far away as possible from these kinds of friends.

"I said 'I'm on parole'. Not that I was interested in getting involved with anything anyway. I just used that as the reason." He didn't hear from them again.

Still, Jerome Taub was convinced Mel was up to something. He didn't know what and he didn't know how, but he felt it in his gut. Maybe all those years of bending the rules had left its mark on Mel, and Jerome picked up on it. Or maybe it was the way Mel treated Taub as if he were stupid; the notion that Mel's housekeeper had thrown away an address book was as absurd as the claim that his housekeeper misplaced a $20,000 Oriental rug. Whatever it was, Jerome Taub didn't like what he saw.

There was no explicit conflict, but says Mel, "I definitely got the impression that it would be his pleasure if I was working at a gas station. I think he liked very little about what I was doing. I could tell by his actions. I could tell by his questions. I used to tell my father and a couple of other people, 'I really believe this guy's got it in for me.' And they always told me I was imagining it or exaggerating.

"I was already in the wholesale telecom business by then, and I was running lines to Jamaica, and he didn't really understand what I was doing."

Not only was the telecom business booming, telecommunications and digital technology was one of the leading high-tech industries, exploding with innovation. Mel's new business thrived.

Dr. Vishwananth introduced Mel to another Indian gentleman named Robby Josh – originally Raamesh Joshi. "We ended up starting a telecommunications company. We approached AT&T and got a rate for Mexico for twelve cents a minute. We contacted a guy by the name of Chris Edgecomb from Star Telecommunications out in California and told him that we had a top-tier route to Mexico, and we were going to be able to give him some very good rates. And we gave him reduced rates starting at twenty-one cents a minute, and as he did more and more volume, his rates would come down. If he did a million minutes his rate would drop to eighteen cents."

Mel was becoming a successful wholesaler of telecom routes around the world.

In the early days of telecom and VoIP or Voice-over-Internet Protocol, long-distance minutes were one of the industry's main products. Good rates and quality to certain countries were in demand. Companies like Global Crossing and Star Telecom, known as "second-tier carriers," would buy and sell minutes to other carriers around the world in reciprocal arrangements, sending and receiving long-distance traffic.

People like Mel would contract with top-tier carriers like Sprint, AT&T, France Telecom, Deutsche Telecom and others, to buy routes or, to put it another way, the right to "terminate calls" in desirable places like Jamaica, Mexico, Egypt, India, or Nigeria. He would then sell those routes to second-tier carriers.

"I had aggressive, attractive, and good quality routes to sell to Global Crossing, Star, and IDT. I would, for example, get a good rate from AT&T and I would sell it to these carriers." The industry was unregulated at the time, and there was no limit to how much Mel could buy and sell, or to whom.

The amount of money generated by the industry was staggering. With their rate to Mexico, Robby and Mel were sitting on a huge amount of money. Chris Edgecomb was interested. "He said he's going to fly in to meet with us and sign a contract. So I was thinking, it wouldn't look very good if I had this meeting take place at this desk in a travel agency to sign up a multi-million-dollar telecom contract. So Rob and I went over to a building on Park Avenue, the Bank of Montreal building, and we spoke to them about renting half of the top floor which was about 8,000 square feet. It was vacant at the time, and they were working on producing a lease for us. In the meantime, we spoke to the super in the building. Chris Edgecomb was coming in on Tuesday and we had made an appointment for 5:30 pm.

"We asked the super if we would be able to use one of the conference rooms in the building, since we're waiting on the lease for offices up at the top, which, of course, I would never have been able to pay for, because I think the rent was about $15,000 a month in those days.

"He let us use one of the conference rooms. They had conference rooms on every floor, and we brought Chris in to one of the high floors and met him and his lawyer. We signed the contract, and with the security deposit he gave us, we could actually rent the offices. Chris understood that it was after hours, and people had left already. He flew back to California and scaled up, and started hooking up 'T1s'"–the hardwired transmission and switching system that allowed the routing of calls.

The telecommunications business, ironically, had a great deal in common with another of Cooper's earlier enterprises, collecting cans on Rockaway Beach. A mark-up of a penny is all you need to make your fortune. On the deal with Chris Edgecomb, they were making 6 cents a minute with a million and a half minutes terminating each day.

Star Telecom did spectacularly well with their rates to Mexico; so well, in fact, that AT&T decided to lower their own rates to Mexico, and go after some of the same business themselves. Mel and his partner began to run routes to India, using the lines of Worldcom.

Unfortunately, Cooper's taste in partners had not improved much while he was away.

"Robby always dressed in black, he looked like the devil. He drank constantly, straight scotch, and never slept. He drank more liquor than anybody I've ever met. I mean this guy was purely evil. He would drink and then would do things, like, be in a restaurant and walk up to two young girls and tell him that he's a movie producer, and just snow them. He had an accounting background, so he was very sharp. He would do business with somebody, and then just bury them if he could, I mean bury them completely. I mean, just to gain a few extra dollars, or whatever, he would just run you over if he could, and he would figure out how he could do it right from the beginning. He was the type to plot right from the start how he was going to hurt you, and benefit from you financially."

Mel's focus on getting up the ladder had once again kept him from seeing his partner's poor character. Robby Josh, who always focused on exploiting someone's weak spot, suddenly found Mel's; he learned about Mel's criminal record from sneaking looks at Mel's private papers. He didn't hesitate to put the knowledge to use. Josh began holding meetings behind Mel's back. Slowly, he found ways to shut Mel out of his telecom cash cow.

Eventually, after a confrontation, Josh agreed to buy Mel out, and take over the company. He began paying Mel out.

With the money he got from Robby, Cooper started up again with yet another set of partners. It seemed Mel couldn't stay away from partnerships, and the dream that the whole can be greater than the sum of its parts. Or perhaps he was trying to create the family that had never quite worked. This time he found a group of men with capital, already in the telecom business: two Israelis, a Russian, and an American. Once the business was up and running, he brought in his son David who was now twenty-five years old.

Says Mel, "I liked telecom. It was unlimited. It was steady. Once the minutes are running, you go to sleep and it's still running. It's almost like real estate. It had tremendous potential."

Using the money he saved from selling minutes to India and Mexico, Mel put a deposit down on a condo in Trump Tower. It was a two-bedroom apartment on the fiftieth floor facing lower Manhattan. This time, he created an LLC and made sure the LLC owned the condo.

Having made a commitment to live "triple time" and recapture the years he lost in prison, Mel ravenously began hooking up T1s to Panama, Trinidad, Haiti, Jamaica, England, France–wherever they could buy minutes. Aware of the value of appearance and a high-profile name, Mel and his partners rented offices in the IBM building on Madison Avenue and 56th Street. "Everything's running smoothly, and money is being made. We're into 1998 now, and I was reporting to my parole officer once a month. The parole was coming to an end that year."

Mel had left Ray Brook almost four years earlier. On June 3, 1998, Cooper's parole ended. "We had a party in my place. It was a good feeling to know I don't have to look over my shoulder anymore. I asked the parole officer if there's any kind of paper showing that it's finished, and he said no."

It was over. No more Jerome Taub. No more answering questions or reporting on his activities like a child. Mel Cooper was finally free. Without the shadow of his parole officer over him, his efforts and activities had new depth and possibility.

Two weeks after parole ended, he was still savoring the feeling of freedom as he sat in his spacious office, a relaxing symphony of light and glass overlooking Manhattan's East side. He could see the East River in the distance. A clear glass panel along the side of the door let Mel see what was happening just outside his office. At a certain moment, he looked up from his meeting with one of his partners and noticed two unfamiliar men outside his door. Just as they were about to knock, Mel opened the door.

"We'd like to talk to you for a moment," said one of them. They were neatly dressed, wearing suits. The receptionist had let them in, but these were no salesmen. From his years of dealing with the law, Mel knew exactly who they were. He also knew it would be best to step outside. After walking a discreet distance away from his office so they would not be overheard, they gave him the news.

"We're U.S. Marshals," said one, showing Mel his badge. "We're going to take you in for parole violation."

"My parole was finished two weeks ago," said a stunned Mel Cooper.

"Look, we're just the messengers. If you don't give us any problems, you can make some phone calls."

Mel went back into his office and asked his partner if he could have a few moments alone. Then, with the Marshals standing near the door, he called his lawyer. He then called his son into his office. Says Mel, "I said to him, 'here's my keys to the car, to the house, I'll talk to you.'"

He followed the officers out. They took him downtown, back to MCC where once again, he was booked, searched, and re-imprisoned.

"It was like starting the whole thing over again. You just got your life together, you bought a place, you're getting things going, and here they go, taking it away. Because if they take you away, it's not going to be there when you come out. It's devastating, thinking what you'll have to go through again."

Mel was brought to Brooklyn MCC where the parole board needed to review the charge. "As it turns out, Jerome Taub filed a complaint the last day of my parole, and it took the marshals two weeks after to pick me up. He filed what's called a 'complaint of association.' He probably did it afterwards and backdated it because it doesn't take two weeks to find me. They know what time I go into my office every day. So my guess is, what he did is he filed it a week and half late and he just backdated it and had them pick me up."

Officer Taub accused Mel of associating with ex-convict Kevin Trudeau, based on the address book incident. Why did Taub do it? "Because he felt that he should, because there must be something wrong if I'm doing what I'm doing. I would come in and tell him what I was doing because I wanted him to understand how I'm making a living, and I would explain, 'I'm doing lines to Jamaica, we're doing this and that.' He's sitting there saying, 'Something has got to be wrong.'

"I remember he tried to catch me with regard to my lawsuits. I still had lawsuits against the Bureau of Prisons on violating the laws of kashrut, so he was trying to see if I ever ate in a restaurant that wasn't kosher, or something. He's working for the government, but he's not supposed to be doing that."

Guesses aside, whatever was bothering Jerome Taub, as Cooper says, "They can lock you up. They don't need a reason." Two weeks later found himself on his way to the Federal Correctional Institution in Otisville, New York.

"It's like a merry-go-round that you can't get off, Dante's Inferno. It's not so much the one time, it's how many times you have to go back and confront it, and each time it takes a piece out of you. It's not like you do it and then you're finished. It's over and over and over. It's horrifying."

FCI Otisville has both a minimum and medium security facility. It's only ninety miles from New York City, and it has the distinction of housing some of the state's high-profile white-collar criminals due to its proximity to the city. It was also home to New York's Chassidic and Orthodox lawbreakers, since it has the strictest kosher kitchen in the nation. With two lawsuits already in the works, this time the Bureau of Prisons didn't want to deal with Mel Cooper's diet.

"The Bureau of Prisons had a rabbi stationed in Otisville, which was very unusual." It was to Otisville that the government sent people who would prefer to starve rather than eat a non-kosher roast beef sandwich.

Mel's prison routine began again. Working out. Drawing. The library. He had more freedom than before thanks to Otisville's more relaxed regulations. This time he remained focused on business on the outside.

From Otisville, he guided his son David through the minefield of serving as his proxy in the business. David had only joined the business a month or two before the visit from the US Marshals. From Otisville, Mel spoke to his son every day, discussing events in the office. At twenty-five years old, David found himself a full partner with "the same slimy guys"

Mel had left behind when he went to Otisville.

David would call and report on the partners' activities, informing Mel, "They're doing something with Mexico, they don't want me to hear, they're running traffic."

With a predictability you could bet on, Mel's partners did not turn out to be strong in the character department. Or, according to his assessment, "they were basically snakes who would cut each other's throats, never mind mine. They were stealing, they would have stuff billed to the company but the profits would go to some other place, and David already knew this. So within a period of time I said, 'Listen, we're going to start again without these guys.'"

From Otisville, Mel and his son began to work on plans for yet another new business, staying within the field of telecommunications.

He also focused on the upcoming hearing to review Jerome Taub's charges. "What I did in my spare time is try to figure out how I'm going to get out of this. At best, I know they got me for something that's bullshit. But it takes 90 days or 120 days or six months to be able to prove it, to have your final hearing, and then you wait for an answer."

Mel's appeal unfolded in the usual glacial time frame. It took six months, but after all the hearings and review, in early January of 1999, they dismissed the association charge. "They don't call it a lie. They call it an 'uncorroborated accusation.' Oh no, they never 'lie.'" At which point the Department of Justice decided to keep Mel in jail anyway. Mel had still not paid his original fine. He owed the government almost $160,000. Though he had been out for four years, working, traveling, and spending, he had only paid a little over one thousand dollars.

According to Mel, it was Jerome Taub who kept him in. "My parole officer came to see me when I was in Otisville. He said, 'we have not established as a fact that you were meeting with Kevin Trudeau. Therefore, we're not keeping you for that purpose. But we are going to keep you because you didn't pay your fine.' I saw that this guy just wanted to keep me there."

And so Mel remained in FCI Otisville as a new year got underway.

23

DOWN AND OUT IN OTISVILLE

It takes a certain amount of *chutzpah* to tell the government you want to take a pauper's oath when you own a condo in Trump Tower. A pauper's oath is an affidavit in which one swears he or she is unable to pay court costs and fines. It means you are destitute, perhaps even indigent. In 1999, Mel's apartment was worth a million dollars. Nonetheless, he submitted his request to the US Attorney's office asking that he be deemed a pauper and, once again, released. He claimed the condominium was owned by partners, and that he had no cash to pay his fine.

Mary Jo White, United States Attorney for New York State's Southern District sent a letter back to Cooper stating, "Defendant is not eligible at this time to take the pauper's oath because it is undisputed that he owns an apartment at 721 Fifth Avenue (Trump Tower). Indeed, it is undisputed that he has a substantial amount of equity in the apartment."

From Mel's point of view, it made perfect sense to factor his condo out of the equation and just call himself a pauper. As far as he was concerned, he had paid enough for his crimes, with his businesses shut down, millions in loans never paid off by his "victims," his belongings gone. He had been unjustly busted for parole violation and put back in prison—another business sunk as a consequence. Now the government wanted more. It wanted him to sell the one thing he had acquired for himself, the only thing he owned after year away: his home. He wasn't going to do it.

"They wanted the money. I just wasn't liquid. I said, 'I'll put my condo on the 50th floor up as security, I have access to money.' I just couldn't do anything about it while I was in Otisville. They said no." The government wanted its money and it was entitled to it.

His request was rejected in January. What happened next was the most painful experience of his entire prison saga. Mel asked his family for help. He asked his father and his brothers if they could loan him the money to get out of prison. How hard could it be for four working brothers and his father to scrape together $160,000?

He would have been released after the dismissal on January 19, in the winter of 1999, were it not for the fine. Now he was just killing time. A week went by, then another. January became February. February became March. Nobody paid his fine.

According to Mel, "At first everyone said 'we're working on it, we're having meetings.' Then it became 'Dad should pay it.'" But his father didn't pay it, and Mel remained in prison as spring came to Otisville.

"It's very hard to sit there and accept this. Because I know that if the shoe was on the other foot, I really believe that they would not have to wait ten minute if it was up to me to help them."

The government had the legal grounds to keep him in Otisville indefinitely, and it looked like they planned to do it. Mel's family was of the opinion that he should sell his condo and lay out the money himself. Why should they pay again for Mel's problems when, according to them, just like Mel, they had already paid so much? And whose fault was it that Mel bought a flashy condo in Trump Tower but didn't pay his fine?

As he sat in Otisville waiting for someone to get him out, what particularly obsessed Mel were the memories he thought he had put behind him. Again, he thought about the belongings and property that had disappeared when he was in before. The West Hampton condo alone could have paid his fine. Within a few months in Otisville, Mel looked ten years older, his face drawn and sunken.

"I was thinking, I'm going to stay here for a long time. This was a very negative feeling, a futile feeling. It was a terrible, terrible feeling. But somehow when you do a number of years, I can't say you get used to it, but you tolerate it. But it's a negative feeling, especially when you feel you don't belong here now."

Mel did not ponder the irony of the situation. His current predicament had been set in motion by his conviction for loansharking. Now, because of the money he owed the government, he was trapped by a system that asserted its legal right to keep him, just as he had trapped his customers in a net of legal documents years before. They owed money. Now he owed money. But irony or karma wasn't what Mel was thinking about.

Over the months, various people came forward who claimed to want to help him. Again, rabbis featured prominently in his efforts.

"One rabbi wanted me to sell my condo. All he wanted to do was have his friend, the broker, take the listing and sell it so they'd make a big commission. I didn't want to sell it because I knew I had gotten a good buy, and it was going to go up in value. And he was just pushing to sell, sell, sell."

He finally got the help he needed from another rabbi, a man named Mendy Katz. Rabbi Katz was involved with an organization called Aleph, which helps incarcerated Jewish prisoners. Aleph gives assistance of all kinds, from spiritual to educational. "I met him when I was in Terre Haute. Maybe I called him, or I talked to him on the phone but I definitely met him at one of the institutions, and he came to visit me every so often. Rabbi Mendy Katz went to see my father.

"They were helpful, they used to send the food for the different holidays. Aleph would send *tefillin* – elements of Jewish prayer – for people who didn't have, prayer books if you didn't have. I found a lot of people misused their trust. And that bothered me because they allowed it to happen, but the way they look at things is they say, 'we don't care if someone's coming to a service for just for the food, eventually maybe they'll come without the food.'

"Rabbi Katz went to see my father in Miami right before Passover." It was March. Mel had been in Otisville for nine months. "My father was staying right on the beach in Florida at that time so the Rabbi asked him how he thought his son felt, not being able to see the waves. Something like that. He said something that got my father to say, 'Okay, I'm going to put up the money.' So a couple of days later he paid it, and I got out very quickly. I paid him back three months later."

24

TIME SERVED

"First you forget what things look like. Everything melts into a drab gray color. Then you forget faces. You actually start to block things out when you leave prison. Even people you like, your friends, start to fade away, and when you think of them, there's just a whiteness where their face should be. That's the period that's the most vague for me, my memory of prison," says Mel.

"Once I got out, it didn't take me long to get back on track. I was behind a lot, it was starting to get into foreclosures, and I had to catch up and pay everything off. I paid everybody off. My father got his money, I paid him all the money I owed him.

Mel had a feeling of freedom he had not known before. There was no way they could put him back in. Prison was truly behind him. He went back into telecommunications. This time, however, there were no strangers, only family and old friends. He started a business and brought in his son David and one of his son's friends, a young man named David Berson.

"While I was in prison, I was giving David and his friend instructions on how to get a business started on a very small basis without a lot of capital. And it started growing from there. Money came in, they took an office, and by the time I came out, they had an office downtown on Water Street. Certainly, it wasn't much to look at, it was dirty, small, and depressing, so we were there for another year, then we moved to 58th Street, to nicer offices."

Mel was still a wholesale carrier. "We had customers like Verizon who was sending traffic through us. We had another division where we got retail customers to go on our service and use our networks for long distance. They can go through us."

Within a few years of exiting prison, Mel was using networks around the globe and installing T1s by the dozen. In the bullpen of his telecom office, Mel installed a large whiteboard that his staff of salespeople used to track sales. It looked like a roster of exotic travel destinations, with young men and women selling long-distance minutes to Johannesburg, Rio, Bangalore, Cairo, Buenos Aires, Tel Aviv, Abidjan, and more.

Mel Cooper lives by the motto, "You can always start again." Still, even he has had enough of starting again. Since his release from Otisville, he's staying on the right side of the law, "dotting the 'i's' and crossing the 't's,'" as he says, refusing opportunities that could lead to trouble.

As for his past behavior, Mel sticks to his story. "I would say we had some very overzealous prosecutors, and there were a number of reasons why the government did an overkill here. I mean, I was in Terre Haute with people that were there for murder doing half the time I was.

"We were clearly on the edge. We obviously didn't take it seriously enough because it was a situation where nobody was beaten up to get money back, there were actually mortgages set up with each loan. So it wasn't our intent to go out and collect money with a bat. But the government, in their enthusiasm to tie in the Mafia, came after us."

There are some things Mel has just decided to accept. The government was doing its job. Until a few years ago, he still thought Doc Hyman was a great guy. They each did what they had to do. And if he had it all to do again, he probably would.

But as article after article appeared in newspapers about Jesse Hyman's decision to "flip"—articles with headlines like "Mob Still Feeling Dentist's Bite" and "Dentist-Turned-Informant Worries Mob"—Mel revised his view of Doc Hyman. Today Mel acknowledges, "His whole existence was corrupt. His dental practice, his involvement with Teamster pension money, his loans to Las Vegas—everything he did was corrupt and dirty, from the bottom of his foot to the top of his head."

Beyond that, Mel doesn't think about it. After spending ten years in prisons, holdovers, and correctional centers, not dwelling on the past has a certain appeal. The past is over. He is also not one of those people who want to talk about how much he has learned, nor is he grateful for the experience. "I would say it was a hideous experience, and that you should make every attempt possible not to go through it. Prison is the worst, most humiliating thing."

Meanwhile, Mel continues to scale up. "We have a new vendor in Austria, and he's bringing our networks into Eastern Europe, the Middle East, and Africa. The business is multiplying very quickly. In New York right now, we have fifteen or twenty people, and we're just going to add on eight or nine salesmen. It's going to grow substantially."

Mel may be living three times as fast, as he likes to say, but you can never catch up. You can't get back years. Even if you do exactly what you would have been doing had you not been away, and try to fit in everything you missed, it's not the same. Starting a business at age fifty-five isn't the same as doing it at age thirty-eight. Falling in love or starting a new relationship isn't the same. Your kids are grown up. Seeds of resentment have been sown.

Yet making up for lost time is all you can do. Since Mel has been out, he's put every penny he's made back into living. "You understand what it means to do things fast and get a lot of things done and try to do more than you normally might do. We're doing quite a number of things here, not just one thing, because I don't have fifty years to develop something. Right now, I want to make up for the lost time, and we're doing that. It's a matter of mostly common sense but you need the drive and a little luck.

"I want to show that when you come out, it's not the end necessarily. You can get started again. You can make things happen. When you come out, life is not over."

What is it that makes someone self-destruct, only to return with determination to climb higher than before, and why has Mel Cooper, so far, succeeded?

He answers without hesitation. "Because I want to." It might as well explain everything Mel Cooper does. "I have a need to. I want to. I have a drive."

But Mel was not done with his cycle of spectacular success followed by equally spectacular failure; he had one more dramatic rise and fall to act out, one more act of self-sabotage, this time in the realm of the personal. Sometimes even the steeliest determination and chutzpah are no match for a well-developed drive to self-destruct.

By the mid-to-late 2000s, Mel was doing well in telecom and accumulating cash. He transitioned seamlessly to the next digital revolution, VoIP, or voice-over-internet protocol. Telecommunications had taken a huge leap and now, instead of hooking up physical T1 lines with a hard switch, the industry had moved to a software switch. Mel likens it to a shift from "candles to electric light bulbs." The time it took to hook up carriers went from days to minutes. He made a deal with Sprint that gave him excellent rates to Western Europe, and soon he was selling five million additional minutes a day.

Mel began purchasing real estate with the money he made. He sold his condo on the fiftieth floor of Trump Tower and upgraded to a two-bedroom on the forty-fifth floor facing Central Park. He invested in a property down in Miami, a new building that was part of the Fontainebleau Hotel complex. He bought eight condos.

Though he was busy in telecom, Mel remained dedicated to his habit of weightlifting and working out. He joined the New York Health and Racket Club near his apartment and visited the gym several days a week.

One day, a trainer at the gym, a Russian woman he saw often, called him over.

"Are you dating anyone?" she asked.

"Not right now," Mel answered. He had stayed decidedly single since his last relationship had ended in a public blowup, when he sued his ex-girlfriend for the diamond ring and BMW he gave her. Since that time, Mel had enjoyed his solitude.

"I have someone I want to introduce you to," she said.

Mel agreed to meet her.

Her name was Polina, and after a phone call, they planned to meet for dinner at the Pierre, one of New York's iconic hotels. Mel walked from his 58th Street office to the hotel on Fifth Avenue opposite Central Park.

Mel remembers the first date. She turned out to be young, much younger than he expected. She was gorgeous, tall, and dressed like she had just stepped out of Town & Country Magazine. And she was Russian.

"We went into the dining room, and we started talking. We had a couple of drinks and an appetizer, then I yawned because I had been up since 6:30 a.m. and it was 10:30 now, and I looked at her, and she gets up to leave. She walks out, and she walks down Fifth Avenue. So I follow her out, and she's there looking to get a cab. I said, 'What's going on, why did you leave?' She said, 'In Russia, when someone yawns it's a sign they're not happy with the person they're with.' So I said, 'In America, when someone yawns it's a sign that we're tired.'"

So began a predictable cat-and-mouse game that ultimately produced a baby daughter.

After the date at the Pierre, Mel called her again. Says Mel, "It was my flaw that I called her again, I shouldn't have called her, just based on the way she walked out. I wasn't so crazy about her, but I figured, oh, let me call again. It's like I can't stand to lose. I invited her to Jersey Boys, and she said, 'I don't go to shows like that, I go to Lincoln Center and Carnegie Hall,' and I said 'Excuse me, this is a Broadway show.' She ended up going and she loved it.

"So I'm driving her home—I think I had a Jaguar at that time—and she said 'I'm having a problem, I live in a two-bedroom apartment, the owner lives there, and the woman is having her son coming over for two weeks. Would you mind if I stayed at your place for two weeks?'

"So I'm thinking, this is not a good idea, but I said, alright. I knew once someone is in, it's hard to get them out. So she came over for two weeks and then after two weeks I said, 'It's time to go.' She asked if she could stay two more weeks. So I said, 'You stay in the living room, I'll stay in the bedroom.' Five days later, I find out she's pregnant. I didn't want to have anything to do with her at that point, I said this is a complete trick."

But it wasn't a trick. Mel let her stay in the apartment until the baby was born. When the baby was born, he had her DNA tested. It was Mel's.

The next seven years were a nightmare of court battles, accusations, fights, police visits, and interventions. Cooper claims Polina was part of a group of several women and a lawyer who engineered profitable relationships with American men. According to Mel, they helped and guided one another, coaching each other on what to say in court. "They try to find a rich guy, get pregnant, and then they try to trap them."

But it's hard to imagine she enjoyed the situation any more than Mel, since explosive fights and conflict followed the baby's arrival. The only positive outcome for Polina was that she ended up with Mel's cherished Trump Tower condo.

"Eventually, she was living in the apartment, and I couldn't go to the apartment anymore. She had a restraining order and they let her stay in the apartment."

By 2014, Mel's apartment in Trump Tower was gone. At the end of years of turmoil, it went into foreclosure. In a perfect repetition of a past trauma, once again, Mel's belongings disappeared. "There was a million dollars' worth of furnishings, chandeliers, artwork, antiques, crystal, silverware, a Chagall. She sold it all.

"It's because of a major flaw in my character that I have to take advantage of a situation. If that wasn't my mentality, I would not have called her after the first date. But I did because I had to win. I had to have a victory, I can't lose. It's based on a desire to be powerful. This was my excitement in life, I thought. Going up. Winning. But later, a girl I knew, a psychotherapist, explained to me it wasn't just about going up. She said it was about the falling. 'You get excited by the free fall.'"

At 72 years old Mel is still trying to get something going. "I was up to the sky and down to the ground, and this is the third time. It's the third time I'm on the floor. And I'm going back up to the sky."

But it's different now. The telecom business as Mel knew it no longer exists, replaced by smart phones and apps. And he has his daughter.

"She's the best thing that ever happened to me. She goes to school, she plays piano, she's an artist. She's a very bright girl, there's no end to her talent. She comes to me on weekends. She doesn't stop saying 'I love you' and hugging. I try to get her things that she likes, she has friends around her that she plays with. You start to realize what's important in life. You sit there and one day you say, my goodness, what have I been doing? Is money the most important thing in life, or is living and appreciating and being happy with what you have more important? It's a whole different life now. You start to open your eyes and you see, 'This makes me happy, that makes me happy,' it can be a very simple thing. And your feeling of happiness is a lot more than when it was a little shallow, because it's coming from dollar bills. It's a different kind of happiness.

"I would like to have more so I can take care of my daughter and do things. I'm working on a number of things now, the way I used to do. But this is so I can get things for my daughter."

Losing his apartment and belongings again was not simply reminiscent of what happened to him in prison. When it was all gone, it was like what he felt leaving prison. "There's a feeling of freedom now. You're not tied down by anything, not chained up. You're actually free. Your responsibilities are a lot smaller. Things just tie you down, they're chains on you.

"Seventy-two is a good age. That's an important number in the Kabbalah. If you have seven and two, that adds up to nine. Nine multiplied by any other number, again adds up to nine." The significance? "Everything returns to itself. That age is a sign that things are coming back. This is going to be an incredible year for me. This will be a year that will encompass many things.

"My past is behind me and everything that's gone is coming back—the positive things, like success in business. The negative stuff, I know how to close that out now. I'm going to try to keep that away from me. Now I see what's important in life."

Mel has arrived at perhaps his most life-changing concept: "Now I don't say 'yes' that fast."

Mel lives a quiet life in Brooklyn where, instead of overlooking Manhattan from the high floor of a Fifth Avenue condo, he rents the ground floor of a private house. There, he works on his projects, occasionally going outside on a small porch to smoke a cigar or feed kosher chicken to the cats that gather in the backyard in the evenings. During the day, he feeds the birds in the front of building. "I throw a lot of bread out there."

Mel still spends his days trying to "get something going," as he puts it. Like before, he wants to and needs to, he has a drive. But this time he's doing it for someone else.

www.ingramcontent.com/pod-product-compliance
Lightning Source LLC
Chambersburg PA
CBHW020536030426
42337CB00013B/875